Waging Peace

Other books by Jim Wallis

Agenda for Biblical People

The Call to Conversion

WAGING PEACE

A Handbook for the Struggle to Abolish Nuclear Weapons

Edited by Jim Wallis

HARPER & ROW, PUBLISHERS
SAN FRANCISCO & SYDNEY

1817

Cambridge, Hagerstown, New York, Philadelphia
London, Mexico City, São Paulo

WAGING PEACE: A HANDBOOK FOR THE STRUGGLE TO ABOLISH NUCLEAR WEAPONS. Copyright © 1982 by Sojourners. All rights reserved. Printed in the United States of America. No part of this book may be used or reproduced in any manner whatsoever without written permission except in the case of brief quotations embodied in critical articles and reviews. For information address Harper & Row, Publishers, Inc., 10 East 53rd Street, New York, NY 10022. Published simultaneously in Canada by Fitzhenry & Whiteside, Limited, Toronto. Published simultaneously in Australia and New Zealand by Harper & Row (Australia) Pty. Limited, P.O. Box 226 Artarmon, New South Wales 2064.

FIRST EDITION

Designed by Tony Agpoon Design

Library of Congress Cataloging in Publication Data
Main entry under title:

WAGING PEACE.

  Bibliography: p. 288
  Includes index.
  1. Atomic warfare—Religious aspects—Addresses, essays, lectures.　2. Peace—Addresses, essays, lectures. I. Wallis, Jim.
BR115.A85W33　1982　　　　　　261.8′73　　　　　　　82-47759
ISBN 0–06–069240–5 (World except Australasia)
ISBN 0–06–312051–8 (Australasia)

82 83 84 85 86 10 9 8 7 6 5 4 3 2 1

To Dorothy Day

CONTENTS

CONTENTS

ACKNOWLEDGMENTS

Many people contributed to this book. Grateful thanks go to the authors, who made the writing of their articles a priority, often in the midst of busy schedules. Mernie King helped in the initial selection of articles and authors for *A Matter of Faith* handbook. Many of these articles have been revised or reproduced for this volume. Dana Mills-Powell provided valuable editorial input in the selection and arrangement of material for *Waging Peace*. Jim Rice compiled the glossary and resources. Dana and Joe Lynch wrote the study questions. Susan Masters typed much of the manuscript. Special thanks go to Lindsay McLaughlin, who did all the copy editing and worked with me throughout in putting the whole project together and bringing it to completion.

"Ultimate Terrorism," by Richard Barnet. A shortened and updated version of an article reprinted with permission from *The Progressive,* 408 West Gorham St., Madison, WI 53703. Copyright © 1979 The Progressive, Inc.

"Hysteria Is Coming! Hysteria Is Coming!" by William Greider. Reprinted with permission from the September 28, 1980, *Washington Post.*

"The Medical Consequences of Nuclear War," by Howard Hiatt. Reprinted with permission of the author. Shortened version of a speech delivered by Dr. Hiatt at a symposium on the medical consequences of nuclear weapons and nuclear war in New York on September 27, 1980. Copyright © Physicians for Social Responsibility, 639 Massachusetts Ave., Cambridge, MA 02139.

"A Family Sees the Light, Again and Again," by Elizabeth Wright. Reprinted with permission of the author from the April 11, 1980, *Los Angeles Times.*

"The High Cost of Insecurity," by Ruth Leger Sivard. An updated version of an article reprinted with permission from *The Nation,* June 17, 1978.

"Reconciling Our Enemies," by Ronald Sider. Originally published in the January 1979 issue of *Sojourners*. Now part of a book by Ronald Sider, *Christ and Violence*, published by Herald Press.

"A Biblical Call to Nuclear Non-Cooperation," by Helmut Gollwitzer. Shortened version of an article reprinted with permission from *Therefore Choose Life: Essays on the Nuclear Crisis* (International Fellowship of Reconciliation, 1961).

"The Central Murder," by Dale Aukerman. Originally published in the March 1980 issue of *Sojourners*. Reprinted with permission of the publisher from *Darkening Valley: A Biblical Perspective on Nuclear War*, by Dale Aukerman, published by Seabury Press. Copyright © 1981 by Dale Aukerman.

"The Work of Prayer," by Jim Wallis. Originally published in the March 1979 issue of *Sojourners*, and supplemented with material from *The Call to Conversion*, by Jim Wallis, published by Harper & Row. Copyright 1981 by Sojourners.

"The Canadian Churches Respond to Militarism," by Ernest Regehr. Originally published in the July 1982 issue of *International Review of Mission*. Reprinted with permission of the Commission on World Mission and Evangelism of the World Council of Churches. Copyright © 1982 by the World Council of Churches, Geneva.

HOW TO USE THIS HANDBOOK

The nuclear arms race has emerged as a central issue for Christian faith in the 1980s. Protestants, Catholics, evangelicals—representing both pacifist and traditional just war positions—are all responding to the threat of nuclear war. The issues of faith raised by the nuclear danger are being addressed in the churches as never before. The need for evangelistic and educational resources that both explore the state of the arms race and give a political and moral perspective rooted in Christian faith is growing.

To meet this need, Sojourners in 1981 published *A Matter of Faith: A study guide for churches on the nuclear arms race.* Our initial supply of these study guides was depleted rapidly, and it seemed we could not keep up with the demand. An emerging and deepening commitment to peacemaking was evident in the life of the church.

As the military budget increases and the arms race escalates, more and more Christians are being awakened to the nuclear issue. Others who have opposed nuclear weapons for some time are wanting to take further steps in their peacemaking journeys. This new handbook, *Waging Peace,* is offered both for those who are just developing a concern over nuclear weapons and for those who want to become more thoroughly informed and involved. It is an updated and newly expanded version of *A Matter of Faith* and includes some of the material from that study guide as well as new articles, some taken from *Sojourners* magazine and others written for this handbook. The format for the book, and its study questions, are based on *A Matter of Faith.*

Arranged in three major sections, *Waging Peace* gives a thorough assessment of the present state of the arms race, biblical and theological responses to it, and a discussion of what can be done. Together these articles tell of the need to put our faith into action in response to the nuclear danger.

Waging Peace has been conceived as a basic educational and formational tool for individuals, local churches, college and seminary classes, and prayer and study groups. It is divided into twelve study sessions, each followed by questions drawing upon the essence of each article and asking for individual and corporate thought and discernment.

Groups using *Waging Peace* may want to allow two hours for each session and a week between sessions, so people can read the material and reflect on it beforehand. Participants may want to take turns at starting the time together with brief reports on the articles. Most of the time should be left for discussion. Feel free to use the questions throughout the book in whatever ways would be most helpful.

The hope is that this handbook, in all the ways in which it can be used, will help many to probe the meaning of the current nuclear crisis and find ways to make a faithful response.

INTRODUCTION:

A Time to Wage Peace
by Jim Wallis

It was May 1978. About 140 people had begun to occupy the railroad tracks leading to the Rocky Flats Nuclear Weapons Facility. Located in a desolate area about 16 miles northwest of Denver, this stark bomb factory makes the plutonium triggers for every nuclear warhead produced in the United States.

The plutonium is shipped along the railroad tracks on which we were sitting. We were there to block those trains with their deadly freight. Our purpose was to present, with our bodies, a nonviolent obstacle to the continued production of nuclear weapons.

Ten minutes after we walked onto the tracks, a rain began to fall that continued through the night. We were all soaked through our clothing when a quick mountain weather change caused the temperature to plummet and the rain to turn to sleet. I couldn't remember when I had been so cold.

Throughout that wet and bitterly cold night, I thought about what it means to "wage peace." I first pictured centuries of soldiers sitting in rain and cold as we were that night. People have always been ready to leave their families, go to faraway places, endure incredible hardships, and even die in order to wage a war. Is it conceivable, I wondered, that the cost of peace could be less? What if we were willing to sacrifice for peace as others have sacrificed for war?

It is time to wage peace. The momentum of our technology, the genius of our science, and the human capacity for evil have combined to bring us to the precipice of total war. Our weapons are now ultimate. Our world, our children, and creation itself will not likely survive their use.

Either we turn our hearts and minds to the making of peace or we will face certain disaster. If we wage peace with at least the same commitment that we have waged war, the chances for our survival will increase. If we do not, or if we remain silent,

1

cynical, or paralyzed, our prospects are most grim.

As I huddled under wet blankets on the railroad tracks that night, I felt a deep and pervasive fear. It was more than the rain, the cold, or the possibility of arrest. It was even more than the heavy military security around us; we had been told that armed guards were all over the facility, with tanks and artillery on hand.

A presence of evil lies at the heart of nuclear weaponry; my fear was of the evil that pervades Rocky Flats. The passage from Scripture that went through my mind again and again during the night was from Ephesians 6: "We wrestle not against flesh and blood but against principalities and powers, against spiritual wickedness in high places." If we merely understand the struggle against nuclear weapons on a political level, we are in great danger.

At 7 o'clock the next morning, there was a service in celebration of life at which I had been asked to speak about hope. After feeling fear all during the night, I still knew that the one thing we have that the powers of evil cannot defeat is hope. Hope is our mightiest weapon, the strongest resource we have to bring to the peacemaking struggle. Hope can be described as believing in spite of the evidence, and then watching the evidence change. This book is an offering of hope in the face of the overwhelming evidence of destruction in our midst. It is a gathering of voices all committed to the waging of peace in the face of nuclear war. It is not a collection of abstract intellectual treatises, but a handbook of faith and action in the struggle to abolish nuclear weapons.

The nuclear age began almost four decades ago. It was a warm, clear morning on August 6, 1945, when the *Enola Gay* appeared in the sky over Hiroshima, Japan. Out of her belly fell the most awesome force the world had ever seen. In a flash, almost 100,000 people were cremated and a whole city obliterated. The heat of the firestorm that swept Hiroshima left the imprint of human shadows on stone as memorials of that dreadful day, and perhaps as a foretaste of what might be ahead.

The Hiroshima event signaled the start of the mad race toward nuclear oblivion. The world will never be the same, for now it faces the possibility of total war. Albert Einstein, who later regretted his role in the development of the atomic bomb, said, "The unleashed power of the atom has changed everything except our way of thinking."

The invention of nuclear weapons has put the nations of the world on the edge of catastrophe. The United States and the Soviet Union now possess more than 50,000 nuclear weapons, the equivalent of more than one million bombs the size of the one dropped on Hiroshima. The bomb that destroyed Hiroshima represented a huge escalation in explosive power. But today a bomb its size would be considered only a small nuclear warhead.

Today the United States and the Soviet Union each have the capacity to totally destroy the other in less than half an hour. And neither side can do anything to defend itself.

One Trident submarine, one of the United States' newest nuclear systems, when fitted with Trident II missiles, will be able to destroy more than 400 Soviet cities. The Navy plans to build 30 Trident submarines. Any one of the 100 missiles of the new MX system will contain more explosive capacity than all the bombs dropped in World War II and Korea combined. The world is clearly capable of its own suicide.

In spite of the nuclear ability to destroy everyone in the world many times over, the arms race continues to gain speed. Each day the United States adds three new nuclear warheads to its stockpile.

The Trident and MX are part of a new kind of nuclear system being built by both sides. They mark an escalation that will radically increase the likelihood of a nuclear exchange. These weapons, called "counterforce," exhibit increased accuracy, power, and effectiveness in targeting capacity. They are created with the capability to destroy the other side's missiles before those missiles are launched.

Regardless of the stated intentions of either side, counterforce provides the option of a first strike. Once these weapons are in place, fear of first strike will dominate U.S.-Soviet relations, and nuclear war will have a hair trigger.

Nuclear strategy is shifting away from the old idea of deterrence, in which each side is supposed to be restrained from using nuclear weapons by the fear of retaliation. This dramatic change in strategic nuclear doctrine has plunged us into a world in which nuclear war has become more thinkable.

Our government refuses to pledge that the United States would never be the first to use nuclear weapons. Now we hear the Pentagon talking of fighting and even winning "limited nuclear wars." Military strategists plan for such wars, in which a death toll

of tens of millions of Americans is regarded as an "acceptable loss," as if "victors" exist in a world laid waste by nuclear conflict.

Many political and military experts now describe the prospect of nuclear war, either by design or accident, by the end of the century as "probable" or even "inevitable." The *Bulletin of Atomic Scientists'* doomsday clock, which registers the probability of nuclear war, now ticks away at four minutes before midnight.

Further, we are entering what some describe as "the second nuclear age." The commercial export of nuclear energy has given scores of countries the technological capacity and the material to make atomic weapons. Between 35 and 40 nations will be able to make nuclear weapons by 1985, and the figure could hit 100 by 1995. The momentum of a worldwide nuclear arms race is building. Can this momentum be stopped and reversed before it's too late?

Dr. Howard Hiatt, dean of the Harvard University School of Public Health, has described nuclear war as the final epidemic, a health problem that medicine cannot possibly treat. The only cure he prescribes is prevention.

But the arms race is already responsible for widespread suffering around the world. As President Eisenhower said in 1960, every dollar spent on war is robbery from the poor. It is now estimated that a billion of the world's poor go hungry every day. It has been calculated that, to provide adequate food, water, education, health, and housing for everyone in the world, $17 billion would be required every year; that is the amount of money that the world spends on arms every two weeks. The Congressional Budget Office has estimated that from 1982 to 1986 the United States will spend $1.635 trillion on the military.

The rationale for the U. S. nuclear buildup has always been a need to respond to the threat from the Soviet Union. Yet it is the United States, and not the Soviet Union, that started the nuclear arms race and has led in every step of its escalation. Even today, the United States still leads in the number of total warheads, submarine-launched warheads, and targeting accuracy.

The specter of the Soviet threat is the justification for every new U.S. escalation, and it has become a self-fulfilling prophecy. While the Soviets have been playing catch-up in this race for many years, it now seems clear that in the last decade they have made great strides toward closing the gap. Many military experts agree that the United States and the Soviet Union have reached nuclear

4

parity. This simply means that neither side can keep one from destroying the other.

The superpowers have reached a stalemate, but both sides are still racing to gain an "advantage." The nuclear spring is being wound tighter and tighter. How much more pressure will it take before the world is sent hurtling toward oblivion?

With the possibility of nuclear war, all the old political notions of war are obsolete. Before nuclear weapons, war was thought to be winnable, giving the "winner" some economic or political power. But nuclear war has no winners. It can offer no advantage; it brings no protection. It can only assure the destruction of both sides and possibly all life on earth.

All the old theological notions of war have passed as well. By whatever traditional standard of teaching the church has used to evaluate its relationship to war and violence—whether pacifism or the "just war" theory—the conclusion is the same: Nuclear war can have no Christian theological justification.

For the first three centuries of the church's life, no Christian writer ever justified the participation of believers in warfare. The members of the early church identified so deeply with Jesus and his way of the cross that they would not kill in the emperor's wars. When called upon to take life, they said they could only give their lives, for this was the way of Jesus.

In the fourth century, after the conversion of the emperor Constantine, theologians gradually abandoned their pacifism and adopted the notion of "just war." A doctrine still held by many Christian traditions today, the just war allows that under certain specific circumstances, violence can be justified if a greater good or justice is accomplished. But the means of violence has to meet particular criteria, including a prohibition against the taking of innocent lives or killing noncombatants.

The nuclear age has rendered the traditional just war theory obsolete. Nuclear war is indiscriminate by definition. Uncontrollable in their devastation, nuclear weapons destroy everything. Any cause that might be used to justify their use would lose all meaning after nuclear war broke out. After all, can any justice be achieved in a global holocaust?

But certainly the question of Christian response to nuclear weapons is more involved than simply reaching a clear theological position. The Scriptures teach us that evil is rooted not only in the

human heart but also in social and political structures. Often we are involved in destructive arrangements without being aware of it. A kind of spiritual blindness operates, which brings us to a condition that the Bible calls "hardness of heart."

The Bible describes hardness of heart as the loss of the ability to distinguish between good and evil. It is like having deadened nerves that can no longer feel. Reason becomes clouded and hearts closed, and a callousness to the pain of others sets in.

The fact that we have finally acquired the means for our own total self-destruction seems no longer to shock anyone. It's simply another fact of life. Living with the everyday potential of annihilation has become normal. We know that nuclear weapons exist. Yet, on a deeper level, we don't seem to believe that they are really there or will ever really be used.

The nuclear danger has come upon us gradually, over a period of four decades. Perhaps that is why we have been lulled into a false sense of security so that we passively accept such weapons of ultimate destruction. We have become accustomed to feeling helpless.

By accepting the presence and threatened use of the bomb, American Christians have already become captive to the spiritual death it brings. The choice to make nuclear weapons a part of our national life has made hardness of heart a national necessity. We can live with nuclear weapons only by allowing some very basic moral values to die.

While the arms race has many complicated political and economic causes, its root cause is fear. The bomb is the political result of fear. It is the logical and social extension of our personal fear and anxiety. We have allowed our faith and security in God to be overcome by fear, the greatest enemy of faith and its final contradiction.

People feel a need to be saved from all the things that frighten them, so we are susceptible to anyone or anything that promises to save us. We fear our enemies and believe our way of life needs protection. So we bow before our nation and its military might, which literally promises us salvation. We fear the Russians, and the Pentagon promises to save us, so we do what it requires of us, including the surrender of our faith.

But the one whom we proclaim as Lord had some very direct and simple words that apply in this historical moment in which the

danger and challenge are so overwhelmingly clear. Jesus said, "You have heard that it was said, 'You shall love your neighbor and hate your enemy.' But I say to you, Love your enemies and pray for those who persecute you" (Matthew 5:44).

For centuries, most of the church has refused to make Jesus' command to love our enemies historically specific. We have said, "Love your enemies . . . unless they are Russian, or Cuban, or Iranian," or whomever the government identifies as our adversary at the moment. We say, "Love your enemies . . . unless they threaten you." And if they do, you are released from the command to love and you may hate, acting it out in any form necessary.

Recently, I spoke to a conference on "The Soviet Threat." The scene was the Cannon Office Building on Capitol Hill. The words from Jesus' Sermon on the Mount about love for enemies seemed starkly out of place in a congressional conference room filled with the trappings of power. To speak of loving enemies there was to risk being thought naive, unrealistic, even foolish.

I confessed my insecurity and proceeded to raise the question of where all of our realism had brought us. The tough and pragmatic approach, so common in those hallowed halls of Congress, has brought us to the brink of nuclear war and the increasing likelihood of a destruction none of us can even begin to imagine.

"But what about the Russians?" continues to be the most commonly asked question when I begin to talk about the nuclear arms race. Even in the churches, the Soviet threat gets more attention than the words of Jesus. The question may indeed be the right one, but it is being asked in a tragically wrong way.

What *about* the Russians? What about the Russian people and their children? What would become of them in a nuclear war? They are among the hundreds of millions of God's children whom we seem quite ready to destroy in the name of freedom, democracy, and national security. What will our causes mean to us after they and we are all dead?

I recently received a letter from an Iowa farm woman, a mother of five, who described herself as a "seeking parent and citizen." The letter was filled with struggle around this question. She had supported President Reagan because of her fear of communism, but was now questioning that support because of an even greater fear of nuclear holocaust.

About the same time, I received a letter from a Catholic sister

who wrote of receiving a Christmas card from a friend studying in Moscow. On the card was a country snow scene in which children made snowmen, skated, and pushed sleds. Only the postmark made it clear that these were Soviet children and not American. These children too are our "enemies," or in current political jargon during a nuclear attack, "collateral damage."

The second letter began to answer the first. It is indeed the children—ours, the Russians', and the world's—who are most important in all this. Their future weighs most heavily on us as we watch the frightening escalation of nuclear arms.

But we've been taught not to think of Soviet children and families, but only of "Russians" and "communists," as if they have no children. Our enemies have become only fearful and threatening images.

Of course, the Russian people view us in America in much the same way. If they are the lumbering bear about to devour the world, we are the reckless cowboy willing to start a war for a fast buck. Both governments have behaved in a way that often adds substance to the caricatures.

The two giants play the same game with the nuclear arms race. Each accuses the other of escalations, each continues to escalate, and each uses the other's escalations as the justification for its own. It is a very old story—two superpowers out to shape the world in their own image, each accusing the other of doing what they themselves are doing. Neither cares much for freedom, for truth, or for peace. Each pursues its own self-interest through manipulation, power politics, and violence, then arrogantly proclaims its cause as righteous.

The gospel says, "Why do you see the speck that is in your brother's eye, but do not notice the log that is in your own eye? Or how can you say to your brother, 'Brother, let me take out the speck that is in your eye,' when you yourself do not see the log that is in your own eye? You hypocrite, first take the log out of your own eye, and then you will see clearly to take out the speck that is in your brother's eye" (Luke 6:41–42).

The people of El Salvador weep with the people of Poland and Afghanistan, as do the poor of South Korea, the Philippines, Chile, and every other place where military rule has been imposed, human rights trampled, people imprisoned, tortured, and killed, all with the support of the United States government or the Soviet Union.

8

We can expect the superpowers to slaughter the innocents and then attack each other for doing so. But we must refuse to take sides in this horrible and deadly hypocrisy, because behind the frightening images of Russians and Americans put out by both governments are real people—much more alike than they are different.

That's what the two governments want to keep their people from seeing. It's far easier to build fear and justify an arms race when we're facing threatening images of one another. It would be much harder to stir up popular support for increasing military budgets while showing people pictures of their enemies' children.

Life on a farm in the Ukraine is probably not too much different from life in Iowa. Mothers and fathers probably have the same concerns. Families in both places are likely to be more interested in living and building a better future for their children than they are in taking over somebody else's country.

Yet the farmers of the Ukraine are afraid of American imperialism just like farmers in Iowa are afraid of Soviet expansionism. They remember Vietnam as we do Afghanistan. They are told about U.S.-backed dictatorships in Latin America as we are told about Soviet domination in Eastern Europe. Both Ukranian and Iowan farmers worry about reports of how the other side is building up its nuclear arsenal and seeking military superiority.

Both look at their children. But what if they could see each other's children? What if they could work each other's fields, sit in each other's homes, eat at each other's tables? Their governments wouldn't want them to do that; because if they did, and if they laughed while watching their children play together, they might decide their differences weren't worth killing each other over—much less destroying the whole world for.

The question we should be asking is, "What has become of us?" What does it say about a people when they are prepared to commit mass murder against "enemy populations," whatever the reason? For some things, there are no reasons good enough.

In the Netherlands, where the European Peace Movement had its birth, the church's leadership has been clear. In a "Pastoral Letter to All Congregations" issued in November of 1980, the General Synod of the Netherlands Reformed Church stated:

Religious freedom and freedom of speech are among the essential achievements of our society for which we are thankful.

9

We have no illusions about political systems from which we wish to remain free and which we fear. But as believers we can say: We can live with our Lord no matter what the political system may be. In no case does the defense of our freedoms justify basing our security on the possible destruction of everything dear to us and to our opponents and on an assault on the creation.

We American Christians have elevated our nation, our system, and our principles above everything else, even the survival of the world. National loyalty has preempted our loyalty to the body of Christ. We have allowed thousands of nuclear warheads to be aimed at millions of Christians in the Soviet Union, with whom we share a common faith and Lord.

It is a historical irony that there were Catholics on the bombing crew that dropped the atomic bomb over Nagasaki, the first and largest Catholic city in Japan, and that ground zero—the target chosen for the bomb—was the prominent Urakami Cathedral, in which hundreds of worshipers were killed. That day thousands of Christians, including three orders of Catholic sisters, were destroyed.

Jesus never said that we would have no enemies nor that they would never be a threat. There is no lack of realism here. What Jesus offers is a new way to deal with our enemies, a different way of responding that has the potential to break the endless cycle of violence and retaliation that now threatens us all with ultimate violence.

The New Testament assures us that God loves us and has prepared a way for our reconciliation. Jesus gave his life on the cross that we might be made one with God and our fellow human beings. God chose this particular strategy for reconciling enemies. As Christians who have been made one through the sacrifice of our Lord, how can we be willing to kill sisters and brothers in a nuclear war?

The "realistic" approach has not worked so well. What is realism now, in the face of nuclear war? Which strategy must we now call naive? To continue to think that both real and imagined threats can be successfully countered with nuclear weapons is the height of unreality and naivete. Nuclear weapons cannot defend us; they can only destroy us. We have reached a dead end. To continue down the same road is to court disaster.

10

In the past, Jesus' simple exhortation to love our enemies has been given a place of reverent respect and then summarily dismissed as politically irrelevant. Some theologians have called it "a necessary but irrelevant ideal."

But in a time when all other solutions have brought the world to the brink of destruction, Jesus' plan for reconciliation may be our only viable option. If we fail to see a neighbor in the face of our enemy, the consequences will be unthinkable. To ignore Jesus now, in the name of political realism, is to allow our realism to destroy us.

The God of the Bible hungers for reconciliation and justice among all people. The people of God are to be known in the world for the same things for which their God is known. We are a people called to bear the very likeness of Christ in our life together and to reflect his character in the world. When we understand this, the nuclear question no longer remains a debate over political policy, military strategy, or national security, but for Christians it becomes a test of our worship.

Worship calls us back to the roots of our identity as the people of God. When we worship, we make a statement about where our security ultimately rests and we can stand before the world free of its false securities.

Since the earlier days of the church, an integral relationship has existed between worship and politics. Both raise the same questions: Whom do we love? Where is your loyalty? What is your deepest identity? Where is your security finally rooted? The central affirmation of the early Christians was, "Jesus is Lord." Their worship was understood politically by the authorities: If Jesus is Lord, then Caesar is not. If Jesus is Lord, then his followers have no other lords.

If we lose sight of this, we become uncertain of who we are and are easy prey to forces from the surrounding culture that are stronger than anything happening within the community of faith. In biblical language, we become vulnerable to false gods and have no strength to resist the idols that dominate our culture.

A church that places its trust in nuclear weapons is a church that no longer trusts in the Lord. We live in a nation in which we are told that to be secure we must place our faith in systems designed to incinerate the globe. Can we possibly agree with that and still say, "We are God's people, we belong to the Lord, and we place our security only in him"? The question in a nuclear age is

11

whether the church will demonstrate to whom it ultimately belongs.

The arms race is a crisis of faith because it presents a pronounced conflict between competing lords and rival saviors. It is at base a question of which lord we will serve—the God of the Bible or a national god that promises nuclear protection.

The clearest explanation of the church's long accommodation to nuclear preparation is that we have fallen into idolatry. We have forgotten who the true God is. An idol, in the biblical sense, is a false security. It can be anything or anyone that blocks our relationship to God and makes us feel secure in that which is not ultimate reality, not of God.

Biblically, the prophetic task is to name the idols and to call people back to the Lord. In order to free the captives, the captivity must be named. The prophets helped the people return to the Lord by reminding them that they were the people of God.

In both the Old and the New Testaments, conversion meant a change of Lords. It meant turning from idolatry to the true God. Such conversion never happens in a vacuum. People in the Bible turned to God in the midst of concrete historical events and choices: Moses resisting Egyptian bondage, Esther responding to threats to her people, and Paul speaking to the sin of racial separation. Repentance means to stop, turn around, and go in a different direction, and it was the call of the prophets, from the Old Testament to John the Baptist.

Genuine conversion and faith in God will always be tested in each new historical situation. The gospel must always be addressed to the particular time in which we live. There are always historical issues that shape the life of the church and in which the gospel is most truly at stake. Christian faith in our day must include a complete turn away from nuclear weapons.

It is a sin to build nuclear weapons. Yet, in this country, it is often the Christians who have their fingers on the nuclear button. The members of our churches are our generals and politicians, nuclear scientists and engineers, and the workers in the military industry. We pay for nuclear weapons with our taxes; we support the government's military and foreign policy grounded in the nuclear system; and we vote for politicians who will declare their willingness to use nuclear weapons.

Everyone is playing his or her small part in the arms race, and the small parts add up to a whole. Few Christians have thoroughly

appraised their responsibility for the consequences of their work, and the church has shown little pastoral concern for members' vocational ties to the arms race.

If the Christian's relationship to the nuclear system is at heart a spiritual issue, then it must be occasion for the church's pastoral care and discernment. To bring the nuclear question into the center of the church's life is not only a prophetic task; it is a pastoral obligation and an evangelistic necessity.

What is the church's pastoral responsibility for its members who are making, for example, Trident submarines that are capable of murdering millions? What was the responsibility of the German churches toward their members building the ovens for Auschwitz? If we love our brothers and sisters making the Tridents, and if the integrity of the church's worship is crucial to us, we cannot ignore this situation. Our spiritual lives are at stake.

Sin is a barrier to faith that impedes the Spirit's work and it must be confronted. The pastoral task is to offer a healing ministry to those who exhibit broken places and divided loyalties. Sin cannot be ignored or its pain and sorrow will come home both in its perpetrators and in their victims.

The willingness to produce, possess, and use nuclear weapons must be named for what it is: the chief manifestation of human sinfulness and rebellion against God in our age. The nuclear arms race is not just one issue among many: it is the overriding idolatry of our time.

Several years ago, a story appeared in a U.S. newspaper about the response of German children to the television docudrama "Holocaust." According to the report, the children were appalled and felt betrayed by the revelation of the murder of the Jewish people. They asked two kinds of questions of their parents. First: "Where were you when this was going on? What did you do? What did you say?" And then: "Where was the church? Where were the Christians? What did they do and say?"

A more massive holocaust is now being threatened. At some point in the future, if there is a future, the children may ask us, "What did you do about nuclear weapons? Where was the church?" What will our answer be?

For the church to change how it lives and relates to nuclear weapons will require more than well-intended words and fine statements. Already there are numerous statements and declarations

from almost every church body condemning nuclear weapons and calling for peace.

Unless Christian statements are accompanied by noncooperation at every level, our concern will have no credibility. What we say to our government should be rooted in what we ourselves are first of all willing to do.

The bright spot in the darkening picture of the nuclear arms race is the growing opposition to it. Christians in many places are being led to the firm conviction that repentance in a nuclear age means noncooperation—an absolute refusal to cooperate with the nation's preparations for nuclear war.

One veteran political reporter told me recently, "There is no question that a peace movement is emerging in opposition to nuclear weapons. And the foundation of it is in the churches." It would be a divine irony if an evil as great as the prospect of nuclear war would become an occasion for the renewal of the church. Yet that seems to be exactly what is happening.

We are witnessing the beginnings of a conversion in the churches—a conversion to peace. The signs of it are everywhere. It is a movement of faith and conscience, not just a political phenomenon. Where the commitment to peace is emerging, so is Bible study, prayer, the renewal of worship, and community. What began as a few lonely voices crying out in the wilderness has become a visible movement in the life of the church.

The new Christian peace movement is taking hold at the local level and is deeply ecumenical. Catholics are working beside Mennonites, evangelicals with mainline Protestants. The urgent matter of peace has the potential to unite the denominations more than anything has in years. It is increasingly important that this unity of Christian conscience be demonstrated publicly.

Church leaders are speaking out, many for the first time. Local congregations are reexamining their life and ministry in light of the nuclear question. Christians are leaving military-related jobs. More are refusing to pay war taxes. Many are becoming involved in nonviolent direct action. Some are committing civil disobedience and are going to jail.

The prospect of many Christians and their churches turning to peace would certainly pose a powerful political challenge to current government policies. A great opportunity for collective Christian witness is emerging. The convergence of a number of significant events and plans suggests that some Spirit movement is afoot.

14

A comparable movement took root in the United States in the last century. Little more than a hundred years ago, black people in this country were considered nothing more than property to be bought and sold. This system of owning other human beings was not believed by the vast majority of people to be inconsistent with their most basic human and religious values.

In the 1840s and 1850s, however, many people came to understand slavery as immoral and a contradiction of their faith in God. During those years a revival, marked by many conversions and a mighty outpouring of evangelical faith, swept the United States. Central to this revival was an unswerving opposition to slavery.

Christians began to preach that to turn to Christ meant to turn from slavery, a principal sign of rebellion against God in their time. Opposition to slavery came to be seen as a fruit of Christian conversion. For these Christians, slavery was an evil so great that it challenged the very integrity of their faith. They came to be called abolitionists.

Like slavery in the 19th century, the nuclear arms race challenges everything we say we believe about Jesus Christ. As the danger of the nuclear arms race steadily grows, the need for this movement of Christian conscience to oppose the deadly momentum is increasingly clear.

In the winter of 1980, a small circle of Christians who saw that need began to meet together. We came from five different groups: the Fellowship of Reconciliation, New Call to Peacemaking, Pax Christi, World Peacemakers, and Sojourners.

Our gathering was truly an ecumenical event: from Protestant, Catholic, and historic peace churches; evangelical and liberal theological traditions; both pacifist and nonpacifist. The sessions were centered in prayer and theological reflection on our perilous situation. We asked how the new stream of Christian peacemaking now flowing here and there might become a mighty river of fervent prayer and costly action for peace in our time.

It became clear that we needed more than another statement. The idea of a "covenant" emerged, perhaps because that was what was occurring among us. We were becoming bound together for the sake of abolishing nuclear weapons. The covenant would not be a new organization but a new relationship among Christians for the sake of peace.

The historical precedent of the 19th-century abolitionist

movement had become a great inspiration to us and served as an example of how faith could be applied to a fundamental moral question.

What emerged we called the "New Abolitionist Covenant." It expresses the deep conviction for peace that many of us feel. In its first year, more than one million covenants have been ordered, printed, and distributed. I offer it here as the summation of my hope that the power of the gospel might turn our nation away from its present destructive course and take us a step closer to peace.

THE NEW ABOLITIONIST COVENANT

In the name of God, let us abolish nuclear weapons.

The Christian faith must be demonstrated anew in each historical moment. The gospel is always addressed to the time in which we live. Christians must find ways to relate timeless but timely faith to their own situation, showing what they will embrace and what they will refuse because of Jesus Christ.

Some historical issues stand out as particularly urgent among the church's fundamental concerns. These overarching moral questions intrude upon the routine of the church's life and plead for the compassion and courage of God's people everywhere. Slavery was such a question for Christians in the 19th century. The nuclear arms race is such a question today.

Thousands of Christians from diverse traditions came to see that slavery was an evil that challenged the very integrity of their faith. They believed that for any person to claim ownership of another human being denied that each person is loved by God and made in God's image. These Christians began to preach that to follow Christ meant to turn away from the institution of slavery, to refuse to cooperate with it, and to work for its abolition. Though this seemed like an absurd, unattainable goal, they insisted that God required nothing less. They came to be called abolitionists.

Christian acceptance of nuclear weapons has brought us also to a crisis of faith. The nuclear threat is not just a political issue any more than slavery was: It is a question that challenges our worship of God and our commitment to Jesus Christ. In other words, the growing prospect of nuclear war presents us with more than a test of survival; it confronts us with a test of faith.

Nuclear war is total war. Unlimited in their violence, indiscriminate in their victims, uncontrollable in their devastation, nuclear weapons have brought humanity to a historical crossroads. More than at any previous time in history, the alternatives are peace or destruction. In nuclear war there are no winners.

We are Christians who now see that the nuclear arms race is

more than a question of public policy. We believe that the wholesale destruction threatened by these weapons makes their possession and planned use an offense against God and humanity, no matter what the provocation or political justification. Through deliberation and prayer we have become convinced that Jesus' call to be peacemakers urgently needs to be renewed in the churches and made specific by a commitment to abolish nuclear weapons and to find a new basis of national security.

As the foundation of national security, nuclear weapons are idolatrous. As a method of defense, they are suicidal. To believe that nuclear weapons can solve international problems is the greatest illusion and the height of naivete.

The threatened nuclear annihilation of whole populations in the name of national security is an evil we can no longer accept. At stake is whether we trust in God or the bomb. We can no longer confess Jesus as Lord and depend on nuclear weapons to save us. Conversion in our day must include turning away from nuclear weapons as we turn to Jesus Christ.

The building and threatened use of nuclear weapons is a sin against God, God's creatures, and God's creation. There is no theology or doctrine in the traditions of the church that could ever justify nuclear war. Whether one begins with pacifism or with the just war doctrine, nuclear weapons are morally unacceptable.

The God of the Bible loves the poor and demands justice for the oppressed. To continue to spend hundreds of billions of dollars in preparation for war while millions go hungry is a grievous failure of compassion and an affront to God. But by God's grace our hearts can be softened in order to heed the biblical vision of converting the weapons of war into instruments of peace.

When nuclear war is thinkable, folly and madness have become the accepted political wisdom. It is time for the church to bear witness to the absolute character of the word of God which is finally our only hope in breaking the hold of the political realities in whose name we march to oblivion.

In times past, Christians from many traditions joined together to oppose great social sin and point the way to change. We believe the growing prospect of nuclear war now calls for such unity of Christian response.

Our response as Christians begins with repentance for almost four decades of accepting nuclear weapons. Repentance in a nu-

clear age means non-cooperation with preparations for nuclear war and the turning of our lives toward peace.

Whatever we say to the government must be based first on what we have publicly committed ourselves to do and not to do in the face of a nuclear war. The fruits of our repentance will be made visible in our active witness and leadership for peace.

No longer trusting in nuclear weapons, we refuse to cooperate with preparations for total war. Trusting anew in God, we will begin cooperating with one another in preparations for peace. We covenant to work together for peace and join with one another to make these vital commitments.

1. PRAYER

We covenant together to pray. Prayer is at the heart of Christian peacemaking. Prayer can change us and our relationships. Prayer begins in confession of our own sin and extends into intercession for our enemies, bringing them closer to us. We will pray, asking God to hold back the nuclear devastation so that we may turn from our folly. Through prayer the reality of Christ's victory over nuclear darkness can be established in our lives and free us to participate in Christ's reconciling work in the world.

2. EDUCATION

We covenant together to learn. Our ignorance and passivity must be transformed into awareness and responsibility. We must act together to dispel our blindness and hardness of heart. We will ground ourselves in the biblical and theological basis for peacemaking. We will become thoroughly and deeply informed about the danger of the arms race and the steps to be taken toward peace. We will become aware of the churches' teachings on the matter of nuclear warfare.

3. SPIRITUAL EXAMINATION

We covenant together to examine ourselves. To shed the light of the gospel on the nuclear situation, we will examine the basic decisions of our personal lives in regard to our jobs, lifestyles, taxes, and relationships, to see where and how we are cooperating with

preparations for nuclear war. The church should be concerned with the spiritual well-being of its members whose livelihoods are now dependent on the nuclear war system. We will undertake a thorough pastoral evaluation of the life of our congregations in all these matters.

4. PEACE EVANGELISM

We covenant together to spread the gospel of peace. We will speak out and reach out to our friends, families, and Christian brothers and sisters about the dangers of the nuclear arms buildup and the urgency of peace. We will take the message to the other churches in our neighborhoods, to our denominations, and to the decision-making bodies of our churches on every level. The cause of peace will be preached from our pulpits, lifted up in our prayers, and made part of our worship. We will offer faith in God as an alternative to trust in the bomb.

5. PUBLIC WITNESS

We covenant together to bear public witness. Our opposition to nuclear weapons and the imperative of peace will be taken into the public arena: to our workplaces, to our community and civic organizations, to the media, to our governmental bodies, to the streets, and to the nuclear weapons facilities themselves. A prayerful presence for peace needs to be established at all those places where nuclear weapons are researched, produced, stored, and deployed, and where decisions are made to continue the arms race.

The gatherings, events, and institutions of the churches will also become important places for our public witness. We will make our convictions known at all these places, especially on significant dates in the church calendar and on August 6 and 9, the anniversaries of the bombings of Hiroshima and Nagasaki.

6. NUCLEAR DISARMAMENT

We covenant together to work to stop the arms race. In light of our faith, we are prepared to live without nuclear weapons. We will publicly advocate a nuclear weapons freeze as the first step toward abolishing nuclear weapons altogether. We will act in our

local communities to place the call for a nuclear weapons freeze on the public agenda. We will press our government and the other nuclear powers to halt all further testing, production, and deployment of nuclear weapons, and then move steadily and rapidly to eliminate them completely.

We recognize a call from God to make these simple commitments and, through the grace of God, we hope to fulfill them. Rooted in the gospel of Jesus Christ and strengthened by the hope that comes from faith, we covenant together to make peace.

HOW TO USE THIS COVENANT

The purpose of the covenant is to place before the churches the abolition of nuclear weapons as an urgent matter of faith. The nuclear threat is a theological issue, a confessional matter, a spiritual question, and is so important it must be brought into the heart of the church's life.

This is not a statement to sign but a covenant to be acted upon. In other words, the purpose is not to gain signatures, but to encourage response. Find at least two or three others to spend an hour, a day, or a weekend with this covenant. Gather with your friends to make the covenant and then take it to your congregations, groups, and communities. We hope to see the covenant distributed widely, used locally, and result in action.

The covenant should be dealt with in a community process. These commitments cannot be carried out alone. Therefore, we encourage people to enter into supportive relationships with others for the purpose of prayer, reflection, and action. Our hope is that the covenant can strengthen existing groups working for peace and help create new ones.

For more information about this covenant and for a guide on how to use it, contact any one of the following groups, whose addresses are listed in Appendix A of this book: Fellowship of Reconciliation, New Call to Peacemaking, Pax Christi, World Peacemakers, and Sojourners. An inter–faith version of the covenant is available from the Fellowship of Reconciliation.

PART I.

OUR PERILOUS SITUATION:
The Nuclear Arms Race and Its Consequences

From only two nuclear weapons in 1945 to over 50,000 in 1981, the nuclear arms race has escalated out of control and threatens human survival. Intense debate surrounds issues of security, defense, and power. What are the answers? Who is the leader of the arms race? What is the Soviet threat? How does the international political climate affect nuclear strategy? What can be done about proliferation? What are the human and social costs of nuclear weapons? Articles in this section explore the facts and fictions and suggest directions for response.

ULTIMATE TERRORISM:
The Real Meaning of Nuclear Strategies
by Richard Barnet

The era of nuclear terrorism began with an attack without warning on the civilian populations of Hiroshima and Nagasaki. The threat to keep killing hostages ended World War II in a matter of days. Now, every American is a hostage and a target, and so is every Russian. According to estimates of the National Security Council, 140 million Americans would probably die within days after a full-scale Soviet nuclear attack, and more than 100 million Russians would die in a U.S. retaliatory attack. Hundreds of millions of defenseless men, women, and children in the Soviet Union and the United States have no control whatsoever over the decisions of their leaders to go to war.

When a man with a gun threatens to shoot the passengers of an airplane unless some prisoners are released or a ransom is paid, we call that terrorism. When leaders threaten millions of deaths—and every nuclear weapon targeted on an enemy city is just such a threat—we call it strategy.

Thirty-five nations possess nuclear weapons or can acquire them within months. The Ford administration predicted that more than double that number would have nuclear weapons by the end of the century. There is no secret; a Princeton undergraduate designed a bomb that could be built with parts available from a local hardware store. There is no shortage of fissionable material; significant amounts have already been diverted from "peaceful" reactors. The only secret to the atomic bomb is the actual number such countries as Israel, Egypt, South Africa, and Taiwan may have.

There is a private market for nuclear weapons just as there has been for all other kinds of weapons. We must expect they will soon be in the hands of terrorist groups and criminal syndicates—anyone who has ready cash and a strong motive to terrorize others.

For the present, however, the practitioners of nuclear terror-

ism are concentrated in Washington and Moscow. The nuclear arsenal contains thousands of weapons more than 50 times the size of the Hiroshima bomb, designed to incinerate or poison the population of any large city. The Soviet Union has somewhat fewer than the U.S., but the killing power on both sides is so enormous that, despite the professional alarmism of the military in both countries, the difference is without military or political significance.

The United States has about 3,000 of these weapons in submarines deployed off the Soviet coast. According to former Secretary of Defense Robert S. McNamara, 100 such weapons would kill 37 million Soviet citizens and destroy almost two-thirds of Soviet industry, so there is no way the Soviet Union could "win" a nuclear war even in the unlikely event that it could destroy all our land-based missiles and airplanes in a surprise attack. But despite the fact that the United States long ago ran out of large Soviet population centers and major military installations that could be added to the target list, our government continues to turn out three nuclear weapons a day. The steady Soviet buildup also continues.

President Reagan has called for an annual 7 percent increase in military appropriations above the inflation rate, which means that between now and 1986 American taxpayers will have spent $1.5 trillion on preparations for war. Most of this money is for "conventional forces"—the B1 bomber, the M-1 tank, a new generation of battleships, and pay raises for soldiers. But nuclear weapons, such as the cruise missile, are becoming standard equipment throughout these forces too. The Soviets will spend comparable amounts.

Both superpowers are poised at a new stage of the arms race that promises to make the world of the 1970s look, in retrospect, like a Quaker village. The peril arises not so much from the numbers of new weapons being stockpiled, but from their character. Far more than their ancestors (most of which are still around), the new weapons are specifically designed to fight and win a nuclear war. Improved accuracy of guidance systems and advanced computers foster the illusion of "controlled nuclear warfare."

According to the 1977 Strategic Survey of the International Institute for Strategic Studies, a London research organization with close ties to military and intelligence circles, the "greater theoretical ability to fight a strategic nuclear war at controlled levels may increase pressure to launch a preemptive counterforce strike in a

crisis"—that is, a surprise attack might "prevent" the other side from making war.

The fear is real. Military planners interpret the deployment of counterforce weapons as evidence of an intention to strike first, since such weapons have no use unless they are used first. If the United States builds 300 new mobile MX missiles (at a cost of $25 billion) it will, theoretically, have the capability by the mid-1980s to knock out 90 percent of the Soviet land-based missiles—even after a Soviet surprise attack. And it will still have 6,000 city-busting warheads left to drop on the Soviet Union.

The Pentagon regularly provides Congress with equally frightening scenarios of what the Soviets could do. Such a situation makes both sides extremely nervous and provides the impetus for hair-trigger responses and desperate searches for technological breakthroughs that might finally promise victory in the nuclear age.

As land-based missiles become more vulnerable to attack, the response is not, as one might have supposed, to abandon them and rely on much less vulnerable submarine-launched missiles. Rather, the response is to consider digging hundreds of expensive holes to confuse the enemy, and to adopt "launch on warning" strategies. If our radar is again confused by a flock of geese, as it has been in the past, the Strategic Air Command may start World War III out of an excess of caution.

So after 35 years of nuclear terrorism—the conventional term is "balance of terror"—the American people, the Russian people, and the hundreds of millions of potential victims of nuclear war in other countries are far worse off than they were when it all began. After spending almost $2 trillion on the military since 1945, the United States has much less security than it had at the end of World War II. The Soviet leaders have sacrificed the hopes of their people by choosing to divert scarce resources to building a formidable nuclear war machine. Seeing no alternative, they have managed to match every major technological development of the United States, and they proclaim every intention to keep matching us in the future. When we have spent the next $1.5 trillion, we will have no more security than we have now; we will almost certainly have less, for the world will have become even more dangerous than it is today.

How did it happen? Albert Einstein, who persuaded President

27

Franklin D. Roosevelt to build the atom bomb and regretted it for the rest of his life, had the answer. At the dawn of the nuclear age, he declared, "The unleashed power of the atom bomb has changed everything except our way of thinking."

Most people on the planet have no notion of what a nuclear war would be like. Americans have not experienced a war of any kind on this continent in more than a century. Russians old enough to remember the incredible destruction of their country in World War II have a better intimation of the catastrophe towards which we are drifting. But everyone who contemplates the future depends on historical analogies from simpler times and falls into the trap of thinking about stockpiles of city-destroying bombs as if they were protection: If only we have enough of them, we will be safe.

But everything has changed. There is no defense. There is no place to hide. There is no victory. There are some in the Reagan Administration, however, such as Richard Pipes of the National Security Council and Deputy Under Secretary of Defense Thomas K. Jones, who have argued that a nuclear war is fightable and survivable. Pipes has stated that a nuclear exchange "would be like an amputation—traumatic but not necessarily fatal." Jones has suggested that if civilians "dig a hole, cover it with a couple of doors, and then throw three feet of dirt on top," then "everyone's going to [survive] if there are enough shovels to go around." But anyone who cares to seriously ponder the effects of a single nuclear bomb exploding over a city cannot help but conclude that even a "small" nuclear war would be a catastrophe beyond imagination.

"Mankind must put an end to the arms race or the arms race will put an end to man," John F. Kennedy said, and every other recent president has echoed his words. Why, then, does the arms race continue? Powerful political and economic forces support the arms race in both the United States and the Soviet Union: millions of bureaucrats in and out of military uniform who go to their offices every day to build nuclear weapons or to plan nuclear war; millions of workers whose jobs depend upon the system of nuclear terrorism; scientists and engineers who are hired to look for the "technological breakthrough" that can finally provide "security"; contractors who are unwilling to forego easy profits; warrior intellectuals who deal in threats and count on wars. But undergirding the entire military-industrial complex are the myths that can kill us—that peace requires preparation for war, that leaders are too

sensible to start a war in a world armed to the teeth, and that the more terrible the weapons, the more sensible the leaders will be.

If the United Nations were to install lie detectors in the Oval Office and the Kremlin and test each day for secret intentions to start a nuclear war, our leaders and their leaders would doubtless pass with flying colors. But the absence of intent provides no assurance that it will not happen. Neither the Kaiser nor any other national leader bargained in 1914 for the devastation of World War I. Hitler did not have the denouement of World War II in mind when he attacked Poland in 1939.

The fact is that nuclear weapons are now integrated into every phase of the U.S. and Soviet war machines and that in the United States, at least—we don't know much about Soviet planning—the use of such weapons has been considered or proposed at the highest levels:

• In 1954, according to former French Foreign Minister George Bidault, Secretary of State John Foster Dulles offered "one or more atomic bombs to be dropped on Communist Chinese territory near the Indochina border" and two atomic bombs for use against the Viet Minh at Dienbienphu.

• Former President Eisenhower later disclosed that on entering the White House in 1953 he had "let it be known that if there was not going to be an armistice [in Korea] we were not going to be bound by the kind of weapons that we would use. . . . I don't mean to say that we'd have used those great big things and destroyed cities, but we would use them enough to win and we, of course, would have tried to keep them on military targets, not civil targets."

• At the time of the 1962 missile crisis, the United States initiated a blockade of Cuba and prepared for invasion, knowing that there were substantial risks of escalation that could lead to nuclear war. "We all agreed in the end," Robert F. Kennedy said afterward, "that if the Russians were ready to go to nuclear war over Cuba, they were ready to go to nuclear war, and that was that. So we might as well have the showdown then as six months later." President Kennedy thought the risks of nuclear war were considerable and that such a war would produce "150 million fatalities in the first eighteen hours."

• In the summer of 1961, the Kennedy Administration seriously contemplated the use of nuclear weapons in the Berlin crisis.

Presidential Assistant Arthur Schlesinger, Jr., wrote that "everyone agreed that the Soviet blockade of West Berlin would have to be countered first by a western thrust along the Autobahn. But there was disagreement between those, like General Norstad (Supreme Commander of NATO), who wanted the probe in order to create a situation where the West could use nuclear weapons, and those, like Kennedy and McNamara, who wanted the probe in order to postpone that situation. . . . Everyone agreed that we might eventually have to go on to nuclear war. . . ."

• In 1968, General William C. Westmoreland, commander of the U.S. forces in Vietnam, convened "a small secret group" in Saigon to "study . . . the nuclear defense of Khe Sahn, a besieged Marine base then in imminent danger of being overrun." Although he recognized "the controversial nature of the subject," the field commander who ran the war for so many years still believes that "the use of a few small tactical nuclear weapons in Vietnam—or even the threat of them—might have brought the war to an end."

• General Douglas MacArthur proposed using nuclear weapons in Korea; the Joint Chiefs advised Eisenhower that Quemoy and Matsu, two islands off the coast of China, could not be held without using nuclear weapons, and such an option was seriously considered by the National Security Council; in March 1961, according to President Kennedy's closest aide, Theodore Sorenson, a majority of the Joint Chiefs "appeared to favor the use of tactical nuclear weapons on the ground" in Laos: "If massive Red troops were then mobilized, nuclear bombings would be threatened and, if necessary, carried out. If the Soviets then intervened, we should be prepared to accept the possibility of general war."

• On October 25, 1973, President Nixon put all U.S. military units on standby alert in what he called "the most ominous big-power test of will and nerve since the Cuban missile crisis in 1962." Though the alert was widely viewed in the United States as a political ploy to divert public attention from the Watergate scandal, the placing of nuclear forces in an advanced state of readiness was precisely the sort of situation that could invite a preemptive strike.

Any of the above crises could have resulted in nuclear war had the Russians reacted differently, or had the president not rejected military advice. There is no reason to be confident that the inhibitions of U.S. and Soviet leaders, which caused them to pull back from the brink of war on these occasions, will prevail in all

future circumstances. As presidents become weaker—we have not had a two-term president since Eisenhower—they are likely to find it difficult to resist unanimous military advice, especially if the country is awash in hawkish propaganda and no peace movement exists to offer resistance. (If we are to believe H. R. Haldeman's memoirs, the massive antiwar demonstrations in Washington were a major factor in dissuading Nixon from issuing a nuclear threat against Vietnam in 1970.)

The turmoil of Southern Africa, the Arab-Israeli conflict, the internal struggles of strategic Iran, and potential crises in many other places around the world provide the makings of new U.S.-Soviet confrontations. When these occur, we will not always be able to count on the Soviets to back down; their remarkable record of restraint in crisis—even in those crises they provoke—reflects the relative military weakness they suffered in the past.

Having achieved rough parity with U.S. military power, their national security managers are now much more likely to think like their U.S. counterparts: "We can't afford to back down and be exposed as a pitiful, helpless giant." "If they want war, we might as well have it now as later."

Twenty years ago, thousands marched to protest atmospheric nuclear testing because people feared that strontium-90 was contaminating their children's milk. After a period of complacency, public concern has been rekindled by the U.S.'s refusal to ratify SALT II and the Reagan Administration's belligerent rhetoric, and the people are once again organizing en masse to protest the nuclear arms race. Not a single missile has been dismantled, weapons stockpiles on both sides have continued to grow, and most of us no longer accept the notion that the "experts" are in control.

There is no hope of reversing the arms race until the American people reject the myths of "national security," regain contact with reality, and reinstate the question of nuclear terrorism as a political and moral issue.

It will take an intellectual leap to recognize that nuclear terrorism is a system to be abolished, not one to be tinkered with. U.S.-Soviet arms negotiations have failed because they began from the premise that the nuclear arms race should be controlled rather than ended. Nuclear terrorism, like slavery in the last century, is an evil system that cries out for abolition.

THE DEADLY RACE:
A Look at U.S.–USSR Nuclear Capabilities and Intentions
by Robert Aldridge

As of 1982, the United States has about 10,000 strategic nuclear bombs and another 22,000 tactical nuclear bombs. At the same time, the Soviets have approximately 7,000 strategic and 15,000 tactical.

Strategic nuclear weapons are those which would be used in a major confrontation between the United States and the Soviet Union. Tactical nuclear weapons are intended for theater conflicts as might occur in Europe, Korea, or on the oceans. The dividing line is becoming fuzzy, but basically the difference between strategic and tactical nuclear weapons has to do with the range from which they can be delivered. Explosive power is not a differentiating factor, because many tactical weapons are more powerful than strategic weapons.

It will confine this discussion to strategic weapons because they are the most capable of destroying the homelands of the Soviet Union and the United States, and have the most influence on the so-called balance of power. This is not to minimize the danger of tactical weapons, however, because even the most limited of nuclear exchanges would most likely escalate to total thermonuclear war.

The three aspects of the strategic nuclear triad are land, sea, and air. In the U.S., as of 1982, the land leg consists of 1,052 intercontinental ballistic missiles (ICBMs) in underground silos, 550 of which are the Minuteman III vehicles, which were originally equipped with three 170-kiloton warheads that can be directed against separate targets. (A kiloton is the explosive force equal to 1,000 tons of TNT.) But 300 of those missiles are being updated to carry three 335-kiloton warheads each.

The air wing consists of 316 intercontinental B-52 bombers. More than 200 of these aircraft are the later "G" and "H" models

which comprise the backbone of the Strategic Air Command. Each bomber can be equipped with up to 20 nuclear-tipped missiles which can be launched against ground targets, the latest of which are the air-launched cruise missiles.

The sea leg is comprised of 31 Poseidon submarines, each carrying 16 submarine-launched ballistic missiles (SLBMs). Twelve of these subs have been converted to carry the new Trident-1 missiles loaded with eight 100-kiloton warheads each. The remaining 19 boats carry Poseidon missiles equipped with 14 individually targeted 40-kiloton bombs. These submarines carry over half the United States's inventory of strategic warheads. In addition, the first Trident submarine is scheduled to be operational during late 1982, and it will carry 24 Trident-1 missiles.

This vast array of power does not satisfy the American military. Its thirst for bigger and better weapons is supported by a significant number of large business firms that reap lavish profits from weapons contracts. Virtually every leg of the strategic triad is undergoing modernization.

A historical review of the nuclear arms race in any public library will reveal that it has been an action/reaction cycle, with the United States leading in virtually every escalation. It has been fraught with fictitious gaps—the bomber gap, the missile gap—which have frightened Americans into supporting further arms buildups. But contrary to what we have been led to believe, the United States holds a five-year lead over the Soviet Union in most technologies and even more in others. This has been true for almost four decades, as illustrated in Table 1.

Up until the mid-1960s, the arms race focused mainly on quantity. Just as the Soviet Union was starting its strategic missile buildup in earnest about 1966, the Pentagon initiated a strategic exercise study which eventually led to the B-1 bomber, Trident submarine and missile, cruise missile, and the MX mobile ICBM.

In 1968 the defense secretary announced that enough was enough as far as quantity was concerned. He said that henceforth the U.S. effort would be on making the weapons work better. This sounded much more plausible to Congress and the public, who were beginning to question the wisdom of building more missiles when both superpowers had the capability to destroy each other many times over. And so the arms race continued.

The first U.S. "quality" improvement was to put many bombs

Escalation of the Arms Race

	U.S. (Action)	USSR (Reaction)
First nuclear chain reaction	12/2/42	12/24/46
First atom bomb exploded	7/16/45	8/23/49
First H-bomb exploded	11/1/52	8/12/53
European alliances in effect	8/24/49 (NATO)	5/14/55 (Warsaw Pact)
Tactical nuclear weapons in Europe	1954	1957
Accelerated buildup of strategic missiles	1961	1966
First supersonic bomber	1960	1975
First ballistic-missile-launching submarine	1960 (Polaris)	1968 (Yankee)
First solid rocket fuel used in missiles	1960	1968
Multiple warheads on missiles	1964	1973
Penetration aids on missiles	1964	None to date
High-speed re-entry bodies (warheads)	1970	1975
Multiple independently targeted re-entry vehicles on missiles	1970	1975
Computerized guidance on missiles	1970	1975

on one missile so it could destroy numerous targets. Thus the U.S. nuclear stockpile of bombs actually continued to increase, while the missiles remained constant. The Soviet Union continued to produce missiles in quantity until the Strategic Arms Limitation Talks (SALT) I agreements were signed in 1970. Nonetheless, the U.S. maintained a numerical lead in actual warheads.

Since 1970 the United States has been forging ahead in the race to improve arms "quality" and developing maneuvering warheads that can "see" their target as they approach and correct course as necessary; navigation satellites that will be able to give missiles very precise fixes to correct course during flight; and miniaturized cruise missiles that cannot be verified due to their small size and low-flying ability.

The Pentagon is also expending a herculean effort to monitor, globally, all Soviet forces by means of every conceivable type and location of sensor, and to develop communication systems of every frequency, technology, and location. These and numerous other programs are leading America toward a disarming first-strike capability over the Russians. The Soviet Union, of course, is trying to keep pace.

Miniaturization is the key to much of the latest "quality" dimensions of the arms race. Miniaturization of nuclear components made it possible to put many bombs on one missile. Multiple individually targeted re-entry vehicles, more commonly called MIRVs, were put on the land-based Minuteman III and submarine-launched Poseidon missiles in 1970. It was the MIRVs for Poseidon on which I started working in 1965.

Miniaturization of electronics led to installing computers in missiles to attain better accuracy. That has given the smaller American warheads a greater potential for destroying enemy military targets than their bigger but less precise Soviet counterparts. Although some of the latest Soviet missiles have been reported to have achieved the same accuracy as the U.S. Minuteman III, that was during tests when ideal conditions were chosen. When that date is extrapolated to an operational accuracy during a wartime environment and tension, the precision would be very much less.

Maneuvering re-entry vehicles (MARVs), like MIRVs, were at first justified to evade enemy interceptors during the final seconds of flight. But it was on this project that I first recognized the trend toward greater accuracy.

In addition to MIRVs and MARVs, warhead miniaturization has led to replacing the bomb on Minuteman III re-entry bodies with one of twice the power without increasing overall weight and size. The guidance platforms on Trident-1 submarine-launched missiles use a fix on a star to correct trajectory after being launched. The NAVSTAR Global Positioning Satellite network will soon provide very accurate in-flight corrections for missile navigation computers. The command date buffer computer controller allows changing targets for the entire Minuteman III force in just about twenty minutes. That used to take a day and a half.

A new dimension to the strategic triad has also quietly slipped into development and production: the cruise missile. This species of weapon has been described by one U.S. senator as a "fourth leg of the triad" which is a "provocative arms control problem."

Cruise missiles are an outgrowth of the German buzz-bombs of World War II and are similar to small, pilotless aircraft after the wings and tail unfold. A miniaturized jet engine propels them at subsonic speeds for distances that can exceed 2,000 miles. They can be launched from airplanes, trucks, and surface ships as well as from submerged submarines. They avoid obstacles while flying at treetop height to defeat radar. Cruise missiles will be so numerous they will saturate enemy defenses. A guidance system that follows the earth's terrain like a map gives this missile almost 100 percent kill probability against hard targets. New versions under consideration include a supersonic concept that will be able to outrun and outmaneuver interceptors if it is detected.

To supplement present silo-based ICBMs, the Air Force wants to build a huge mobile missile called MX. It will be more than twice as big as present Minuteman missiles. The problem seems to be in how to obtain that mobility that is supposed to keep it hidden from the Soviets. Numerous schemes for basing this weapon—ranging from air-launched to shell games on the desert and even strapped to sides of submarines—have been going on for over a decade with still no solution in sight. MX is a missile without a home.

Another aspect of MX unrelated to mobility is the zero-miss accuracy proposed. It will be able to destroy Soviet missile silos over intercontinental range.

The Trident missile/submarine combination is the most deadly weapons system ever designed. The Trident submarine looks not

unlike a Polaris/Poseidon boat from the outside, except that it is much larger. Rather than carrying 16 missiles, it will contain 24. Construction has been plagued with problems, and the first ship is more than two years late. It will be operational in 1982. Fourteen have been approved, and Navy charts indicate that the U.S. will have 30 by the end of this century.

There are two generations of Trident missiles. These are being built near my home in Santa Clara, California. Trident I is the same size as the Poseidon: 34 feet long and 74 inches in diameter. Whereas Poseidon can fly 2,500 nautical miles with a full load of re-entry bombs, Trident I can carry its warheads a distance of 4,000 nautical miles. (One nautical mile equals 1.15 statute miles.) Although Trident I does not now have the accuracy to destroy missile silos, the technology has been developed that will allow it to do so. It will be backfitted into at least 12 of the Poseidon submarines by late 1982, as well as placed on the new Trident submarines.

Development has started on the Trident II missile. Being much larger than Trident I, it will fit only in the new Trident submarines. Its range will be 6,000 nautical miles or more. Trident II will be able to carry approximately 17 precision maneuvering re-entry bodies with an explosive punch of 100,000 tons of TNT.

Let us consider what all this means. On each Trident submarine equipped with 24 Trident II missiles, which in turn have 17 warheads capable of being individually targeted and with terminal homing, there is the capacity to destroy 408 different hard targets or cities, each with a blast five times that which devastated Hiroshima. That is a lot of death and destruction to put under the control of one submarine commander.

The Trident II missile in the Trident submarine will be the ultimate weapon, though a similar argument can be made for the mobile MX missile. In conjunction with a profound system of computer-integrated antisubmarine warfare weapons and sensors, Trident will give the United States first-strike capability.

In the years since the nuclear age dawned with a blaze of light across the New Mexico desert, we Americans have been led to believe that our country would use nuclear weapons only "defensively," to deter aggression. In reality, however, Pentagon ambitions have been seeking the capability to fight and win a nuclear war, an offensive posture. This fact is evident from the developing nature of the weapons described above.

A deterrence or defensive strategy is based on threatening massive and unacceptable retaliation against an aggressor if the aggressor strikes first. It is based on the ability to strike back against cities and factories that are sprawling targets and are vulnerable to any nuclear blast. The weapons do not have to be accurate or sophisticated.

On the other hand, an offensive strategy for winning a nuclear war is based on striking the enemy nuclear forces first. It is called "counterforce," which means to counter the enemy's military forces. The ability to inflict a disarming or unanswerable "first strike" is the ultimate in counterforce. Extremely accurate missiles are needed for such a war-fighting strategy because the military targets are often underground and protected by concrete and steel. These missiles also require very intricate systems for timing, target reselection, navigation, and control.

War-fighting was accelerated under the Nixon administration. In 1974, when he was secretary of defense, James Schlesinger alluded to the need for a better war-fighting capability while implying that the U.S. strategy provided only for massive retaliation against Soviet cities. But when questioned during Senate hearings, he said, "We have no *announced* counterforce strategy. . . . We have a new targeting doctrine that emphasizes selectivity and flexibility" (emphasis added). He also admitted that most of the 25,000 strategic targets were not cities at all, but were military targets such as bomber bases and missile silos, and that that had been the case for some years. This counterforce (renamed "countervailing") policy was most recently confirmed at the highest level, by the Carter administration's 1980 Presidential Directive 59.

"Selectivity and flexibility" has opened the door for limited nuclear war by making it appear acceptable. It sounds more humane to be aiming at military targets, but, for the short period of time a nuclear war would last, that is an aggressive stance. There is no point in destroying missile silos, underground command posts, bomber bases, submarine pens, and the like unless they are destroyed before they serve their one-shot purpose. That means striking first, which is a gross departure from deterrence. Furthermore, the types of weapons needed for limited nuclear war are the same as those which would make an all-out first strike possible.

The first requirement for war-fighting is a missile force accurate enough to destroy enemy land-based military targets. That is

especially significant because 75 percent of the Soviet Union's nuclear weapons are in missile silos. Its intercontinental bombers are based on land, and 85 percent of its missile-launching submarines are always in port. In addition, destroying land-based command and communications centers would severely hinder getting launch instructions to weapons commanders.

To make war-fighting weapons fit into the *announced* strategy of deterrence, Pentagon officials have provided a scenario to justify them. It postulates that if the Soviets should launch an attack on U.S. Minuteman ICBM silos but hold back sufficient ICBMs to threaten American cities if the U.S. retaliates, then U.S. forces must be able to destroy those remaining Soviet missiles when it does retaliate. This, according to Pentagon officials, assures that the deterrence policy will still work and is the reason war-fighting weapons must be built.

That scenario will not stand close inspection. Only 25 percent of U.S. warheads are in silo-based missiles. As long as these ICBMs are not accurate enough to threaten Soviet missile silos, Kremlin planners would see no advantage in attacking them, especially when 50 percent of U.S. warheads are safe in submarines with any one of those submarines alone able to destroy the Soviet Union as a political/economic/social entity. But when the U.S. develops weapons that can destroy silos, based on this illogical scenario, we provide the missing logic to make that hypothetical attack more likely to occur during the heightened tensions of some future international crisis.

Other military technologies are also being refined to support a disarming first-strike capability for the United States. They include antisubmarine warfare, ballistic missile and bomber defense, space warfare, and what is known as command, control, and communication. In what follows, I will address only a portion of the latter, which pertains to the control of nuclear weapons.

As the United States and the Soviet Union continue to make their nuclear forces more capable for war-fighting, it becomes increasingly urgent that response to a nuclear attack be executed before the weapons for response are destroyed. Seconds become critical when as little as nine minutes of time elapses from the moment a missile leaves a submarine to when it hits the target.

"No human being can enter the real time decision-making loop and control the system," the former director of Ballistic Mis-

sile Defense, Dr. J.B. Gilstein, has pointed out. "It has to be pre-programmed with logic so the computer can make decisions and run the game." This frightening rationale has evolved because of the massive amount of data that must be instantaneously processed and evaluated during a crisis.

Here is a preview of what can happen. During 1979 and the first half of 1980, U.S. early-warning computers, designed to announce when the U.S. is under attack, have set off 147 false alerts, four of which actually escalated the strategic forces to a higher state of readiness. Some have lasted from three to six minutes. Had the U.S. been operating under a launch-on-warning strategy, requiring it to fire endangered missiles immediately, the consequences would have been disastrous.

Similar false alerts have occurred in the more distant past. But even more worrisome is the thought of what will happen when highly automated networks operating under sensor control are put into operation. Compounding that will be the volatile atmosphere existing when both the U.S. and USSR see the military advantage in any confrontation lying with the country that shoots first.

Public peace of mind that nuclear weapons will not be accidentally or illegally launched rests chiefly in the belief that the President must personally approve their use. But a 1975 Library of Congress study revealed that, although under existing law the President alone is responsible for the use of nuclear weapons, he can lawfully delegate that authority virtually without restriction. Moreover, there is ample testimony that such authority has been delegated to military commanders down the chain of command.

Even if the President did have personally to approve use of nuclear weapons, today's complicated electronics and sophisticated technologies make any presidential launch decision an academic exercise. One former deputy director of research and engineering for the Defense Department pointed out that you cannot just present the chief executive with a room full of maps and charts and expect him to make an instantaneous decision. He said, "It has to be boiled down to a scale—for example, green, yellow, and red—and he can decide by how far the needle moves what he should do."

Punching the nuclear war button when the needle hits red can hardly be called a presidential decision. The actual decision-making responsibility goes back to the Pentagon's war room, where movement of the needle is controlled. Dr. George Heilmeier, former di-

rector of the Defense Advanced Research Projects Agency (DARPA), once indicated how movement of that needle might be planned: "Human limitations in formulating and communicating commands will be a central difficulty in increasingly complex command, control, and communications systems . . . DARPA has initiated research aimed at developing and demonstrating a new type of command system cybernetics. . . ." That research is aimed at imbuing the computer with the ability to infer and deduce, as opposed to its traditional logic task of numerical processing.

It does not take much imagination to recognize the catastrophic consequences of future false alerts when electromechanical fallibility is honed to a quick edge by war-fighting weapons.

Aside from the danger of accidental or unauthorized use of nuclear weapons, and the delusion that nuclear war can be kept limited, merely possessing war-fighting, silo-killing weapons indicates a capability to strike first, however unintended such a strike may be. We can expect Soviet strategists to look at capabilities rather than announced intentions.

Former President Carter reported in one of his arms control impact statements that building silo-killing weapons is destabilizing because "under extreme crisis conditions, Soviet leaders, concerned that war was imminent, and fearing for the survivability of their ICBMs if the United States struck first . . . might perceive pressures to strike first themselves."

What I have tried to illustrate here is that the United States is taking the lead in pushing toward the most dangerous step yet attempted in arms race history. We are on the threshold of a first-strike standoff when twitching fingers will be poised over the nuclear button as strategists on each side try to outguess the other's intentions. Meanwhile, we are being told we must build more weapons to insure our safety.

This is a replay of history, albeit a more dangerous one. The past has been replete with "gaps." We had a bomber gap in the early 1950s that was later proven false—but only after U.S. production of B-52 bombers was well under way. In the late 1950s and early 1960s, we were warned of a missile gap, and again it was later shown to be fictional—but only after the Pentagon had accelerated production of ICBMs and SLBMs.

Let us take a lesson from history. Again we are being told of another gap: a counterforce gap, a Soviet lead in the ability to de-

stroy our strategic missile force. It is simply not true that the Soviets are closer to an unanswerable first strike than we are. But if we are deceived into allowing our country to acquire a decisive advantage in destroying missile silos and other strategic targets, we can be sure the Soviets will hold up their end of the race. Even if they do not catch up, they could still be pressured into firing their missiles before they lose them, when it looks like a confrontation is imminent.

United States nuclear policy is frightening. The American public has been deceived for reasons of power and profits. It is true that Soviet weapons are a threat to us, but our response should not be to panic and make more weapons that further upset stability.

What is called for is a clear-headed approach toward a solution based on consideration for all people and not influenced by corporate profits or Pentagon prestige. Meaningful steps toward disarmament are possible, but we must first show sincerity by divesting ourselves of war-fighting weapons. Only then will we be able to negotiate treaties that will actually reduce arms. Toward that end there is an unmitigated urgency for people to start questioning nuclear policy.

THE STRATEGIC NUCLEAR TRIAD

Both the U.S. and USSR operate with a triad of strategic weapons which are delivered by land, sea, and air. The first to be developed was the air wing: the intercontinental bombers to deliver nuclear weapons in the same fashion as was done at Hiroshima and Nagasaki. As we advanced into the missile age during the late 1950s, the land leg was established: the intercontinental ballistic missiles (ICBMs) which were eventually housed in underground silos. Not too long after that, the sea leg was established to fire submarine-launched ballistic missiles (SLBMs) from underwater.

In the Soviet triad, the modernization presently taking place is deployment of SS-17, SS-18, and SS-19 ICBMs and SS-N-17/ 18 SLBMs.

On the U.S. side, upgrading of the land leg is now comprised of Minuteman III improvements (a more precise guidance system, more powerful warheads, and the ability to select targets rapidly from remote locations) which are now taking place and development of the new MX missile. The Trident I now being deployed and the Trident II SLBM in development are the sea leg updating. The B-1 bomber has returned, and the air wing is being modernized with air-launched cruise missiles.

While the Soviet Union has more missiles, the U.S. has more ready to launch at any given time, and more that will work as intended after being fired. Whereas the USSR has bigger bombs, miniaturization and accuracy make U.S. warheads more effective.

SPREADING MADNESS:

The Proliferation of Nuclear Weapons
by Sidney Lens

The nuclear arms race is fearsome in two respects, first in that at least two powers already have the capability of killing every human being on earth, and second in that it spawns a rampant technology which develops ever more frightening weapons and proliferates them to many of the least advanced nations on earth.

In 1945 there was just one nuclear power with only enough warheads on the racks to destroy two Japanese cities. Then in 1949 there were two (add the Soviet Union), in 1952 three (add Britain), in 1960 four (add France), in 1964 five (add China), in 1974 six (add India), and along the way at least one other power, Israel, and perhaps two more, South Africa and Taiwan. In the coming years it is certain that Pakistan will have the bomb, and that a total of 40 nations by 1985, and 100 by the year 2000, will have the capability as well as the material, plutonium, to make nuclear warheads.

"Up to this point," Fred C. Ikle, Director of the Arms Control and Disarmament Agency, told a Cleveland audience in February, 1975, "I've been talking about arms control matters between ourselves and the Soviet Union. . . . But this relationship may not always pose the greatest danger. The nuclear age, from the very first day, confronted us with a more distant danger, a danger that may make us look back on the present as a safe and easy time by comparison. I refer to the possible risks involved in the *inevitable* worldwide spread of nuclear technology" (emphasis added).

Ikle admitted in another speech (as have many other experts) that "we are basically defenseless against threats of nuclear attack that could come from a great many different sources rather than from one or two principal adversaries."

This, then, is the second nuclear age. The first one was terrifying enough, with a thermonuclear blowout seriously considered on at least 15 occasions, beginning with Truman's 48-hour ultima-

tum to the Soviet Union in 1946 that he would use fission bombs if their troops did not evacuate Azerbaijan (in Iran). On at least five occasions the world came close to nuclear exchange between the superpowers because there was a misreading of radar. Seven times the U.S. seriously weighed limited nuclear engagement, and twice an all-out nuclear war seemed imminent (in the October 1962 missile crisis and again during the 1974 Yom Kippur War).

But the second nuclear age is far more dangerous because proliferation threatens to put the arms race entirely out of control. Unless that race is ended soon, no people anywhere will be secure again; "little wars" will have an inherent tendency to escalate into nuclear confrontations, and "limited" nuclear confrontations into worldwide ones.

Technology, pulled by its own momentum, causes two forms of worldwide proliferation: one whereby great powers in addition to the Soviet Union and the United States acquire the nuclear capability to destroy any adversary on earth; another in which as many as 100 weaker powers may possess nuclear bombs within the next two decades.

Moreover, the prospect is that all of these warheads will be launched from missiles or bombers that are progressively more accurate. That is significant because accuracy greatly increases the kill capability of a nuclear weapon. As a former chief engineer for Lockheed, Robert C. Aldridge, notes: "Making the warhead twice as accurate has the same effect as making the bomb eight times as powerful."

Great power proliferation creates the possibility that within the next decade or so there will be six, or possibly seven, nuclear superpowers instead of two. China has tested a missile with a 7,500-mile range and already has a stockpile of missiles capable of hitting targets as far away as 3,500 miles. Within a decade, some experts believe, China will have enough nuclear instruments to seriously threaten the Soviets, and China says that war with "social-imperialist" Russia is inevitable.

In addition, the cruise missile may become the vehicle by which France, Britain, Germany, and perhaps Japan become major nuclear powers, not on a par with the Soviet Union or the United States, perhaps, but still capable of totally destroying any single adversary. According to Flora Lewis of *The New York Times,* France, Britain, and Germany have been pressuring Washington to

let them produce a cruise missile arsenal of their own. "The low-flying pilotless drones," she wrote in late 1977, "promise cheapness, accuracy, and an ability to penetrate Soviet air defenses that no existing weapon can offer."

All three powers are evidently hesitant to start such a program without American concurrence, at least under present circumstances. But that might change in the not-too-distant future, if America's position were to deteriorate further and its allies begin to play a more independent game. In any case, as Flora Lewis notes, "Both Britain and France have the capacity to develop their own version of the cruise missile, and there has also been some talk of a possible joint development project with West Germany."

Perhaps more unsettling than great power proliferation is the pernicious spread of nuclear capability to secondary powers: Pakistan, Israel, Argentina, South Korea, Libya, Brazil, South Africa, Spain, Taiwan, and many others. Oddly enough, the primary impulse for this aspect of the second nuclear age has come from the much heralded spin-off of bomb technology: the nuclear reactor that generates electricity.

"It is ironic," the late Senator Stuart Symington told Congress in 1975, "that the United States, which in the first instance sought to limit membership in the nuclear weapons club, has made possible through its sharing of atomic technology additional membership in that fearsome club."

Had there been no nuclear power reactors, all but a few nations would have found it impossible to manufacture nuclear bombs, at least for many decades. That is because the technology for making the bomb material is both complicated and expensive.

The more plentiful isotope of uranium, U-238, cannot be fabricated into nuclear warheads because it is not fissionable. But in every hundred pounds of natural uranium there is seven-tenths of a pound of a fissionable and radioactive isotope, U-235. The uranium must be "enriched" by a complicated and sophisticated chemical process so that the U-235 constitutes three or four percent of the uranium for power reactors, and as much as 90 percent for bombs. This is no simple matter, since present enrichment plants cost one, two, or more billion dollars each and demand a high degree of skill.

As of January, 1975, there were only seven uranium enrichment plants in the world, three in the United States, and one each in the Soviet Union, China, Britain, and France. A half-dozen other

nations have since joined or are about to join the uranium enrichment club, but the number of countries that will make atom bombs with the U-235 from their own uranium enrichment facilities is likely to remain relatively small.

The greater prospect is that dozens of nations will soon have access to large supplies of plutonium from another source: the "waste" from nuclear power reactors. Unlike U-235, plutonium does not have to be enriched. Nine pounds of plutonium 239, or 17 pounds of plutonium extracted from reactor "waste," can be fabricated into a nuclear bomb without further modification. And there are thousands of people spread throughout the world who now have the basic know-how to do it.

Plutonium is the primary material for most fission (atom) bombs, as well as for the "trigger" in fusion (hydrogen) bombs.

Unlike uranium, which appears in nature, plutonium is a human invention. During World War II, the U.S. government built a huge complex of three plutonium-producing reactors at Hanford, Washington, and in the 1950s added another complex of five reactors on the Savannah River in South Carolina. As long as the manufacture of this element was under the control of the Atomic Energy Commission or the military, there was little danger that other nations would acquire the necessary amounts to produce atom bombs.

The commercialization of nuclear power, however, has changed all that. The supply of plutonium from research reactors and breeder reactors is very limited, but the same cannot be said for the couple of hundred nuclear power reactors that generate electricity. About 500 pounds of plutonium can be extracted annually from the "waste" of burned-out fuel rods in the average reactor, enough for 30 to 50 bombs like the Nagasaki bomb, depending on the purity of the plutonium. All that is needed is a reprocessing plant to separate the plutonium from other material, and that is a technology much less complicated than uranium enrichment.

Eleven nations now have "significant reprocessing capability," according to the Stockholm International Peace Research Institute (SIPRI), and at least two others have contracts to build such facilities. In addition, the technology is already available for small reprocessing plants that cost a few million dollars each and provide enough plutonium for five or 10 bombs a year.

Thus, as estimated by former President Gerald Ford, by 1985

47

there may be 40 countries with plutonium and know-how ready to enter the nuclear club. The expected worldwide avalanche of plutonium is staggering. In 1970, by SIPRI's estimate, four tons of plutonium were being produced annually; by 1974 it was 18 tons, and by 1990 it was expected to be 450 tons.

Scientist Bernard T. Feld, editor of *The Bulletin of the Atomic Scientists,* estimates that by the end of the century, less developed nations will be able to produce 30,000 nuclear warheads a year from part of this plutonium stockpile (as much as the United States has accumulated in more than three decades), and developed nations 210,000. These figures must be trimmed, perhaps by half or more, because of the severe drop in reactor sales, but Dr. Feld's claim that "there are many who believe that we have passed the point of no return as far as nuclear weapons proliferation is concerned" cannot be dismissed lightly.

The United States continues to express its horror and shock that this mad momentum isn't checked, but Washington is in the dilemma of trying to persuade others not to manufacture nuclear weapons while it plans to more than double its own stockpile in the next decade.

The United States, it is true, was a leading force in pushing through the Non-Proliferation Treaty (NPT), signed in 1968 and since ratified by more than a hundred nations. The treaty was a compact not to spread nuclear weapons beyond the five nations that had them in 1968. The five nuclear states (the United States, the Soviet Union, Britain, France, and China) were to pledge not to transfer nuclear weapons or the capability to make them to non-nuclear states. The non-nuclear states were to pledge not to produce or purchase such weapons, provided in return that the "haves" commit themselves "to pursue negotiations in good faith" for "cessation of the nuclear arms race at an early date," as well as for nuclear and total disarmament "under strict and effective international control."

Unfortunately two of the five nuclear states (France and China) refused to sign. India, which would explode a bomb in 1974, also held out. So did a host of nations which did not have the bomb but had a potential for producing it. The biggest obstacle, however, was that the two superpowers, the United States and the Soviet Union, showed no inclination for a "cessation of the nuclear arms

race at an early date." On the contrary, even the SALT II agreement provided that each side would increase its arsenal of strategic warheads by more than 4,000, and there was no limit placed either on tactical nuclear weapons or on accuracy improvements.

No wonder, then, that when India was bitterly criticized by the U.S. and Canada for exploding a 12-kiloton device in May, 1974, the director of its Institute of Defense Studies and Analyses, K. Subrahmanyam, responded with equal rancor: "In this world you and I are asked to accept the credibility of the structure of peace built on 7,000 strategic nuclear warheads, in addition to another 7,000 tactical nuclear weapons capable of incinerating all of us on this globe many times over; the credibility of a Non-Proliferation Treaty since the signing of which nuclear weapons have quadrupled in number; the credibility of deterrence which means a non-stop arms race. . . . Therefore, before we answer the question how credible India's [peaceful] declaration is, we have to ask for a definition of credibility in international politics." If America can do it, in other words, why can't we?

The rationale for proliferation is as mystifying and invincible as fission itself: China needs the bomb because America (later Russia) threatens the Asian continent; India needs it because China has it; Pakistan wants it because India has it, and so it goes. An Argentine journalist, Marianna Grondona, aptly expressed the psychology of proliferation in a 1974 article for *La Opinion:* "Now with India the Atomic Powers are six in number. They would like to remain six. If we [Argentina] come to be the seventh, we would of course like to see no more than seven. The last one to arrive tries to close the door. That is only natural."

Clearly, the problem of proliferation cannot be solved without draconian steps and a heavy measure of international integration. In June, 1946, the United States submitted a plan to the United Nations calling for an International Atomic Development Authority which would assume "various forms of ownership, dominion, licenses, operation, inspection, research, and management" of everything associated with atomic energy throughout the world, from the uranium mine to the bomb. It was an excellent idea and would have ended the arms race immediately but for the fact that it was crammed with jokers.

The plan was long on inspection but short on disarmament. It

required the Soviet Union and other nations to turn over control of their uranium mines and open their doors to geological surveys immediately, whereas the United States would not be required to end its production of atom bombs, divest itself of its arsenal, or communicate its secrets to the international authority until the machinery for inspection and control was in place and functioning throughout the world.

Today, of course, the problem is more difficult to resolve. In 1946 there was barely a baker's dozen of atomic weapons to destroy and in just a single country; today there are tens of thousands and in at least six, perhaps eight, countries.

More recently, the late Secretary-General of the United Nations, U Thant, called for international bodies with power to deal with the four "P's": proliferation, population, pollution, and poverty. "I do not wish to seem overdramatic," he told the U.N., "but I can only conclude that the members of the United Nations have perhaps ten years left in which to subordinate their ancient quarrels and launch a global partnership to curb the arms race, to improve the human environment, to defuse the population explosion, and to supply the required momentum to development efforts."

So far none of this has been taken to heart by the great powers. Instead, the world slogs along doing little to meet the dangers ahead. There have been 130 "little wars" since 1945, killing about 30 million people. We can expect that, in the absence of effective international machinery, such wars will continue at the rate of three or four a year. So far none has expanded into a nuclear war, because none of the powers involved, except the United States, has had nuclear armament.

But what will happen when scores of nations have nuclear weapons? The tendency then will certainly be for the losing power to use everything it has, including nuclear weapons, and for the winning power to try to checkmate its enemy by delivering the coup de grace first.

Thus technology and establishment politics exacerbate the problem of proliferation and drive us toward the dreaded nuclear exchange. It will take a very loud popular voice and a steady drumbeat of protest, in this country especially, to turn matters around.

WE ARE ALL HOSTAGES:
Questions for Thought and Discussion

1. In Barnet's view, "Every American is a hostage and a target, and so is every Russian." In what ways are the citizens of the U.S. and the USSR victims of terrorism? When you think of yourself and your family as hostages of the arms race, how does it affect your reaction to government policy?

2. What kinds of weapons and strategies does Aldridge refer to when he speaks of "first strike" or "war-fighting"? How do these weapons and strategies differ from those for "deterrence"? As decision-making about nuclear war has become increasingly computerized, who controls the decisions and how sensitive are they to error? What effect does this have on international security?

3. Lens states that "proliferation threatens to put the arms race entirely out of control." How is control complicated when more nations have nuclear weapons? Do you find the U.S. position with respect to nuclear proliferation credible? If you were a non-nuclear nation, how do you think you would respond to U.S. nuclear escalation?

HYSTERIA IS COMING!
HYSTERIA IS COMING!

Producing the Born-Again Cold War
by William Greider

I don't blame ordinary citizens for ignorance in this matter of the Red Menace of 1980. Life is too short to spend it reading *Foreign Affairs* and the other turgid journals where the Cold War is fought out in dense, bloodless theory. Normal people have better things to do.

I do blame ordinary citizens, though, for being so easily seduced by the new hysteria over national defense, a collective obsession of 1980 politics that is going to prove outrageously expensive and, if God isn't looking out for us, dangerous.

If Americans kept closer tab of their history, they would remember that they have been duped before by the cold warriors, stampeded by apocalyptic warnings that proved false. The Russians are coming. The Reds are superior. We are vulnerable. Armageddon is just around the corner. Unless, of course, we spend a trillion dollars. Yes, we intend to spend a trillion dollars on defense in the next five years.

Well, the Russians are not coming, folks, so keep your shirts on (if you have them left). The fundamental truth, in fact, is that *they* are weak, and getting weaker, and we are strong. We are not vulnerable. In the present season of martial music, that assertion marks one as irresponsible or, worse, craven. But I am confident that history is on my side.

A few years hence, I predict, the same learned theoreticians who are now exciting national fears will be writing thoughtful articles about how we misinterpreted and overestimated to produce the born-again Cold War of 1980. Perhaps they will make discreet comparisons with the "missile gap" of 1960 when a similar hysteria aroused by some of the same experts proved phoney. Except that it resulted in the very real arms buildup of the '60s.

Many Americans seem intimidated by this Cold War priesthood. They needn't be. Anyone of normal intelligence who can understand the strategies and imponderables of pro football on Sunday afternoon can easily grasp the basics of the national security debates. Cold War theories are crude bits of whimsy compared with the thoroughgoing war games of a Tom Landry or George Allen.

The difference is this: Those football coaches must test their game plans every Sunday afternoon. The nuclear thinkers have been indulged by history, never tested by the real thing, never forced to discover what a nuclear exchange would really be like. This should tell us something about how much theory to believe, for in the history of human warfare, particularly in the 20th century, new weapons have always altered warmaking in horrible new ways that were not predicted beforehand. Consider the machine gun in World War I or aerial bombing in World War II.

If any earnest citizen wants to understand, the relevant information is not top secret. Much of it has been printed in your daily newspaper. But first one has to cut through the general noise of alarm bells and define the three different arguments contained in this new wave of fright (next, one can go to the public library and read a few old articles, all written in plain English).

"The Russians have us outnumbered in tanks and troops and planes—they could sweep across the Rhine and reach the English Channel in a matter of days and we wouldn't be able to stop them."

This is the favorite spectre invoked by those arguing for a big buildup in conventional arms. Sometimes, these days, they substitute the Mideast for Western Europe. The argument regularly invokes deceitful comparisons—our tanks vs. their tanks—which even the densest senator must know is a phoney numbers game.

The U.S. military opted for the best and most expensive model of virtually every weapons system, including antitank wizardry; the Russian tank is crude and simple compared with our million-dollar electronic marvels. The Soviets, out of their own necessities, build on the cheap and build many more. Nobody, as far as I know, is seriously proposing to change our development strategy or even to match the Russians tank-for-tank, plane-for-plane. Yet they still play the numbers game because it sounds so scary.

A reasonable question about the crossing-the-Rhine scenario is why the Europeans, who would be the immediate victims, are less

alarmed than we seem to be. Indeed, a reasonable citizen might ask: If we are headed toward disaster, why are our allies spending so much less on defense than we are?

One reason might be that nobody seriously believes the Russians are planning such an offensive or that they could pull it off without starting World War III, last in a series. The crossing-the-Rhine theories presume or pretend that neither the United States nor our allies would respond with the big one: nuclear weapons. We are pledged to do so. It would be a rather desperate gamble for the Soviet leaders to roll the dice and find out if we meant it.

But why then do the Russians have all those tanks in Eastern Europe, if not to threaten us? Recent headlines provided one of the main answers: to threaten their own satellites and keep them in line.

U.S. conventional forces do have serious and costly problems: the replacement of worn-out equipment, inadequate maintenance, the technological escalation of weapons and their soaring price tags, the shortage of pilots and experienced technicians in the ranks. But none of these problems is a function of Soviet hegemony; none will be solved by scaring folks.

"For the next four or five years, the United States is in a dangerous window of vulnerability—the Soviet Union could start a nuclear war and win it."

This is the notion that launched the $80 billion MX missile "racetrack" scheme, a proposal so dubious that even some conservative hawks oppose it. The fear is that the Soviets now have enough megatonnage in place, ready to fire, to knock out all our land-based missiles in one strike. Though this is theoretically true, no one should be surprised by the development; the Soviets have been building toward nuclear parity with us for the last decade. Anyway, the "window of vulnerability" theory depends on two very flimsy assumptions.

First, that the Soviet leaders, in some sort of crazy desperation, must be prepared for 100 million dead Russians if their gamble is wrong. This is what's known as "war-winning capability." The Soviet leaders are a brutish, hostile lot, but I don't believe they define 100 million dead comrades as victory.

Second, that the U.S. president will surrender without a fight. Our land-based missiles are destroyed, tens of millions of Ameri-

cans have been killed, radiation death is spreading across our land, but the president decides not to retaliate with our thousands of protected bombs on submarines and bombers. Why? By the logic of vulnerability, he would conclude that it wasn't worth it, that more lives would be lost, ours and theirs, and we would wind up in total devastation. A humanitarian view.

Do you believe that? Nothing in American history suggests a precedent for surrender. Indeed, the history of modern warfare, in which many nations have faced similar choices, is filled with eloquent stories of leaders and peoples between devastation and surrender who chose terrible suffering before defeat and subjugation. Would Americans somehow be different?

The "vulnerability" issue evades the larger and now-permanent reality. Both sides have overabundant nuclear arsenals, sufficiently protected from attack, to obliterate the other after absorbing a first strike, if necessary. Together, by 1985, we will have more than 35,000 warheads; we already have 14 billion tons of explosives, three tons each for every living mortal.

"We're not really talking about actual strengths and weaknesses—we're talking about the perception of weakness. If it looks like Russia's arsenal is bigger than ours, it will influence world politics. Therefore, build we must."

This "perception of weakness" is the core anxiety, I believe, a spiritual malaise which infected cold warriors at the fall of Saigon. The argument is really a kind of self-fulfilling theology which lies beyond proof. To prevent the "perception of weakness," we should commit a fixed percentage of our growing national wealth to the military and argue later about how to spend it. This is roughly what the government is now trying to do, and it resembles the primitive rite of offering sacrifice at the altar of the war god.

What's more scandalous is this: The so-called "perception of weakness" is fundamentally wrong. The Soviet Union, as every scholar knows, is in deep trouble, at home and abroad, in the long run and in the immediate future. The scary image of Soviet hegemony, so familiar to American consumers, simply doesn't fit the facts.

The popular rebellion in Poland. The quagmire in Afghanistan. The Islamic reformation, which is much more threatening to the USSR than to us because a growing portion of the Soviet popu-

lation is Moslem. The new tactical nukes in Germany which threaten from the West. And, from the East, the new U.S. alliance with China.

The list goes on. While Americans never seem to see these as ominous for the Soviet leaders, the Soviet leaders do. Their perception is almost a perfect reverse mirror of the U.S. cold warriors' perception: The Soviets see themselves encircled, threatened, endangered.

The long-run outlook for the Russians is even worse. The basic problem, after all the ideological rhetoric has been brushed aside, is simple: Their system doesn't work. The Soviet economy can't grow fast enough to buy all the military hardware and, at the same time, provide elementary consumer goods. It has to buy food from America. It has to borrow technology. Satellite nations like Poland have to borrow capital from Western bankers to stay afloat. Still, the Polish workers go on strike. That's why all those Russian tanks are in Eastern Europe.

These historic contradictions will become more intense in the 1980s because the Soviet population is changing in adverse ways. Because of abortions, a rising rate of infant mortality, and a declining birth rate, the age group of young workers is shrinking as a proportion of the society—and shifting, incidentally, away from the urban centers of industry and toward provincial minorities like the Moslems. None of this is expected to undo Lenin's revolution. But, at the very least, the Commies are facing hard times that make our difficulties seem benign and manageable.

Everything I have said here has been said before, has been printed in newspapers and articles. Yet I would guess that much of it will be news to ordinary Americans. They don't pay close attention to the undramatic and tedious details, but they sit up and listen when someone cries "war."

I don't blame them for selective inattention, but I do think this: If Americans don't get smarter about themselves and the world, someday they are going to get hurt by what they don't know.

LIES CLEARER THAN TRUTH:

A Look at the Russian Threat

by Richard Barnet

Behind every war there is a big lie. Reality is much too ambiguous, much too complex to elicit the popular enthusiasm needed for modern mobilization. So things must be made "clearer than truth," as Dean Acheson once put it.

The nuclear arms race, with its proliferation of missile stockpiles and its even more expensive supporting cast of aircraft carriers, unilateral strike forces, and aging armies in the center of Europe, is a Thirty Years' War going on forty. To keep it going in the United States it has been necessary at strategic moments to raise the spectre of the Russian horde. The Soviet threat is the big lie of the arms race.

The Soviet Union does indeed pose a threat to the United States. Any power that aims thousands of nuclear warheads at our people is making and intends to make a threat. It is the same threat which the United States in more diverse and more sophisticated ways has been making against the Soviet Union for a longer time.

But the Soviet threat, a national myth used as the rationale for an ever-escalating arms budget and a policy of U.S. military intervention over two generations, is something more than an official dramatization of Soviet missile strength. The Soviet threat pre-existed the Soviet missile arsenal. It is rooted in an analysis of Soviet intentions. The essence of the Soviet threat is this: The Soviet leaders, bent on world domination, will stop at nothing to defeat the United States, by bluff, if possible, by nuclear war, if necessary.

As the years go by, the characterization of the Soviet threat has changed. In the early postwar period, the Soviets were dangerous because their ideology was a powerful virus. They were, as one of our ambassadors put it, a cause rather than a country. There was nothing they were not prepared to do, even if they had nothing to do it with.

The threat salesmen of our day stand these ideas on their heads. The Soviet Union is now dangerous because its ideology has been discredited and its economy is a failure. Therefore all it has is military power, and with that power it intends to frighten us into submission.

As World War II ended, the Soviet Union lay prostrate, 73,000 cities and towns smashed, 20 million people dead. The Soviet army was in the heart of Europe, but the Soviet economy was in ruins. In order to build a Center-Right political coalition in Western Europe against the Left (until 1947 French and Italian Communists participated in the cabinets), the spectre of the Soviet invasion was raised.

Winston Churchill stated in 1950 that but for the atomic bomb in America's hands the Russian hordes would be at the English Channel. Most of the panicky public in Europe and the United States agreed. But one searches the historical record in vain for any responsible official of the West who privately shared that belief. James Forrestal, who was obsessed with the Soviet challenge, wrote in his diaries that the Soviets would not move that year—"or at any time." At the founding of NATO, John Foster Dulles, then a senator, underscored his view that the Soviets did not pose a military threat to Europe. The Joint Chiefs of Staff testified in a similar vein.

George Kennan, the architect of the containment policy, has written that NATO was to be a "modest shield" behind which the West could restore its economy. It was not intended as a permanent standing army in the heart of Europe because there was no danger of a Soviet attack. Neither the roads nor the railroad track for a Russian blitzkrieg in Europe existed, even if the still-bleeding Soviet society could have supported one. "The image of Russia poised and yearning to attack the West and deterred only by our possession of atomic weapons was largely a creation of Western imagination, against which some of us who were familiar with Russian matters tried in vain, over the course of the years, to make our voices heard," Kennan has asserted.

By 1955, the Soviet Union had about 350 bombers capable of delivering atomic bombs on the United States; the United States had four times the number, many located in bases close to the Soviet frontier. This was the era of the bomber gap, when Paul Nitze

and many of his colleagues in the Committee on the Present Danger first began to sound the alarm.

Then came the famous missile gap. Now Nitze and his friends accused President Eisenhower of being soft on the Russians, and John F. Kennedy campaigned for the White House in 1960 on this theme. In fact, the United States had a huge superiority in nuclear striking power. The Soviets had built very few missiles. But the new Kennedy administration ordered huge new missile programs anyway, increased the military budget 15 percent, and "won" the eyeball-to-eyeball confrontation over the emplacement of missiles in Cuba in October 1962.

One result of the United States "victory" was the ouster of Khrushchev, who had tried to substitute bluster and bluff for spending money on missiles, and the beginning of a serious Soviet rearmament program. It is that program which is the basis for the current hysteria about Soviet intentions.

At that time, the United States military, eager to ward off pressure for an arms moratorium, concluded that the Kremlin was resigned to being a permanent underdog. (The Pentagon has two rules for negotiating arms agreements: One is "Don't negotiate when you are behind." The other is "Why negotiate when you are ahead?") The Soviets had "lost the quantitative race," Secretary McNamara declared in 1965, "and they are not seeking to engage us in that contest."

Unlike the era of the bomber gap and the missile gap, there *is* a Soviet military buildup. It has proceeded steadily since the Brezhnev era began in 1964. The rate of buildup appears to have remained the same over the years. The current version of the big lie is that the Soviets are out to gain superiority over the U.S. The hawks warn that if present trends continue, the Soviets will have "won" the arms race and will be able to dictate surrender.

Talking about "current trends continuing" is like observing in the midst of a spring rain that if it keeps up the Empire State Building will float away. The Soviets are building to catch up. Every missile in the world not located inside the Soviet Union is aimed at the Soviet Union—those of China, Britain, France, as well as the United States. Russia is the only country in the world surrounded by hostile communist powers.

United States generals and Soviet generals genuinely disagree

on how much the Soviet Union needs to catch up. What looks defensive to one looks offensive to the other. The Soviets started far behind the United States. To draw even close in nuclear striking forces their rate of production and deployment over the last 10 years would have had to be greater than that of the United States.

But the huge head start and continued commitment of the United States to the arms race still leaves this country far in the lead. According to a Library of Congress study, the United States leads in strategic warheads, submarine-launched warheads, and heavy bombers. Soviet missiles are less accurate. They suffer from geographical disadvantages. Sixty percent of the U.S. missile-launching submarine fleet can operate away from port at any one time; only 11 percent of the Soviet submarine fleet can.

The famous Soviet civil defense program is modest. The cost has been calculated at $4 per person compared with $50 per person for civil defense in Switzerland and West Germany. The program, a July 1978 CIA study concludes, is one in which Soviet leaders "cannot have confidence in the degree of protection their civil defense would give them" and hence "the program is unlikely to embolden the Soviet leadership to risk a nuclear war."

It is the United States, not the Soviet Union, that is approaching a theoretical first-strike capability. The Soviets have most of their striking force in land-based missiles which are becoming increasingly vulnerable to our increasingly accurate warheads. Their submarine force and their bomber force are inferior copies of the United States originals. The introduction of the cruise missile, with the capability of delivering many more warheads, significantly increases the American threat for the Soviet leaders.

Stalin's death camps, the brutality in Budapest in 1956 and Prague in 1968, and Soviet mistreatment of intellectuals, Baptists, Jews, and dissident workers elicit and ought to elicit moral outrage, but none of these crimes is evidence of an intention to start a nuclear war.

The Kremlin's worries about the United States are not based on vague historical analogies but on painful experience. The United States participated in a military intervention in the Soviet Union after the revolution "to strangle Bolshevism in its cradle," as Winston Churchill put it. The U.S. conducted a 20-year quarantine of the Soviet Union which in part still continues.

Looking from the Kremlin window, a Soviet leader sees the

fast development of a United States-West German-Japanese-Chinese alliance, a collection of historic enemies. He sees a resurgence of anti-Soviet rhetoric and anti-Soviet politics in the United States. He may well be aware of the fact that the reappearance of the Soviet threat always coincides with the emergence of new weapons systems from the drawing boards and the renewed eagerness of one military service or another to make an addition to its bureaucratic empire. (The first wave of anti-Soviet sentiment coincided with the development of the intercontinental bomber, the second with the intercontinental missile, and the present one with the new generation of counterforce technology—MX, Trident, and the rest of the new computerized-war apparatus.) But that is small comfort. The Soviet leader listens to Senator Henry Jackson, who does not speak for himself alone, and he hears the message: We have nothing to negotiate with the Soviet Union.

There has never been a time since the Cold War began when privately expressed and official, public views of the Soviet Union in the United States have so diverged. Public expressions of alarm about Soviet military spending, activities in Africa, and the missile buildup conceal a growing off-the-record assessment of Soviet weakness. CIA analyses point to a serious labor shortage, mounting difficulties in exploiting the rich mineral potential of the Soviet Eurasian land mass, and perennial problems with agriculture. There is mounting dissatisfaction with the system and a loss of ideological elan.

There is a consensus among Sovietologists about the mounting problems of the Soviet Union, but considerable difference of opinion on what conclusion to draw. Some, like former Secretary of State Vance, see the Soviet problems as providing a powerful incentive for the leaders in the Kremlin to press detente, to reduce the expenditures of the arms race, and to turn their attention to their own systemic crisis.

But there are others who still hold the dreams of "rollback" cherished by John Foster Dulles. The Reagan administration apparently believes that this is the time to push the Soviets hard. Perhaps they cannot be physically pushed out of Eastern Europe, but their world of influence can be undercut and they can be pressed hard in an escalating arms race in which all the advantages lie with the United States.

To be obsessed by the Soviet threat in a world in which more

than one billion people starve, half the global work force is projected to be without a minimally paying job by the year 2000, and industrial civilization is close to collapse because political paralysis and greed have kept us from solving the energy crisis is, quite literally, to be blinded by hate.

Every time we read a statement by a general or a senator or a president that we are prepared to threaten or launch a nuclear war in order to keep the Soviet leaders from doing something we don't like, a threat to recreate a hundred Auschwitzes has been made in our name. But we are blind to it. If we do not have the clarity of moral vision to see that the Russian people cannot ever deserve a hundred Auschwitzes whatever their leaders do, then our faith rests not on reverence of God and his world but on power fantasies and fear.

The characteristic of sin is confusion. We become possessed by irrational fears. Our minds stop working. The Russians stop being people and become hated symbols. No one asks what motive they would have to drop bombs on us other than the fear that we were about to do it to them. There is no worldly prize worth the destruction of the world, or the Soviet Union, or the city of Minsk for that matter, and there is a good deal of evidence that the Russian leaders believe that. No one knows how many Russians would die from the radioactivity floating back from a Soviet attack on the United States.

The insanity of the arms race is underscored by the fact that even the most avid hawks do not believe in the eventualities against which we are pouring out our treasure and poisoning our spirit. It seems rather evident that the Russians, however depraved they may be, would rather trade with Western Europe than occupy a smoking and uncontrollable ruin.

This reality puts us very far from the choice with which the arms race enthusiasts taunt us: Red or Dead? But the question does at least force us to examine the values we think we are promoting by posing the threat of a hundred Auschwitzes.

The biblical injunction to love one another does not rest on the idea that people are lovable in a human sense. The mystery and the burden of Christian love can be traced to the stubborn fact that love is difficult—people are hard enough to love one by one, and harder still to love by the millions. Yet the injunction is inescapable because creation cannot be sustained without it.

The choice is between love and hate, and hate is death. Hate demands an enemy. The identity hardly matters. Enemies change, but the spirit of enmity and fear remains.

The big lie behind all murder, from the random street killing, to the efficient ovens of Auschwitz, to the even more efficient hydrogen bomb, is that the victims deserve to die.

TWO BUMBLING GIANTS:
The Superpowers' Outdated Policies in a Nuclear World
by Richard Barnet

The 1980s have begun with a succession of crises for U.S.-Soviet relations: the brutal Soviet invasion of Afghanistan, revolutionary upheaval in the Middle East and Central America, the ongoing Polish crisis, and the Falkland Islands debacle. Detente has collapsed, the arms race has escalated, and the possibility of direct U.S.-Soviet confrontation in one part of the world or another has become dangerously real.

The world seems closer to a major war than at any time since the 1930s. The informal, de facto rules of the cold war have broken down. For a generation, the U.S. conducted military interventions in Iran, Guatemala, the Dominican Republic, Vietnam, Cambodia, and elsewhere. The Soviets invaded Hungary and Czechoslovakia; but outside the area occupied at the end of World War II by the Red Army, Soviet military expansionism was contained. The U.S. was free to dispatch its forces around the world outside the Soviet bloc without courting a risk of nuclear war; the Soviet Union, as the Cuban missile crisis showed, was not.

This operational code of the cold war was based on shared perceptions of power. With the invasion of Afghanistan, the Soviets demonstrated that the old rules no longer apply. The willingness to send military forces outside the Soviet bloc and to brook the predictable consequences is particularly disturbing because it lends credence to the fear that old ambitions in the whole strategic area have been revived. While Poland has been considered within the Soviet sphere of influence since the end of World War II, the Kremlin's pressure on the Solidarity union has exacerbated this fear.

The present crisis has come about because of the poverty of political imagination in both Washington and Moscow. Two bum-

bling giants faced with unprecedented, interlocking crisis can think of nothing but mindless military escalation. These crises have arisen against a background of certain crucial political events during the last years of the 1970s: the sudden emergence of militant Islam, sparked by the Khomeini revolution, which took both Moscow and Washington by surprise; the overthrow of a U.S. client in Central America and the social turmoil there; the collapse of detente in the U.S. due to the failure of the Carter administration to explain what it was and why it served the national interest; the failure of the U.S. to reduce its dependence on foreign oil, the intermittent panic over the possibility that it would be cut off, and the formulation of a military doctrine to protect the petroleum sources in the Middle East; the shocks to the world monetary system due to the phenomenal rise in oil prices and the incapacity of the industrial countries, particularly the U.S., to manage the new economy thereby created.

Of course none of these "caused" the invasion of Afghanistan during the first days of 1980 and none justify it. But if there is to be any creative response to the present world crisis that is moving us toward war, it must be rooted in some theory as to how an event like Afghanistan—still considered a watershed—came about.

The "worst-case" theory is that the Soviets have territorial ambitions in the whole region, as Molotov indicated to von Ribbentrop in 1939, and that the dawn of the new decade was the opportune moment to begin the process of Sovietization of the Persian Gulf. If that is true, it raises in an immediate way the profound moral dilemma nonpacifists have so far refused to face: Is there any value, including containment of an outlaw nation or just retribution for outrageous behavior, that justifies risking the death of everything? Is it morally justifiable to punish the Russian leaders with a punishment that will fall not only on their population and our population, but may well contaminate the whole earth and perhaps lay a horrible curse on every future generation?

Fortunately, policymakers are not yet driven to that moment of ultimate moral discovery because it is by no means clear that the Russians are following a master plan for world domination. If the Russian leaders are reincarnated Hitlers, as columnists and politicians are suggesting, then the lessons of the 1930s dictate that we fight a war now to prevent a greater war later. That is, of course, nonsense, because we have no confidence for the belief that punitive or preemptive war can be kept small.

A much more credible theory for what happened in Afghanistan is that the breakdown of order in the region was perceived by the Soviets as a threat rather than an opportunity. The Soviets moved in a spirit of insecurity and panic rather than overconfidence.

Afghanistan was hardly a ripe plum waiting to be plucked. The ineptitude and butchery of the Amin regime had threatened to turn the whole country into a militant Moslem anticommunist state, making it certain that the Moslem areas of the Soviet Union would be bordered by two fiercely anticommunist states. The bonds of detente were frayed to the point of snapping, and so it seemed there was little to lose. SALT II was already as good as dead. The U.S. had already announced a commitment to a major escalation of the military budget. The decision had been made to emplace in Europe the cruise and Pershing missiles, the latter being a new strategic nuclear weapons system as far as the Soviets were concerned. Brezhnev's October offer to negotiate a reduction of European-based nuclear weapons had been dismissed.

All this signaled a decisive shift in U.S. policy away from detente. As they looked out from the Kremlin, Soviet leaders saw West Germany moving closer to acquisition of nuclear weapons and the U.S.-China military alliance taking shape. The U.S. military programs of the 1980s would restore an overwhelming nuclear superiority to the U.S. unless matched at a fantastic cost.

To be sure, a finding that the Soviets act out of weakness rather than strength is not necessarily reassuring; originally, containment policy was premised on the theory that the Soviets were too paranoid to coexist peacefully with the West. The issue is whether Soviet fears are really a threat to the peace, and whether it is in the U.S. interest to increase or decrease those fears.

It is no secret that a number of U.S. political and military figures have welcomed the Afghanistan crisis as an opportunity to push rearmament, just as an earlier generation welcomed the Korean invasion in 1950. Whatever interpretation one makes of the consequences of the remilitarization and military interventions of the 1950s and 1960s, it is striking how little the planned increments of military power can solve the security crisis we now face.

Before the assumption is made that military and paramilitary moves are required to deal with the crises of the 1980s, policymak-

ers had better take a hard look at what those moves could reasonably accomplish. In Vietnam, the misfit between military power and the political problems the United States was seeking to solve was the heart of the tragedy. The U.S. cannot field an army to fight the Russians in Afghanistan or Iran without drafting millions of men and women, and it could not win such a war. The proposed Middle East-U.S. bases are no military bar to a firm Soviet intention to move into the Persian Gulf. Indeed, they are a political asset for the Soviet Union, for they neutralize the anti-Russian enmity that the Soviet invasion has elicited in the Moslem world by symbolizing the U.S. commitment to the hated status quo in Palestine. Arming Pakistanis to fight in Afghanistan could well elicit a Soviet incursion, Cambodia-style, against the "sanctuaries."

That the U.S. with all its military power was unable to rescue 50 American hostages in Iran should be a clue. In the 1980s, the principal threats to the peace are not monolithic, superorganized dictatorial regimes a la Hitler's Germany but the global breakdown of organization and order. A process of disintegration seems also to be occurring within the Soviet Union. There is still no stable government in Iran. The Falkland Islands crisis is further evidence of the fragility of the existing political order and how unpredictable war has become. (If the United States had contingency plans for a war in which Argentina, Cuba, the USSR, and members of the Latin American community would be arrayed against Britain and the U.S., Secretary Haig's activities in the crisis did not reveal it.) These political facts make the traditional projection of military power counterproductive.

The great danger of the 1980s is that the possibilities for miscalculation have increased enormously. The U.S. miscalculated the negative effect of the NATO missile decision and the Soviet reaction to an emerging U.S.-China alliance. The Soviets probably underestimated the difficulties in pacifying Afghanistan and the political consequences of their act. If President Reagan appears to be a bellicose cold warrior, the Soviets appear to be growing increasingly insecure and therefore more dangerous. With Brezhnev about to leave, it is not clear who is in charge.

The ambiguity of policy in both capitals is the heart of the danger. Old ground rules have broken down and new ones must be put in place immediately. New de facto rules about what the super-

powers can and cannot do will either be forged in the crucible of confrontation or they will be arrived at by explicit agreement. A new world security system is urgently needed.

It is now more important than ever to offer an explicit, simple, and comprehensive agreement for stopping the arms race and prohibiting the further deployment of military forces in other countries. Surely what is needed is a moratorium on the production, testing, and deployment of all nuclear weapons, which would apply to the U.S. and the USSR. Before going ahead with new weapons systems, the U.S. should press the Soviets to accept such a moratorium for at least three years. The Soviets have publicly expressed interest in stopping "all new weapons."

At the same time, we need mutually agreed upon restrictions on what each superpower can do with its military power, including the threat of intervention, which would outlaw future Vietnams, Dominican Republics, Chiles, Angolas, Czechoslovakias, Hungarys, Afghanistans, and possible future Polands, Nicaraguas, and El Savadors. We should offer the Soviets a broad agreement that embodies the principle of equality on which they have long insisted—clear ground rules that inhibit both the U.S. and the USSR and symbolize their mutual understanding that military power cannot be effectively used by the superpowers in the Third World, and therefore will not be used.

Both superpowers seem to lack a minimum understanding of our historical moment. The failure to grasp the power of liberation ideologies is the fundamental weak point of the official view in Washington, and so, it seems, in Moscow, too. In one sense, we are at the "end of ideology." Neither communism nor capitalism remain credible philosophical systems for organizing society in the contemporary world. The existing models are too beset by internal contradictions and failures. There is panic and violence in the world not, as at other historical moments, because of a fanatic belief that one system or another has a monopoly on truth but because of widespread feelings that no one in charge knows what to do.

The failure of both socialist and capitalist regimes to bring liberation or dignity to billions of people has unleashed a profound spiritual reaction—a radical rejection of the dominant international culture. The popular impulse is not so much to build a "nation" in the 19th century sense of the word as to restore a sense of cultural and religious autonomy and to achieve an identity which, as in the

case of the Kurds, for example, may be transnational. But the transforming power of popular passions is real, and in the corridors of power it is hopelessly misunderstood.

The official U.S. worldview ignored Islam in Iran until the mobs were in the streets. The Russians have been more aware of popular passion as a major political force of our time, but they too are so bound by the traditional geopolitical view of the world that their only response is to try to crush it.

Given the realities of world power and the parallel reflex response in Washington and Moscow, there is no way out of the national security dilemma as it is now being defined. The U.S. does have a historical opportunity to help build a new world consensus to contain aggression. It can do that, however, only by identifying more with the concerns of the weak states where the world's majority lives.

To build a world consensus, we need new ground rules that will be equally applicable to the superpowers. To curb proliferation, the U.S.-Soviet competition in nuclear weapons must come to a halt. To build a world consensus to condemn Soviet interventions, the U.S. must commit itself to cease further military interventions of its own. To build a new world majority for reestablishing the minimum international order necessary to survive the rest of the century, the poor countries must have a significantly greater stake in that order.

The fundamental security problem for the U.S. and the whole industrial world is how to restructure our societies so that we use less of the world's product, because it will not be available to us. The rebuilding of an international economy based on a fairer and more stable distribution system for world resources is critical for survival.

The principal security problem for the U.S. in the 1980s is instability; the Russians are indeed a part of the problem, but only a part. The mounting disorder in the world requires more detente, not less. We need more emphasis on human rights, not less; only legitimate governments, not repressive juntas.

We need accommodation with the developing countries on economic issues. We dare not let our obsession with the Soviets define our global security policy. The effort to develop rational security policies appropriate for the 1980s is being abandoned, and we march to catastrophe under the banner of a hopeless realpolitik.

The moment of crisis can, however, be a moment of hope and transformation. If we are to be faithful stewards of the earth whose short-term tenants we are, we must hold out an alternative vision than that of war.

THE FAILURE OF ARMS CONTROL:
Why Government Efforts at Arms Control Have Failed

by Robert Johansen

Several thousand diplomatic meetings during three decades of arms negotiations have failed to reduce a single arsenal or the willingness of governments to use military power in diplomacy and combat. These efforts to reverse the arms buildup have failed for three reasons. First, the leaders of the world's greatest military powers do not *want* to create a world in which their military power will play a diminished role. A careful examination of U.S. proposals over the past three decades, for example, demonstrates that U.S. officials do not favor reducing U.S. military strength except under world conditions that are economically, politically, and militarily so advantageous to themselves that rival governments cannot reasonably be expected to accept them.

But, one might ask, does not the conclusion of a few international arms agreements prove that officials are trying? Yes, they are trying to reach agreements, but not for the purpose of reducing the influence of military power in international relations. When agreements are reached, they seldom impose genuine restrictions on new weapons that military officials want. Arsenals today are no less dangerous than they would be if there were no agreements.

The most dangerous dimension of the arms competition in the 1980s will come not from qualitative improvements that make weapons faster, more deadly, more accurate, and more difficult to detect or defend against. The Strategic Arms Limitations Talks (SALT) II treaty, even if it had been ratified, would not have prevented a single qualitative development on the Pentagon's drawing boards. In this respect, Reagan's version of SALT, START, probably will be no different.

Despite the technological bonanza the SALT II treaty allowed for the Pentagon, Reagan believed the treaty unfairly re-

stricted the United States. So he boasted that if elected he would "tear up" the SALT II treaty and step up U.S. military preparedness. This candor accurately reflects Reagan's attitude toward arms reductions. Yet without acknowledging any contradiction in his actions, he will, like his predecessors, embrace SALT as a pillar of peace.

Second, past and present government efforts are fruitless because there is a fundamental contradiction between two goals of arms control policy: It is not possible to halt the arms competition and at the same time rely on arms for security and diplomatic influence. To be sure, officials might hope theoretically to stop the arms buildup at a point of exact equilibrium between states. But this fails in practice because one government's perception of military equality is seldom the same as its rival's perception. In addition, no government in competition with another is satisfied with equilibrium. Each wants a predominance of power in its favor.

As long as arms are perceived and maintained as the key to security and diplomatic influence, one never has enough. A dynamic technology makes matters worse. If one weapon system, such as the B-1 bomber, is foreclosed, scientists provide a new, as yet uncontrolled weapon, such as the cruise missile, to get an advantage for a few years over one's competitor. Until a fundamentally different approach is taken, one weapon system may come or go, as arms control succeeds or fails, but the arms competition will continue.

Third, arms reductions seldom occur because the people who want them often unintentionally waste their time and money by supporting the government's arms control policies, even though these are not likely to reverse the growth of armaments. As a result, many well-intentioned persons have concentrated their efforts on a journey that turns out to be a political dead end. Not enough people and energies are left over to travel down more promising roads. Disillusionment quickly sets in for those trapped in a dead end. Many give up, reducing the size of the potential constituency for arms reductions. As any social organizer knows, many people who once hoped for arms reduction later think that arms control is hopeless.

When all three of the above reasons are present, the arms buildup gathers almost irresistible momentum—as it has since SALT began in 1969. Again and again arms control negotiations have attracted and then nullified the efforts of citizens who seek an

end to the arms race. Because the contradiction of goals noted above is not acknowledged, the political process attending negotiations often encourages the expansion rather than the reduction of arsenals.

Negotiations, for example, focus more attention than would otherwise exist on the number of missiles and other weapons. As a result, the inferior side steps up its efforts to become equal, so it will not be embarrassed or intimidated by being "behind." The superior side tries to move farther ahead in order to negotiate from a position of such strength that the inferior side will concede points or tire of trying to catch up. But this does not work because the inferior side will not accept a treaty permanently freezing its inferiority. Meanwhile, the superior side will not negotiate away its superiority because domestic hawks would end the political careers of those recommending such policies.

While near equality exists, the parties may agree to stabilize one category of aging weapons while simultaneously stepping up the drive for superiority in another area. As Washington and Moscow moved closer to stabilizing the number of stationary land-based missiles, for example, they simultaneously put many more warheads on each missile. Malcolm Currie, the director of defense research and engineering, explained that because the SALT II treaty set limits on the number of strategic missiles, "the accord . . . re-enforces our need for technological progress." Most officials who favored the SALT II treaty wanted to couple ratification with a five percent annual increase in military expenditures.

The guiding principle of arms control is to limit an existing or unwanted weapon so as to facilitate the movement of money and brainpower into new, more sophisticated instruments of mass destruction. The limits for the SALT II treaty, for example, were set in the Vladivostok agreement of 1974. At that time the United States had deployed 832 multiple, independently targetable reentry vehicles (MIRVs). The Soviet Union had none. That accord was the last easy opportunity to ban MIRVs completely. Being ahead, the United States refused this opportunity.

Later Secretary of State Henry Kissinger admitted that the MIRV ceiling could possibly have been lower but that he made no effort to reduce it below the level that the U.S. had planned to produce without an agreement. Negotiators set ceilings far above existing deployments; these ceilings then become production targets

for new programs. The accord allowed a total U.S. and Soviet increase of 1,808 MIRVed vehicles, or 217 percent. President Ford told the public that this five-year limit was "a firm ceiling on the strategic arms race, thus preventing an arms race. . . ." Kissinger held a press conference to announce that these ceilings would "be seen as one of the turning points in the history of the post-World War II arms race."

The upward pressure on arms levels is further stimulated by the desire to bargain from a position of strength. The more bargaining chips one can produce and then trade away, the argument goes, the more successful the negotiations will be. In practice, new weapons are developed as bargaining threats; later negotiations ratify the deployment of everything previously begun.

This process provides an arms control justification for weapons that lack a military justification. In the early 1970s, for example, no security arguments could be found for the MIRV. It would stimulate the arms race and not increase the ability to deter an attack. But since officials wanted MIRVs anyway, they developed an arms control "need" for MIRV. They claimed that a MIRV force would help induce the Soviet Union to limit its antimissile missiles by making the latter ineffective.

When SALT I limited antiballistic missiles (ABMs) to a militarily insignificant number, there was again no need to proceed with MIRVs. So U.S. officials adopted a new argument to justify U.S. MIRVs as a bargaining chip to discourage the Soviet deployment of MIRVs. Despite Soviet interest in restricting them, U.S. officials lost interest as U.S. deployment proceeded. Similarly, U.S. officials favored development of an air-launched cruise missile as a bargaining chip to trade away if the Soviet Union agreed not to produce mobile land-based missiles. After the Soviet Union agreed to discuss this U.S. proposal, the United States reversed its position. Officials began to argue that it was more important to develop the cruise missile than to ban it. By retaining the mobile missile option, officials also allowed themselves to go ahead with another much larger, totally new ICBM—the MX.

Military officials use the SALT negotiations and liberals' enthusiasm for arms control to entice members of Congress to vote money for new bargaining chips ostensibly to induce the Soviet Union to negotiate seriously. An implicit theme of many congressional discussions has been that more weapons are needed for arms con-

trol than for military security. President Reagan echoes a similar theme in arguing that the United States must build up its forces in order to negotiate a START that is better than SALT II.

Even after the text of a treaty is written, the stimulus for more arms continues. In return for agreeing to accept the SALT I treaty, the Joint Chiefs of Staff extracted "assurances" from the White House that they would get "a very extensive . . . development program and aggressive improvement and modernization programs. . . ." Another payoff to gain Pentagon support was the decision to go ahead with the cruise missile—not then part of the negotiations. The cruise missile later complicated and delayed the completion of SALT II, and now threatens to make the verification of any future ban of nuclear weapons virtually impossible.

Similarly, Pentagon officials made the development of the MX missile their price for supporting the second stage of SALT negotiations, even though there was no need for such a large or accurate missile if one's purpose was deterrence of war. Of several different missiles that officials considered as a way of keeping the land-based missile invulnerable to Soviet attack, the MX was the most threatening to the Soviet Union, rather than the one least vulnerable to Soviet attack.

During the process of building support to obtain Senate ratification for SALT II, Carter attempted to placate Senate hawks with new public commitments to proceed with more Trident submarines; to speed up the deployment of the Mark 12 maneuvering warhead on Minuteman missiles; to proceed with the Trident II missile; to hasten the decision about deploying the MX; to test and further develop cruise missiles capable of being launched from land, sea, and air; to persuade reluctant NATO governments to increase their military spending; and to increase U.S. military expenditures by 25 percent above inflation over the next five years.

Carter also appointed a career military officer and former opponent of arms control to replace Paul Warnke, who negotiated the treaty and was the Director of Arms Control and Disarmament Agency. Carter called for registration for the draft, even against the advice of the selective service. Although the United States could reduce its strategic nuclear arsenal by more than 90 percent and still have enough warheads to destroy the Soviet Union two times over even after suffering a first strike, Carter continued to add several warheads each day to the U.S. stockpile. Despite SALT II's

failure to reduce the number of U.S. warheads at all, Reagan gained in the campaign polls by criticizing Carter for letting the United States get too weak.

If after all the above concessions the SALT treaty still could not be ratified, can anyone believe that the United States has a serious program for arms reduction or that the present approach is effective in leading the public toward a less militarized future?

Surprisingly, the description of the mainstream approach by officials and journalists convinced most of the public that the government was doing everything possible to achieve a disarming world. As a result, except for a few like Senators George McGovern and Mark Hatfield, people's eyes rested on SALT while destabilizing new armaments arose everywhere. What SALT I refused to control—the MIRV—expanded the arms race much more than the treaty limited it.

What SALT II legitimized—the cruise and MX missiles—undermined the future of human security far more than the treaty enhanced it. Even well-informed people have acquiesced. For example, after endorsing the missile ceilings for the SALT II treaty, the editors of *The New York Times* commented that as a result of the agreement, the arms buildup would continue "just about as planned, and possibly a little faster in some areas—legitimized, in fact, by international compact." Upon concluding extensive Senate hearings in the weapons evaluation subcommittee, Senator Edmund Muskie observed, "My suspicion is that the SALT talks actually stimulated the arms race rather than stabilized it." Because the government told the public and the public chose to believe the erroneous idea that SALT represented the best possible effort at arms control, the negotiations actually deterred more promising steps for arms limitation.

To be successful, a plan to reduce arms needs to be based on two understandings: (1) the prevailing approaches to arms control will not halt the arms race; and (2) the arms problem cannot be "solved" until the present balance of social forces and many peoples' values are changed. Success will await those who give less emphasis to mainstream approaches and more emphasis to educating and organizing for basic change of attitudes and institutions.

The first step is to decide whether one is willing to switch one's attention from the agenda set by the government to more

promising, even if less glamorous, tasks. The purpose of present arms control policy is to manage a continuing arms buildup, not to strengthen the attitudes and institutions that will undergird a more secure system of world peace. The latter requires commitment to a different way of life, not to fine tuning of the present international system—which is, ultimately, a war system.

New initiatives should not be misconstrued as a campaign to oppose ratification of SALT treaties. Even if such treaties are a mixed blessing, by the time a treaty is completed, the price, in terms of legitimizing new weapons, has already been partially paid. Rejection of a treaty would not recover those losses. Moreover, it is important to avoid self-righteousness about one's own position and to accept other people's actions at different places on the political continuum.

In deciding where to stand, individuals, lobbyists, and social action committees should consider whether they have not lost ground by giving up the 1950s' commitment to disarmament in order to embrace arms control. This reorientation was an effort to be realistic. But has it been successful? Has any U.S. official in the past decade said anything as promising as the U.S. representative to the UN in 1961: "We do not hold the vision of a world without conflict. We do hold the vision of a world without war—and this inevitably requires an alternative system for coping with conflict. We cannot have one without the other."

To leave arms reduction to militarily powerful governments and publics like those represented in Washington and Moscow is like waiting for a king to lead a revolution for democracy and aboli- tion of his throne. It is like relying on plantation owners of the 1850s to demand the abolition of slavery and the erosion of their economic and political strength. It is like depending on Congress to pass tax legislation that would eliminate tax loopholes which bene- fit those who make the laws and their wealthy supporters. Such legislation never happens unless the government's foundations are shaken from below.

Arms reductions are even harder to achieve than tax reforms, because citizens hesitate to challenge their government out of fear that such action may encourage a rival government to take advan- tage of U.S. domestic pressure for arms reduction. If people are not willing to accept the risk (and take steps to avert any dangerous

side effects), then they must accept an unending arms race and, eventually, the near certainty of irretrievable disaster for the human race. No third, less painful alternative exists.

For people committed to increasing human security, the most logical step is to draw a clear line where the purchase of instruments for distant death and suicide must stop—an across-the-board nuclear freeze with no loopholes and no exceptions. People can, if they will, insist on an immediate halt to the testing and deployment of all new nuclear weapons and delivery systems. This fulfills two goals: (1) it moves U.S. society closer to thinking about practical alternatives to an indefinitely continuing balance of terror, and (2) it communicates to the rest of the world that part of the U.S. public is now moving, for the first time in history, to demilitarize world society, and that other nations can help this antimilitary movement by dampening their own arms buildup.

This "citizens' diplomacy" buttresses but goes far beyond the most peaceful aspects of Washington's diplomacy. Calling for a nuclear freeze has a desirable impact on both the United States and the Soviet Union, even if the United States freezes its deployments first and then invites Soviet reciprocation.

In response to this idea many citizens will ask: "Is that really safe? Will not Soviet armed forces someday threaten us?" To be sure, that is a grave danger. But it is impossible to reduce the Kremlin's feared ruthlessness or its reliance on military power by building more U.S. weapons. Because of the way that the U.S. and Soviet governments imitate each other's armaments, a vote by any U.S. citizen for an increase in U.S. military capability is also a vote for an increase in Soviet military capability as well. One of the most important steps those in the U.S. can take to slow the Soviet Union's production of more military equipment is to stop the growth of U.S. arsenals.

At the same time, non-military defenses and international incentives to avert aggression need to be enormously expanded. Of course these steps involve risks, but they are more promising and less dangerous than the present risks of proliferating weapons.

To act for a nuclear freeze in the short run should be part of a larger commitment to abolish war in the long run. There is no substitute for telling one's government and friends what one really is for. In the nuclear age, prudence must lead people to say that they are for an end to war; that they are for practical steps which will

increase security while decreasing the role of military power in international relations; that they are not for the purchase of new weapons to achieve feeble, temporary limits on old ones.

We must seek not so much to limit arms as to inhibit their use and delegitimize their possession. To own a nuclear weapon, which when used will inevitably harm many innocent people, is no less shameful than to possess a gas chamber for innocents. To call only for a freeze of genocidal weapons is as insufficient as calling for a freeze on gas chambers, meanwhile ignoring the ones already built. In addition to a nuclear moratorium, activists should consider working for the abolition of war by opposing war taxes, military service, and corporate production of war material; by favoring peace education in schools, churches, and public media; and by political action to nurture a demilitarized global security system.

Most people are unaware of the destabilizing changes in weapons that have been occurring during endless talk about arms limitations. In truth, we are squandering the last good, relatively unrisky chance to halt the arms buildup for years to come—perhaps ever. At this moment, we are suffering a massive decline in our security by allowing our government to make its planned innovations in weapons technology, which the Soviet Union and eventually others will imitate.

As the nuclear-tipped cruise missile is deployed, it will become impossible to verify general limits on nuclear weapons without elaborate, intrusive, on-site inspection. The MX is also a step toward greater willingness to use nuclear weapons. U.S.-Soviet competition encourages the spread of nuclear weapons elsewhere. Nearly all nuclear technology—the atomic bomb, hydrogen bomb, intercontinental ballistic missile, submarine-launched missile, MIRV, maneuvering warhead, and cruise missile—could have been easily banned without on-site inspection if they had been prohibited before successful testing of the weapon had occurred. Yet U.S. negotiators have not sought to limit these weapons until after the United States first developed the technology. It is time for Americans to reverse this government pattern.

People are understandably hesitant to oppose their own government on delicate security issues. But the call for a freeze on nuclear weapons is not negative opposition to an effective or legitimate government policy. It could be the first step toward a warless world.

THE BIG LIE OF THE ARMS RACE:
Questions for Thought and Discussion

1. In his article, Greider refutes three myths that create a perception of a Soviet threat. Does uncovering these myths make you feel more secure or less secure?

2. How do you react to Barnet's assertion that "the big lie behind all murder, from the random street killing to the hydrogen bomb, is that the victims deserve to die"? What do you think Jesus would say, in light of how he tells us to treat our neighbors and enemies?

3. Basic to Barnet's thinking in "Two Bumbling Giants" is that the "old ground rules" for international relations have broken down and new ones are needed. He contends that military responses do not solve current political problems, as exemplified by problems in the Middle East. How would you answer Barnet's question, "Is there any value that justifies risking the death of everything?" What would the consequences of your answer be for international politics?

4. In "Lies Clearer Than Truth," Barnet summarizes the Pentagon's rules for negotiating arms agreements as (1) "Don't negotiate when you are behind" and (2) "Why negotiate when you are ahead?" How does Johansen's analysis of the historical situation bear this out, and what is the effect of such a practice on efforts to achieve real disarmament?

THE MEDICAL CONSEQUENCES OF NUCLEAR WAR:

A Case for Prevention
by Howard Hiatt

There are two preconceptions about the medical consequences of nuclear war which take little research to confirm: first, nuclear war is unhealthy; and, second, no effective medical response can be conceived to deal with the human damage that would result. As a physician now concerned primarily with public health, I therefore offer a recommendation increasingly perceived as essential for diseases and epidemics for which there are no cures: namely, that all efforts be directed at prevention.

Planning for the medical and other environmental consequences of a nuclear war is senseless. Little is said about the catastrophe of a nuclear attack, perhaps because it is horrible to contemplate. Surely, little is said about medical intervention because so little that is hopeful can be said. And yet, our very silence permits or encourages the nuclear arms race to continue, making almost inevitable, either by design or by chance, what could be the last epidemic our civilization will know.

Much can be said, however. Two sources of information are available. The first are descriptions of the medical effects of the Hiroshima and Nagasaki bombs. The second are several recent and authoritative theoretical projections of the medical effects of bombing American, or Soviet, cities toward which Soviet, or American, nuclear weapons are now aimed.

The Hiroshima bomb, the explosive power of which was equivalent to 20,000 tons of TNT, is estimated to have killed more than 75,000 out of a total population of 245,000: 25 percent directly burned by the bomb, 50 percent from other injuries, and 20 percent as a result of radiation effects. It destroyed two-thirds of the 90,000 buildings within the city limits. Perhaps even more devastating than the statistics are the descriptions of the individual victims.

Consider this picture presented by John Hersey in his book, *Hiroshima:*

> When he had penetrated the bushes, he saw there were about 20 men, and they were all in exactly the same nightmarish state: their faces were wholly burned, their eyes had run down their cheeks. . . . Their mouths were mere swollen, pus-covered wounds, which they could not bear to stretch enough to admit the spout of the teapot. So Father Kleinsorge got a large piece of grass and drew out the stem so as to make a straw and gave them all water to drink that way.

The destruction wrought by an atomic weapon on Hiroshima provides, along with the similar experience in Nagasaki, direct evidence of the consequences of nuclear warfare, but there are many theoretical appraisals upon which we may also draw. For example, the Office of Technology Assessment of the Congress of the United States last year published a study that described in detail the effects of nuclear attacks on Detroit and on Leningrad.

The description that follows of the effects of a nuclear explosion over New York is taken from materials prepared by the U.S. Arms Control and Disarmament Agency.

The scenario is, you must realize, conservative. While the one-million-ton bomb involved in the attack is more than 50 times more powerful than that dropped on Hiroshima, it is, however, far less destructive than the largest contemporary weapons. And this hypothetical attack involves the detonation of only a single bomb, whereas contemporary military planning and technological capabilities make it far more likely that several will be used in each attack.

New York City's trial by nuclear attack begins with the detonation of a one-million-ton, air-burst bomb 6,500 feet above the Empire State Building.

The area of total destruction, the circle within which even the most heavily reinforced concrete structures do not survive, has a radius of 1.5 miles. That circle extends from the Brooklyn Bridge to Central Park Lake and from Long Island City to Hoboken. Included within it are the Empire State Building, Lincoln Center, and the Stock Exchange. Within this circle, almost all the population is killed.

At a distance of three miles from the center of the blast, past Jersey City and Elmhurst, past the Brooklyn Museum in the south and 145th Street in the north, concrete buildings are destroyed. The heat from the explosion and the spontaneous ignition of clothing cause third-degree flash burns over much of the body, killing most people in this area.

More than four miles from the center, brick and wood-frame buildings are destroyed, and fires caused by the intense heat are fanned by 160-mile-per-hour winds.

In a circle extending to Hastings on Hudson, Livingston, New Jersey, and beyond Far Rockaway to the sea, brick and wood-frame buildings sustain heavy damage. The heat exceeds 12 calories per square centimeter, and all individuals with exposed skin suffer severe third-degree burns. At the outer limit of this circle, brick and wood-frame structures sustain moderate damage.

Miles beyond this last ring, people suffer second-degree burns on all exposed skin and additional burns from flammable clothing and environmental materials. Retinal burns resulting from looking at the fireball may cause blindness. As high winds spread the fires caused by the intitial blast and thermal radiation, the number of casualties grows.

If we assume a population for the metropolitan area of 16 million, more than 1,600,000 are killed. There are 2,800,000 injured. Many of these survivors are badly burned, blinded, and otherwise seriously wounded. Many are disoriented. These are the short-term effects. The problem of radiation sickness, including intractable nausea, vomiting, bleeding, hair loss, severe infection, and often death, will grow in the days and weeks ahead. Fallout from the bomb will spread well beyond the area of impact.

The population is devastated. Many survivors are in need of immediate medical care, food, shelter, clothing, and water. The communities in which they had lived have, in many cases, virtually ceased to exist as physical entities, and as social entities as well. Government is barely existent. The transportation system, including many roads, has been destroyed. Remaining food, water, and medical supplies are dangerously inadequate.

And what of the medical response to such a disaster? In Hiroshima, 65 of the city's 150 doctors were killed in the bombing, and most of the survivors were wounded. Some 10,000 wounded made

their way to Hiroshima's 600-bed Red Cross Hospital. There, only six doctors and 10 nurses were able to help them. John Hersey described the struggle of one of those physicians:

> Dr. Sasaki . . . realized . . . that the casualties were pouring in from outdoors. There were so many that he began to pass up the lightly wounded; he decided that all he could hope to do was to stop people from bleeding to death. Before long patients lay and crouched on the floors of the wards and the laboratories and all the other rooms . . . and in the driveway and courtyard, and for blocks each way in the streets outside. Wounded people supported maimed people; disfigured families leaned together. Many people were vomiting. . . . The people in the suffocating crowd inside the hospital wept and cried, for Dr. Sasaki to hear, "Sensi! Doctor!" and the less seriously wounded came and pulled at his sleeve and begged him to go to the aid of the worse wounded. Tugged here and there in his stocking feet, bewildered by the numbers, staggered by so much raw flesh, Dr. Sasaki lost all sense of profession and stopped working as a skillful surgeon and a sympathetic man; he became an automaton, mechanically wiping, daubing, winding, wiping, daubing, winding.

For New York, we can take as our base a figure of 29,000 physicians in the metropolitan area. Extrapolating from the casualties suffered by the general population, we may project that 3,000 doctors will be killed immediately and some 5,100 will be seriously injured. Thus, 21,000 surviving physicians will be responsible for the care of 2,800,000 patients with grave wounds. It will be essential that these wounds be attended to as quickly as possible, yet for each of these patients to be visited once, for 15 minutes, will require every surviving physician to work a 34-hour shift.

In fact, it is likely that many fewer physicians will survive, for they are concentrated, during working hours, in an area close to the center of the blast. But whether the post-attack physician-to-patient ratio is one to 300 or one to 1,000, where will treatment take place?

The bomb will massively reduce the number of hospital beds within the city alone, and the amount of medical equipment and supplies is similarly inadequate. The New York Hospital-Cornell Medical Center and St. Vincent's Hospital no longer exist. In ruins,

as well, are Bellevue Hospital, Beth Israel Medical Center, Mount Sinai Medical Center, and several others. The geographic distribution of surviving medical facilities will be another problem, some requiring physicians to enter more highly radioactive areas, and thus expose themselves to greater personal danger, in order to treat the injured. The shortage of nurses will be severe.

With a decimated professional community, physical facilities largely in ruins, and a complete disruption of communications, the task of treating the wounded will be hopeless.

If you have any doubts, you will understand my use of the term hopeless after I describe a 20-year-old man who was recently a patient in the burn unit of one of Boston's teaching hospitals. He had been in an automobile accident in which the gasoline tank exploded, and had incurred very extensive third-degree burns. During his hospitalization, he received 281 units of fresh-frozen plasma, 147 units of fresh-frozen red blood cells, 37 units of platelets, and 36 units of albumin. He underwent six operative procedures, during which wounds involving 85 per cent of his body surface were closed with homograft, cadaver allograft, and artificial skin. Throughout his hospitalization, he required mechanical ventilation and monitoring with central venous lines, arterial lines, and an intermittent pulmonary artery line.

Despite these heroic measures, which stretched the resources of one of the country's most comprehensive medical institutions, the man died on his thirty-third hospital day. His injuries were likened by the person who supervised his care to those described for many of the victims of the Hiroshima bomb.

Keeping that one patient alive for 33 days required the extraordinary resources of one of the world's major medical centers. No amount of preparation could provide the human and physical resources required for the care of even a few such patients hospitalized simultaneously in any city of the nation. Yet one must assume that hundreds of thousands of patients would be in that condition in a post-attack New York. At least tens of thousands of such casualties would result in every large metropolitan center hit by a nuclear weapon.

New York is perhaps the most favored American city with respect to resources for burn victims: It has 48 beds devoted to the care of acutely burned patients. Yet at least one-half of these beds would be destroyed in the first seconds after the blast.

This is but one reason that it is futile to suggest a meaningful medical response to the overwhelming health problems that would follow a nuclear attack. Further, only the most limited medical measures can be visualized to deal with the burden of cancer and genetic defects that would afflict survivors and future generations. Temporary evacuation has been suggested as an approach, but radioactivity would make the blast area uninhabitable for months. Most of the area's water supply, sanitation resources, and transportation and industrial capacity would be destroyed.

Note that I have hardly touched upon the equally dreadful intermediate and long-term effects of the nuclear attack on the surviving population.

What is the purpose, one may ask, of describing such almost unthinkable conditions? But the conditions are not unthinkable; rather they are infrequently thought about. Among the painful results of the silence are the continuing proliferation of nuclear weapons and the failure to reject nuclear war as a viable option in the management of world problems.

There is, of course, no reason to consider the consequences of nuclear war in strictly medical terms. But if we do so, we must pay heed to the inescapable lesson of contemporary medicine: Where treatment of a given disease is ineffective or where costs are insupportable, attention must be given to prevention. Both conditions apply to the effects of nuclear war: Treatment programs would be virtually useless and the costs would be staggering. Can any stronger arguments be marshalled for a preventive strategy?

A physician attempts to make a persuasive case for prevention without frightening the patient by describing in clinical detail the most unpleasant aspects of the disease in question. If the patient fails to pay heed, however, the doctor is justified, indeed obligated, to call attention to the consequences in realistic terms, however stark they may be. Our "patients" at present include the political leaders of the principal nations of the world. Many appear not to understand the medical realities of a nuclear confrontation. Therefore, we must inform them and the American people of the full-blown clinical picture that would follow a nuclear attack and the impotence of the medical community to offer a meaningful response. We must paint this picture in its true dimensions, with the horror of a realistic story that has no precedent in devastation and will almost surely be followed by none.

THE DAY THE BOMB HIT:
A Hiroshima A-bomb Survivor Remembers
by Akihiro Takahashi

It was very hot on the morning of "that day," 35 years ago. I was 14 years old and in the second grade of Hiroshima Municipal Junior High School (now called Nakahiro Junior High School, 1.4 kilometers from the point of explosion, or hypocenter). In those days of the war, I was a mobilized student working in the building evacuation program at Koamicho.

I went to school on August 6. I was in the school playground with my classmates lining up for the morning roll call when a B-29 approached over our heads, leaving a vapor trail behind it. Strangely the air-raid alerts had all been canceled. I was watching the blue sky and pointing with my classmates at the B-29.

No sooner was "Get into line!" shouted by a headboy than we were surrounded by dark brown smoke, which was accompanied by a roaring sound as if the ground had been split in two. We could not see even an inch ahead. I found myself thrown back about 10 meters and to the ground. Five minutes, maybe almost 10, passed before it became faintly light around us. Looking around, I found the schoolhouse totally flattened and my classmates lying here and there on the ground.

For a while I was not aware of anything at all; I stood absent-mindedly, and then I looked at my body. The skin of my arms and legs was peeling off just like shreds of cloth, and I could see red flesh. The palms of my hands developed blisters just like the belly of a globefish; my skin had turned yellow.

Several pieces of glass fragments blown off by the blast were sticking into my arms and back. My clothing, which was called "national uniform," was totally burnt. My combat cap had been blown off, and my hair was singed. I felt terribly hot, and I thought that I could not endure the smarting on my back. Suddenly a sense of horror ran through my body.

I thought, "Nothing can be done standing here! I must jump into the river." In the refuge training program we had been instructed to jump into the river in case of an emergency, so I made up my mind to go to the River Yamate that was flowing near the school.

When I happened to turn around, my friend Yamamoto was following me crying, "Mother, Mother. I'm afraid my house in Kusatsu (about 1.5 kilometers from the hypocenter) must have been burned down. What has become of Daddy and Mommy? What will become of me, if they have died?" He was sobbing and mumbling.

Strangely enough, I kept my presence of my mind. No tears were in my eyes. I managed to find a way to the bank of the river while encouraging Yamamoto.

I shouted, "Don't cry! Let's go to the river." Every street was blocked by the ruins of fallen houses, so we went through them on all fours. Our arms and feet were badly injured because of glass fragments, small stones, wood, and nails.

As we crossed over a small wooden bridge, a raging fire started in the fallen houses along the streets we had just passed. If we had been an instant longer in leaving there, we would have been engulfed by a sea of flames.

"Oh, we are saved!" I cried in my mind, and I did not try to stop the tears falling for the first time. I was not aware that Yamamoto had disappeared.

I got to the bank of the river on the side of Yamate-cho and, exhausted, lay down on the sand. As the pain on my back was becoming unendurable, I dipped myself into the water; but each time I dipped my body, I felt an unbearable tingling pain as the sand came between the peeling skin and flesh. On the river numerous dead bodies were floating, one on top of the other.

While I was sitting on the sand, a woman came to me and applied some oily ointment to my body. She told me that there was a first-aid station built by the Army Hospital at Mitaki (about 3 kilometers from the hypocenter).

At the first-aid station, I rested after receiving medical treatment. Then a heavy black rain started to fall in large drops.

When the black rain stopped, I left on foot for Kusatsu where my home was. After walking for a while, I heard a voice calling me, "Takahashi, Takahashi!" Turning in the direction of the voice, I found my classmate Hatta squatting down along the roadside.

Hatta was suffering from burns on the soles of his feet, where red flesh could be seen: "I can't walk; please take me home."

I was at a loss to know how to take him home. Then I got an idea and suggested that he crawl on all fours. Proceeding in this way we did not cover any great distance, so I let him lean on me and walk on his heels. By using these two methods alternately, we progressed towards Kusatsu at a very slow pace.

While we were resting by the roadside, I saw my great uncle and great aunt coming toward us from a Buddhist ceremony. The coincidence made me feel that an old saying had come true: "To meet Buddha in hell."

"Auntie!" I shouted to my great aunt. They were upset to see our burns. I was carried on great uncle's back and Hatta on my great aunt's. I finally reached home, being taken the last part of the way on a stretcher prepared by my grandfather who had come to meet us.

I heard later that Yamamoto and Hatta had died in great pain. I narrowly escaped death during almost one and a half year's struggle against illness, including three weeks in a coma. I have been hospitalized three times in order to have keloids, enlarged masses of scar tissue, removed and to receive treatment for a liver malfunction. Even today, I am obliged to go to the hospital to have treatment for this liver malfunction as I am designated an A-bomb disease patient.

The United States and Japan went through the unfortunate experience of war some 30 years ago. I am convinced that the hatred, the sufferings, and the grief of A-bomb survivors can be overcome. It is my understanding that your people are also still suffering from the deep scars of war, and I sincerely hope that they will be healed by efforts for peace. I would like our two peoples to join each other in speaking out against war and making a step towards the abolition of nuclear weapons.

A FAMILY SEES THE LIGHT, AGAIN AND AGAIN:

Reflections of a Nuclear Weapons Test Victim

by Elizabeth Wright

We couldn't see it, but the desert was there, stretched below. Daddy had parked the station wagon on the western slope of Utah Hill to get a better view. Shivering in the predawn chill, we sat on the tailgate, eating Mama's homemade cinnamon rolls, drinking hot chocolate, waiting.

When it came, it was something that I would never forget, though I was to see it again and again. The sky ripped open with an intense light, the ground trembled, and a mushroom-shaped cloud rose above the horizon. We had witnessed an above-ground nuclear test less than 100 miles away in the Nevada desert.

Little did we know, watching the immense fireball and awed by its unharnessed power, the tragedy that it was to bring, not just to our immediate family but also to our friends and neighbors in the little town of St. George, Utah.

Atomic Energy Commission and Air Force representatives had little trouble in the early 1950s when they sought the cooperation of the citizens of St. George. We manned air-watch stations and met cars at Utah Hill to wash off the "dust" that had settled on them as they drove across the Nevada desert. "There is no danger," the officials told us. "We repeat, there is no danger."

The tests, which often woke us at dawn with their flash of light and tremors, were always made when the wind was blowing away from Las Vegas, the closest "populated" area. Yet twice a day the truck from our dairy cooperative rumbled past my home taking radioactive milk from our cows, which grazed downwind from the test site, into Las Vegas for processing and distribution throughout Nevada.

We children were as sold as the adults on the necessity of the tests. On balmy evenings, my best friend and I would sit on the front lawn and plan where we would run when the Russians attacked us, what we would take, how we would find each other.

On May 19, 1953, the government exploded a bomb from the top of a 300-foot iron tower. The resulting cloud was so full of radioactive dirt, particles from the tower, and other debris that it was—and still is—called "Dirty Harry." When "Dirty Harry" started drifting our way, the alarm went out: "Keep the children indoors for a few hours," even though "there is no danger." The contamination level rose alarmingly, and government officials descended on the town but said nothing. They didn't want to "alarm" the residents further. We took cover for the requested time, then went about our living—and our dying.

On Christmas Eve, 1963, my sister Kay and I were home for a visit from southern California. I had started my first year of teaching, and she was studying design at UCLA. Marilyn and Mike still lived with our parents.

As president of Dixie Junior College in St. George, Daddy was working hard to build the school's reputation, as well as a new campus. At 43 he was in the prime of his life, a large man with an insatiable intellect and love of the outdoors. He had been both president of the Northwestern Association of Junior Colleges and a state park commissioner.

The moment we walked in the kitchen door, we knew that something was drastically wrong. Daddy's skin had a sickly yellow cast to it; he had lost an alarming amount of weight; he shuffled when he walked. He and Mother gathered us in the living room for a family conference. Our family doctor had been there that morning. The tests were conclusive. Leukemia. The disease was progressing so fast that he had a month, perhaps two, left to live. But he managed to stay alive six months, using the time to prepare us and the college for the time when he would no longer be there.

There is nothing graceful about dying from leukemia. His intestinal tract was pitted with ulcers. Hematomas were under the surface of his skin, all over. The pain never ceased. New medications would help for a while and then lose their effectiveness, leaving new complications.

Mother never left him. We all took care of one another. Love held us together—and faith. Daddy died July 5, 1964.

Through it all, my father felt sure that his disease had been triggered in some way by the nuclear testing. He recalled the day that he had been horseback riding on the desert with three friends when a "cloud" drifted overhead from a test detonated without warning that morning. He had commented, "It is like the cloud of doom." Of the four men present that day, three have died of cancer of some form, as have hundreds of their neighbors.

All my life, the one thing that I wanted to be, more than anything else, was a mother. So I was ecstatic to learn, in 1967, that I was pregnant.

During the first three months everything seemed to be normal. Then I began to bleed, and the doctor put me to bed. My husband would come home each day long enough to make certain that I was all right, change his clothes, and go to his second job.

For two months I rested, I read, I bled, I prayed. Twice a week the doctor gave me a cursory checkup. The pregnancy seemed viable, and he didn't want to do anything to disrupt it on the chance that the fetus was developing normally. In fact, my body was destroying my baby, dissolving it cell by cell. After five months a test finally came back negative. The waiting was over.

The strain had been an emotional overload that the marriage couldn't bear, and it too dissolved. I returned home, feeling like a freak. Only in the past year have I found that I was not alone, that my experience was being repeated over and over among my girlhood friends.

My brother Michael is the youngest in our family, but Marilyn had always been our baby, with the touch of fairy gold in her. She developed asthma as a child, and later an enlarged thyroid goiter, further impairing her ability to breathe. She moved to Los Angeles to start a toy company and to be closer to specialists, but she couldn't seem to get better.

One Friday night she had dinner with our sister Kay and her family, then returned alone to her small apartment a mile or so away. Early Saturday morning she called Kay to "come fast." Marilyn was choking. She couldn't breathe. This didn't resemble any other asthma attack.

Two blocks away from UCLA medical center, Marilyn died. Another death, another body to be shipped home to a grieving family, another grave to visit in a cemetery already too full.

I was angry. It wasn't fair. Mother responded to my outbursts with a quiet "It is God's will."

Then one night two years ago, I watched "Clouds of Doubt," a television documentary about the above-ground nuclear testing and its effects on the people downwind. When the show was over, all the anger and rage churned to the surface again, and I wept. All that time our government had known what might happen, yet kept saying, "There is no danger." I felt used.

When a geiger counter is run across my body, it clicks. In the back of my mind is the unspoken dread: When will the bomb inside me go off?

I watch my beautiful little niece, Kay's child, cope with the birth defect that left her with a ganglion that doubled the size of her tongue and wound around, like a weed, inside her neck and down into her shoulder. Three surgeries have removed half the tongue and all the ganglion except the part fastened to the nerves and lymph nodes. At least it wasn't malignant.

Last summer I visited my best friend in St. George. After several miscarriages, she finally delivered two healthy, bright sons, now teenagers. She also adopted a daughter, as I have adopted my two.

She conceived again, too late in life, and gave birth to a third son, a child who shouldn't have survived at all. His tiny body is massed with scars from the skilled but futile attempts to correct all the things that were wrong.

The doctor bills, even after the insurance payments, have mounted into the thousands of dollars. The family's living standard has been cut to barebones limits as it tries to honor the debts. The marriage is teetering under the pressures.

My friend had dark circles under her eyes from the strain of trying to work all day and give her family and baby the attention they need. She is exhausted, yet cradles this diminutive life in her hands and whispers to him how much she loves him, that he is Mama's handsome boy.

At night I leave her and dream about sitting on the lawn and trying to get away, but this time it is my children that I must get to safety. What do I pack, what can we carry, where do we go to hide before the light fills the sky?

THE HIGH COST OF INSECURITY:
Social Costs and the Arms Race
by Ruth Leger Sivard

The images of modern war haunt our memories: the ashes of Hiroshima, London in flames, a napalmed child running in silent agony, the countless scenes of indiscriminate terror and destruction that shock and repel.

An arms race, by contrast, has no visual identity. It moves along quietly, impersonally, a complex phenomenon seemingly remote from daily life and best left to the experts. The financial burden, if we occasionally feel its weight in the tax bill, is to be borne for peace and security.

In its impact on world society, however, today's arms race is neither remote nor benign. The excessive military expenditures demanded by this malign competition are silent killers, taking lives as wantonly as if the weapons they produce had been put to use. The extreme poverty endured by one-third of humanity—the deteriorating cities, the young people without hope of jobs, the children with distended bellies for want of adequate food—is one by-product of an arms race gone wild. It is the ever-present human cost of an obsessive drive for security through weapons.

The first priority of central governments today is military power, and as a whole they spend more on military defense than on any other responsibility to the public. The world's military expenditures in 1982 will exceed $600 billion; on the average, they take $1 in every $6 paid in taxes. But the financial outlay gives only a partial picture of the scope of the military activity. These budgets now support 25 million men in the regular armed forces, another 22 million in the paramilitary forces, and 24 million in the reserves. With an additional 25 million civilians employed in military-related jobs, the world military population has reached an unprecedented number for a time when no major war is being fought. It is larger than the combined populations of Mexico and Canada.

THE HIGH COST OF INSECURITY

Throughout the world, the power of the military bureaucracy extends into all branches of government. In central governments, its workers outnumber all other public employees and account for a major share of public payrolls. They also administer the largest slice of government revenues. In a growing number of governments, military officers hold the key positions of power; more than 40 percent of developing nations are under military control.

The official military power structure has its counterpart in industry. Purchases of increasingly complex military equipment have made the arms-producing industry one of the largest and richest in the world, and the only one with such a sizable representation within government itself. Nor is arms production any longer a monopoly of the industrialized nations—it is the new growth industry of the developing world. An estimated one-fourth of developing nations have acquired indigenous production facilities for arms, some as sophisticated as fighter aircraft and missiles. A growing number of these developing nations have in turn become suppliers to other nations.

Several factors operate to keep this military-industrial-political complex in perpetual motion, spiraling steadily upward in size and strength. To a striking degree, rivalry and antagonism between the United States and the Soviet Union have shaped the military competition in the postwar period. Although representing only 11 percent of the global population, these two nations alone spent about 60 percent of the world's military outlay between 1960 and 1980. Their dominance has diminished somewhat over the years, economically as well as militarily, but in 1980 they still accounted for over half the global military budget.

The arms race has been propelled by an exceptionally heavy investment in weapons research. Between 1960 and 1977, an estimated $336 billion went into research and development of new weapons, almost 80 percent of it spent by the two superpowers. The technological drive among the major military powers has also spurred military budgets and spread weapons across the world. The export of arms—primarily by the United States and the USSR, but also by France, the United Kingdom, and other industrialized nations—was encouraged as a way to ease the balance of payments, spread costs, and maintain the pace of military development. In this competition, governments themselves became the new "merchants of death." By the end of the 1970s, the arms manufacturers were

doing a yearly export business of $25 billion, a rapidly growing proportion of it with the developing nations.

The push for the newest in weapons came from the buyers as well as the sellers. Jet fighters of national prestige, and even nations without the technical personnel to operate them were ready to mortgage their foreign exchange to acquire them. Rapidly rising oil revenues accelerated the buildup of arms in the Middle East, the region where by far the largest buyers were to be found. However, sophisticated weapons have been shipped to every corner of the globe. In 1979, 98 developing nations imported arms, and more than one-fifth of them were among the world's poorest nations, with per capita income averaging less than $200 a year. The military expenditures of developing nations as a whole have increased much more rapidly than has the economic base to support them.

In military terms, the effect of the arms race of the 1960s and 1970s is a sharply elevated destructive potential everywhere on the globe, and an increased threat of global annihilation. The nuclear-weapon nations now include the United States, Russia, Great Britain, China, France, India, and possibly Israel and South Africa. The first two have between them over 16,000 strategic nuclear warheads, enough to destroy every city in the world seven times over, and an estimated 30,000 battlefield and intermediate-range nuclear weapons. Among the other states, there are an estimated 1,000 additional nuclear weapons. But overkill is no longer confined to nuclear stockpiles. The so-called conventional arms, on which 80 percent of military budgets have been spent, have increased dramatically in kill power as well as numbers. Napalm, binary nerve gas, antipersonnel cluster bombs, and other such weapons have narrowed the gap between the destructiveness of nuclear and conventional weapons.

Meanwhile, there is no evidence that this vast expansion of destructive power has made any area of the world more secure. Any national monopoly of modern weapons technology has been short-lived, since a technological advance by one nation is promptly duplicated by its adversary. Change is constant, instability increases, and the whole world has been made hostage to military forces of incalculable power.

In cost to society, the consequences of the arms race have been far-reaching and ruinous. No weapon need be fired: The profligate expenditure of resources for nonproductive use has been

enough in itself to undermine the economy and seriously weaken the fabric of society.

One result has been the spiraling inflation that bedevils every nation. Heavy military spending generates buying power without producing an equivalent supply of economically useful goods for the market. The excess of disposable income adds to pressure on prices and in time becomes a prescription for intractable inflation. A disproportionate number of its many victims are among the weakest members of society: The old suffer more than jobholders, the poor with marginal incomes more than the rich.

The $3 trillion that had been poured into military programs in the 1960s and early 1970s was a significant cause of the 1973 boom in world prices, although the abruptness of the break was attributed to the oil embargo. In that year the worldwide rise in consumer prices accelerated to 11 percent from the annual average of 4 percent that had been common in previous years. In 1974 the jump was 15 percent over 1973 levels. Stimulated by the continuing military strain on resources, the year-to-year increase has fluctuated between 10 and 15 percent ever since.

Productivity gains are slowed as military spending vies with civilian investment for the technology and capital goods that insure growth. It is a competition in which the bargaining power of the military is strengthened by cost-plus contracts. Innovation for civilian needs lags far behind the dramatic advances in weaponry. Military and space programs absorb more public research funds than do all civilian needs combined. As long as military requirements have priority, essential research that could yield new sources of energy, increase food production, provide better housing, improve health, foster employment, and in general improve the conditions of life generally will languish.

The sluggish U.S. economy and the deterioration of the dollar may illustrate these consequences more effectively than would global data. From 1960 to 1979, while U.S. military expenditures grabbed 7 percent of gross national product (GNP) and investment was 14 percent of GNP, productivity grew less than 3 percent per year. In six other major industrialized countries for which data are available, the military burden was less; in all six, investment was higher and productivity rose more rapidly. Japan provided the most striking contrast: only 1 percent of its GNP went to military expenditures in this period; the rate of investment was double the U.S.

rate and the growth of productivity over three times as fast.

· Unemployment is another side effect of the arms race. As military purchases restrict investment and growth in the civilian economy, they limit the civilian job opportunities that are essential for an expanding labor force. Military-related jobs do not provide an adequate alternative. Government spending on weapons yields only half as many jobs as would equivalent funds spent on houses, schools, transit systems, and health services. Weapons production is capital intensive, and the relatively few jobs that it does provide tend to be concentrated in the higher-skill categories. For these reasons alone, weapons production puts an especially heavy burden on developing countries, which typically have large labor surpluses but relatively few trained workers.

Price inflation, a slower growth rate, and rising unemployment give only a partial picture of the impact of the arms race on society at large. Since they compete for finite government resources, military expenditures also have a direct and immediate effect on the allocation of funds to meet human needs. They divert resources from education, health, nutrition, and other basic needs of society, and severely reduce the aid that richer countries make available for the development of the poorer.

As a result, the gap between the rich and the poor of the world is widening at an alarming rate. The children for whom there are no schools, the adults who are illiterate, the people who suffer from chronic malnutrition, unclean water, a shortage of housing and medical care, are present in steadily growing numbers. In a world rich enough to spend $600 billion a year on an oversupply of military power, one person in three lives in painful poverty.

The developed world has one-fourth of the global population and over three-fourths of the global product. It also spends over three-fourths of the world's military budget. The economic aid that the rich, developed nations provide to the poor, developing ones is equivalent to about 6 percent of those rich countries' military expenditures. But in the developing countries, too, budgets are skewed in favor of military programs. Overall, the military outlay of developing nations is almost as large as all their public investment in the education and health care of their 3.2 billion people.

While governments worldwide give priority to military defense, the social deficit grows ever larger. The number of children requiring education increases faster than the schools to house them.

An estimated 500 million school-age children are not in school. Among adults, there are more than 800 million in the world who can neither read nor write. The backlog of facilities for health care is even more pronounced. In developing nations only one person in five has access to medical care; most rural areas are without a single doctor. On the average, the rate of infant mortality is five times greater in developing than in developed nations; in some of the poorest countries it is 20 times greater than in the richest. Life expectancy ranges from 40 years in some of the poorest nations to 75 years in some of the richest.

Perhaps most shocking today of all unmet basic needs is adequate food for all humankind. Malnutrition is still the single most important public-health problem in the developing nations. An estimated 500 million people lack sufficient food to meet their minimum daily requirements of calories. In many areas two-thirds of the children are undernourished.

It is not only in the developing nations that millions are trapped in conditions of extreme want. The United States itself illustrates the appalling dimensions of a social deficit that leaves no nation untouched. In America 32 million people live below the poverty line, 8 million are unemployed, 1 million adults are illiterate, 10 million children are without basic health care. Among Western countries the United States has an exceptionally high crime rate. The death rate due to homicides is several times higher than in other developed nations. Public surveys in 1973 and 1974 indicated that 45 percent of Americans are afraid to walk alone in their neighborhoods at night.

In military strength the United States is the most powerful nation in the world. In the 1982 fiscal year it will spend $188 billion for its military defense; only eight nations can boast a total national income larger than the budget we devote to military defense. Yet we have been unable to buy national security, despite an investment in weapons unparalleled in history. Indeed, no nation has managed to buy security with military spending. On the contrary, by straining the world economy and fostering the neglect of social needs, the arms race has amplified instability and insecurity. It has itself become the major threat to international security.

THE MILITARY ALBATROSS:
How Arms Spending Is Destroying the Economy

by Lloyd Dumas

I believe that over the last several decades military spending has been the predominant cause of the deterioration of the U.S. economy, which has, in turn, been largely responsible for our simultaneously high unemployment and inflation. There are four major reasons why this is true.

The first reason is the economic nature of military goods; the second is the nature of military procurement; the third, the balance of payments problem; and the fourth, the effect on civilian technological progress.

Whatever else you say about military goods, they have no economic usefulness. They cannot be worn, eaten, or lived in; they make no direct contribution to the material standard of living. Nor do they contribute to an economy's capacity to produce goods and services which do contribute to the standard of living, as do products like industrial machinery and factory buildings.

People who produce military goods and services are, however, paid like everyone else, and the money they receive will be spent by the employees on consumer goods or by the business firms on industrial goods. But these people do not produce a corresponding supply of the consumer or industrial goods which would absorb their money. Taxes have not been raised enough to offset this excess spending power, and inflation has resulted.

The second reason relates to military contract practices. Since World War II, these contracts have in practice become "cost plus," which means that the contractor gets paid whatever it costs to produce plus some amount for profit. The higher the cost, then, the higher the revenues. So contractors interested in bringing more money into the firm simply produce inefficiently, that is, at high cost.

Motivated by this kind of incentive system and backed by a very rich customer, the Department of Defense, these firms have bid resource prices up in order to get the resources they needed. That bidding up of resource prices has contributed to the inflation rate. More importantly, though, the purchasing power of the military industry has enabled it to preempt important parts of key economic resources from the civilian sector.

The third reason is the situation surrounding the balance of payments. From 1893 until 1970, the U.S. had a yearly balance of trade surplus, which meant that exports were greater in value than imports. If that had been the only thing going on in the United States' international economic interactions, the U.S. dollar would now be the strongest currency in the world. We know that hasn't happened. The United States' balance of payments has been in deficit for quite a long time. Why?

During the 20 years from 1955 to 1974, U.S. military expenditures abroad alone were 10 percent greater than the entire balance of trade surplus. So the outflow of dollars related to the support of military establishments and military foreign aid helped to destroy what would otherwise have been a positive balance of payments for the United States.

The pressure generated by the balance of payments deficit is first an inflationary pressure. When the dollar is worth less in exchange for, say, the Swiss franc, a product whose price in Swiss francs has not changed becomes more expensive to U.S. consumers. The United States now imports a great many of its important industrial commodities, including oil and steel. By having to pay more for these imported goods, the U.S. is feeding rising costs into its economic system at its base.

The balance of trade has also turned against the United States in the last few years because the competitive ability of U.S. industry has declined as a result of the technological retardation of U.S. civilian industry, which is in turn a direct result of the military emphasis in the economy. Blaming the non-competitiveness of U.S. industry on the high wages of U.S. labor is nonsense. U.S. wages have been higher than wages in most of the rest of the world for 50 to 100 years, and until very recently the U.S. had no particular difficulty in competing in world markets.

The problem is that large numbers of engineers and scientists are required for the design and manufacture of military products.

Estimates of the fraction of all U.S. engineers and scientists engaged in military and military-related work range from about 30 percent to about 50 percent. Pulling this many of them out of civilian work has devastating effects on the rate of civilian technological progress.

Technological progress is critical to an economy's ability to offset the rising cost of inputs; that is, as wages, fuel prices, and the costs of raw materials rise, the only way product prices can be held down is to find more efficient ways of producing.

Technological progress is the result of setting engineers and scientists to work on particular problems to solve those problems and develop improved techniques. A large fraction of the engineers and scientists in this country have been working on military-related problems and looking for military applications and solutions, and that's exactly what they've found.

The U.S. is probably the most technologically advanced producer of nuclear submarines, ICBMs, etc., in the world. But when it comes to things like building trolley cars or better railroad cars or better housing, or even finding better techniques for producing steel, the U.S. is not as advanced as some other countries.

Deterioration of civilian technological progress has meant that much of U.S. industry has lost the ability to offset higher labor, fuel, and materials costs, which are passed along to consumers in the form of higher prices. This process has progressively priced U.S. industries out of world markets, and led to a worsening in the balance of trade. It has also priced U.S. industries out of the domestic markets.

In addition, engineering and scientific educational institutions have oriented their curricula toward training people for the available jobs. Military technology is highly specialized. It is so much at the frontiers of knowledge that it requires many people, each of whom is an expert in a very small area. This overspecialization is carried through into curricula, and now even the people who have been graduated from our major engineering schools, but who do not go into defense work, have not necessarily had the most appropriate kind of training for work in civilian technological development.

For example, in 1974 I met the president of an energy consulting firm which advises businesses in conserving energy. In 1974 his business was booming, and he wanted to hire more engineers to

102

take care of this additional business. He put an ad in *The New York Times.*

He told me later that he thought he could have built a space-craft with the people who applied for the jobs. The master designer of the solar panels on one of the major satellite systems asked for work. But my friend couldn't find anyone in that whole group who knew anything about the design or even the operation of an industrial boiler. In fact, one fellow said to him, "You mean they still use boilers in industry?" He finally got the energy engineers he wanted by importing them from Britain.

Clearly, the non-competitiveness of U.S. industry due to this technological retardation has not only generated inflation, but also unemployment. When U.S. industries lose markets, U.S. workers lose jobs.

Now, the question is what we do about this. A revitalization of U.S. industry is required, which takes a piece-by-piece conversion of U.S. industry from a military to a civilian orientation. This means putting serious money, labor, and technological resources into civilian activity.

How is this done? The first step is to begin contingency planning at all defense facilities (whether they are military bases or production facilities) for alternate, non-military work for the people involved there.

Such a plan requires knowledge of the local situation: who is at the facility in terms of engineers, scientists, and production workers, what their skills are, what equipment is available, and what advantages the site has.

For instance, it would not make much sense for a manufacturing firm that deals with large equipment, such as an aerospace firm which would do a lot of metalworking, to convert to the production of deodorants. It would make more sense to talk about converting to the production of railroad cars or housing modules which would involve the same basic mix of skills.

The next steps are feasibility studies and studies of possible product markets. Probably some people at the firm will have to be retrained and some reoriented; other people will have to be brought in and perhaps others moved elsewhere. Provisions for the interim financial support of these people have to be made.

Conversion for production workers on the whole is not a big

problem. Their skills have not generally been overspecialized to military industry. But engineers, scientists, and managers are more problematic.

I indicated before that military production, research, and design requires an extraordinary degree of specialization. It also requires very little attention to the cost implications of design. The particular design of a product significantly influences the cost of making it. Military engineers haven't had to worry about those costs, since the government has paid whatever was required; but civilian markets will not pay any price for a product.

As a result, it becomes necessary for those engineers and scientists to de-specialize so that they have a broader view of the design problem which enables them to trade off one part against another to keep the cost down. Secondly, they have to have cost sensitivity, to know the cost implications of their designs.

Managers who operate in military-industrial firms operate in a different world than managers in civilian industry. For example, the military-industrial firm's manager doesn't have to know anything about marketing a product in terms of surveying consumers, doing market-feasibility studies, or running a mass media ad campaign. These firms' managers have only one customer, the Department of Defense. What they have to know are the Armed Services Procurement Regulations, the procurement people, and the congresspeople involved. Yet this knowledge has no relationship to what is needed to market a new detergent, piece of furniture, record, or anything else in civilian industry.

With respect to cost sensitivity, that same distinction exists. In military industry, the cost question is not the prime one. In civilian industry, holding cost *down* is one of the primary functions of management. Managers must understand how to do that.

So successful conversion at any given facility requires the retraining and reorientation of the management personnel. If retraining is not done in advance, it must be done in process, and that delays everything and makes it more expensive. For example, Boeing is now producing trolley cars in its Vertol Division. But Boeing didn't retrain in advance. Instead it threw out a good part of the military management in the Vertol Division and brought in management from its civilian divisions. Then it sent its engineers on a world tour to learn how to produce trolley cars in places where they

are still made. (There hasn't been one produced in the United States for 25 years.)

As a result, Boeing is in a terrible financial mess with respect to its trolley car production. It signed a fixed-price contract with Chicago and with Boston, and those cities are not the Department of Defense; they are holding Boeing to these fixed prices, though costs have gone way above the prices. Boeing is losing a fortune. If reorientation had been done in advance, there would have been no reason to throw out the managers; and Boeing would have found itself capable of meeting those contracts or, at least, signing realistic ones: It would have known what it was doing and how to do it.

There is no economic reason why conversion of military facilities to civilian use cannot take place. There is no question of whether enough jobs can be generated. More than enough things that do contribute to the economy need doing in this country and around the world. Labor is one of our most valuable resources. That is not the problem.

The problem is, first of all, developing the political will and, secondly, understanding the economics of this transitional period, in order that the conversion of military facilities to civilian operation can be done smoothly and effectively without seriously disrupting the lives of the people involved, without throwing them out of work until they happen to find a job somewhere that may not even use their skills.

The benefits of carrying out such a conversion are substantial. It is no longer just an idealist's dream or a peacenik's vision. It is the only real hope of revitalizing the U.S. economy on a permanent and enduring basis, of getting us out of the economic mess in which we find ourselves.

WHO ARE THE VICTIMS?
Questions for Thought and Discussion

1. In light of Hiatt's description of the medical consequences of a nuclear war, what are your thoughts about "winning" such a war?

2. Imagine yourself, or anyone else, in Akihiro's situation. How do you find yourself reacting to people who cause that kind of suffering? Are there any situations in which you would feel obliged to inflict such pain?

3. Imagine yourself in Wright's situation. What would be your reaction to the U.S. government? To nuclear testing? What would you do about it? Who are the victims of the nuclear arms race (past, present, and future)?

4. If the global arms race constitutes a war on the poor, as Sivard alludes to, who are the present victors? Which side do you think you are on?

5. Dumas' article contradicts the common aphorism that "war is good for the economy." How is military spending bad for the economy?

PART II.

RESPONSES OF FAITH:
A Biblical, Historical, and Theological Approach

The Christian's faith in Jesus must always be made specific to its place and time. Christians in the last half of the 20th century need to ask what it means to follow Jesus in the face of impending nuclear disaster. What is the biblical basis for our attitude toward war? What can we learn from the early church? From a pacifist and from a just war stance, what are the Christian imperatives for responding to nuclear weapons? What can we affirm about obedience, security, and hope? The writers of this section reflect biblically, theologically, and historically on these and other questions about the meaning of faith for our time.

THE NUCLEAR PRINCIPALITIES:
A Biblical View of the Arms Race
by William Stringfellow

I do not cease to give thanks for you, remembering you in my prayers . . . that you may know . . . what is the immeasurable greatness of his power in us who believe, according to the working of his great might which he accomplished in Christ when he raised him from the dead and made him sit at his right hand in the heavenly places, far above all rule and authority and power and dominion, and above every name that is named, not only in this age but also in that which is to come; and [God] has put all things under his feet and has made him the head over all things. . . .

(Ephesians 1:16, 18a, 19–22)

Finally, be strong in the Lord and in the strength of his might. Put on the whole armor of God, that you may be able to stand against the wiles of the devil. For we are not contending against flesh and blood, but against the principalities, against the powers, against the world rulers of this present darkness, against the spiritual hosts of wickedness in the heavenly places. Therefore take the whole armor of God, that you may be able to withstand in the evil day, and having done all, to stand. (Ephesians 6:10–13)

If human beings today are to realistically comprehend or sanely confront the nuclear issue, it is imperative to expose the mythology—and to dispel the mythological aura—which shrouds the realm of nuclear policy. The prospect of nuclear war must no longer be preempted by military, scientific, or diplomatic professionals or similar putative experts; the subject must no longer be withheld from the scrutiny of the conscience and the common sense of ordinary people. Insofar as the prevailing nuclear mythology inhibits that, it must be exorcised.

The primordial mythology of nuclear power has complicated origins in various aspects of American culture and is compounded by certain historic events. Perhaps the most conspicuous cultural feature has been a profligate idolatry of science, fostering gross overestimations of the capabilities of science and technology together with an uncritical, indeed wanton, imposition of the scientific method, so-called, throughout society. These circumstances have, in turn, issued in a *literally* fantastic attitude that technical capability should be implemented just because it exists, without the exercise of human discretion as to the moral character of any particular venture. Views such as these are secreted in a belief, inculcated profusely in the culture since the start of this century, that science is morally neuter or, to put it in some traditional theological terms, that science as a principality somehow enjoys exemption from the Fall. This naivete, incredible though it be, is commonly associated with the superstition that science can, eventually, supply remedy for any peril or problem wrought from stupid or untimely or inappropriate implementation of any specific technical capability.

The consequences, practically, of these foolish verities have been multifarious, nefarious, and often grotesque in the nuclear realm as well as elsewhere. Thus, to mention a single item only, hundreds of thousands of hapless Americans now await tardy rescue from jeopardies unprojected or, anyway, unforewarned by commercialized science, fomented by reckless, premature, or otherwise improvident disposal of toxic wastes.

In Hiroshima (which is simultaneously the primeval and the penultimate event of nuclear history) such ideas sponsored within the pantheon of science converged with the shibboleths spawned initially by the Second World War. These were quickly enough extended and embellished to suit the "cold war," and they survive still, in substantially this latter form, in the Pentagon, the intelligence apparatus, and the self-styled "national security" authorities. The upshot has been the much-boasted connection between zeal for American nuclear preeminence and a fancied holy destiny for postwar America, the asserted efficacy of superpower in determining history and in domineering the life of creation, and the extraordinary, if nonetheless self-evident, contradiction embodied in the doctrine of nuclear deterrence.

Events have by now intervened and surpassed the heavy

110

myths wrought from Hiroshima: American nuclear preeminence has been dissipated and perhaps was, all along, illusory. The inherent impotence of superpower to feign sovereignty in history and domination over the existence of creation has been verified in one calamity after another befalling the professed superpowers (such has been the redundant lesson in Korea, Vietnam, Afghanistan, Poland, Central America). At the same time, the doctrine of deterrence seems overwhelmed by the ready common public skepticism it entices.

Meanwhile, the fundamental proposition that rendered the making and use of nuclear weapons thinkable in the first place— the curious hypothesis that science is morally innocuous—continues to be categorically refuted, day after day, not only because of the probability of nuclear apocalypse, but also because of the plethora of other perils, contaminations, and plagues produced and promoted in the name of science as safe and beneficial to life. In short, in the present age history itself confirms the radical moral ambiguity of science and of all that science does and claims: history verifies and tells the truth that science is a fallen principality.

The disintegration of the mythology abetting the nuclear weapons race exposes the moral chaos in this world, which *is* the Fall as it affects institutions, nations, systems, regimes, bureaucracies, corporate enterprises, ideologies, and the whole further array (more exactly, *dis*array) of principalities and powers. The collapse of that myth structure seems to have rendered Alexander Haig, erstwhile president of United Technologies, Inc., incurably hysterical, but it is nonetheless liberating for human beings who have harbored throughout the nuclear darkness faculties of conscience and sanity.

To their experience the blunt admonishment of the Letter to the Ephesians sounds familiar wisdom concerning the character of the principalities and powers, their diversity, disparity, and versatility, their virtually irresistible momentum, and, most ominously, their predatory attitude toward human beings and toward human life. Ephesians recites an absolutely crucial insight for anyone worried about nuclear power: the enemy, which is in truth death pervasive throughout creation, is manifest in institutions and nations, thrones and authorities, dominions and realms, administrations and myths, principalities and powers. And even though there be flesh

and blood (that is, human beings) idolatrous of death, the power of death is never *merely* vested in wicked people. I suppose Alexander Haig can take comfort in that fact.

That explains, in part, why the Ephesians designation of the alienation and hostility of the fallen principalities and powers toward fallen human life, and the fallen existence of the rest of creation, is so vehement. Ephesians bespeaks a warfare between the powers and human beings in which human life has no safety and no respite and, finally, no salvation except that which is known in the sovereignty of the Word of God in history as that is acknowledged, upheld, and honored here and now.

Another manner in which to speak of the predatory character of the conglomerate of principalities identifiable as the nuclear reality is straightforwardly in terms of the volume and extremity of violence which nuclear weapons concentrate. This is a violence of such dimensions that it obliterates aggressor as well as victim. Nuclear power is not only utterly destructive; it is, manifestly, utterly self-destructive. Moreover, it is not only visibly, quantitatively, physically destructive; it is psychologically, qualitatively, morally destructive. Actually, I believe any violence is inherently suicidal, but whatever argument there may be about that, the nuclear violence forecloses dispute: nuclear weapons are definitively suicidal.

Surely that has been the message of the Second World War, summed up in Hiroshima. That war involved such sustained, debilitating, and, at last, diabolical violence that it consumed those who commissioned it on each side, ostensible victors no less than notorious vanquished. For America in the Second World War, the means of military conquest became morally suicidal for the nation and politically suicidal for democratic society and constitutional government. The policies of official violence that rule the nation (the paramilitarization of the police, the usurpation of the economy by Pentagon procurement, the unlawful, often criminal, practices of so-called intelligence and security agencies, to mention only a few features of the American technocratic regime that now prevails) in truth were authorized by Hiroshima.

In the nuclear issue, odd as it may sound to say, more than human lives are at stake, more than human survival is at issue. The nuclear principalities and powers threaten human extinction—and indeed the literal ruin of creation—in a way that incarnates the boldest offense of which any creature is capable, namely, *blasphe-*

my (cf. Revelation 13). Blasphemy is much more than a profaning of the name of God. It is more than incantation or curse. Blasphemy is peculiarly the temptation of the principalities—the nations and the corporate powers, science or commerce—in contesting the sovereignty of the Word of God in this world, in challenging and opposing the authority *now* of Jesus Christ as Lord of history, in gainsaying or evading accountability to human life and the life of the rest of creation, and in usurping and disrupting the vocation of the Word of God in judgment of these same nuclear principalities and powers. In this context, the very existence of the nuclear principalities, joined with the weapons in which they trade, is both essentially blasphemous and consummately blasphemous.

This is why a nuclear freeze, so-called, is but a phrase, not a policy. A "nuclear freeze" is not only not enough, as a reaction of nations and persons to the imminent nuclear threat; it is also gravely suspect as an arrogant co-option, at the instigation of the nuclear principalities, of the antinuclear sentiment and of the antinuclear movements. "Nuclear freeze" invites hallucination of a finale to the nuclear weapons proliferations and escalations in circumstances in which, in reality, nothing significant has changed.

On the other hand, even discredited nuclear mythology seems to retain enough influence to preclude American consideration of what is usually called "unilateral disarmament." Though it is seldom elaborated concretely, unilateral disarmament is assumed and asserted to be a radically foolhardy course. I do not know (I forebear to guess) what Alexander Haig and his ilk may mean when they discharge the phrase, but I do not find it foolish to contemplate disassembly of the establishment of nuclear principalities, or disarming of warheads that so poignantly and immediately jeopardize our own lives as well as terrorize others. To my mind, this single allegedly unthinkable option—unilateral disarmament—is the only policy expressing hope. That is because I understand its potential to be penance for blasphemy.

Then, after repentance and its works, Americans might even act upon that wise proposal of Admiral Rickover to dismantle the Pentagon.

A THEOLOGICAL REFLECTION ON NUCLEAR DEVELOPMENTS:
The Limits of Science, Technology, and Power

by Jacques Ellul

The splitting of the atom, whether it is used for the production of energy for industry or for military ends, raises questions of a theological nature, while the "how" of its use raises questions of a moral and ethical nature. I have often challenged the belief that the basic problem with technique is whether it is used for good or ill, but here I do not want to take up that general theme. It is enough to recall it to mind. It seems to me that four issues can be raised: (1) the fundamental one of the limits of science; (2) the spirit of power; (3) human self-sufficiency; and (4) the rigidity of the structures. Despite these seemingly sociological issues, theology cannot be indifferent to them.

THE LIMITS OF SCIENCE

It is with some trepidation that anyone broaches the insoluble question of the limits of science. Put schematically, "If such and such a research is called 'scientific,' is it thereby legitimate and proper?" Do we have the right to do anything and everything? It is quite clear that the modern age, to the extent that it has no criterion for life other than scientific "truth" and is dazzled by research results, will spontaneously answer, "Yes." But the Christian has to phrase it a bit differently. "Do we, *before God,* have the right to do absolutely nothing, simply because it is scientific?" That is the true problem.

Christians are afraid to take a stand, first because they share the prejudices favorable to science held by all and sundry in this era and, second, because they remember the errors committed by the "obscurantist" church in the Middle Ages—e.g., the ban on dissecting cadavers, the Galileo affair, etc. (Let's not forget that the medi-

eval church was not at all as obscurantist as we're led to believe and that Galileo was able to pursue his research thanks only to a pension from the Pope!)

We must get beyond this difficulty. Are there limits? Are there any spheres before which we must remain silent or research must stop? Is it good that science recognize no limit?

Of course, no direct answer is given in the Bible, notwithstanding the hint given in Ecclesiastes 1:18 ("he who stores up knowledge stores up grief"), and the author of that book had Greek science in mind. But his warning is not enough. Can we un-create? Can we go back to the source, to the origin, to the crucial point when life or matter appears? Is that not a forbidden place, an unacceptable action? Don't we see (clearly enough, I think) that here we reach, not God, but the point of an action of God where we tend to substitute ourselves for God?

The comparison is with Genesis 3, when Eve takes the fruit of the knowledge of good and evil—that is, the possibility for us to decide from then on, by ourselves, what is good and evil. Until then, God alone could declare good and evil. At that moment, we had taken over a realm reserved for God.

The question I pose is exactly the same: In laying claim to alter the structure of matter, to transfer matter into energy, to split the atom, so also in claiming parthenogenesis or the artificial "creation of life" and the whole complex of genetic engineering, are we not precisely at the limit beyond which we make ourselves equal to God, where we do what God does—and can we enter into this competition?

I know that here I am broaching a question that is inadmissible for scientists and formidable and apparently insoluble for theologians, who prefer not to hear it discussed. Nevertheless, if we do not dare to pose it, perhaps we'll have to expect, as a result of our trespass, consequences as dire as those following the first transgression. Obviously, I cannot supply a scientific response. Rather than giving a direct answer, I believe that all we can do is reach a certain probability in the answer through an analysis of some of the consequences.

The question of the limits of science seems to me particularly radical, particularly in the area of atomic research. If it were simply a matter of knowing the constitution of matter, I don't think there would be any problem. We all know the traditional answer of

Christian scholars: "The more we come to know about the reality of creation, the more we are led to adore the Creator." Unfortunately, in atomic research we are not dealing with knowledge, so much as manipulation, transformation, and disintegration. Here, there isn't any respect either for the Creator or for the creation—and that is why the question becomes radical.

THE SPIRIT OF POWER

All atomic research is research for power. It is no longer simply "nuclear energy." Some, as in France, must compensate for oil deficiencies; other nations must guarantee continuous growth in energy consumption; still others must escalate nuclear weapons in order to guarantee national security. In all cases power is indeed at stake. We have the fixed idea that matter contains an unlimited amount of power and is completely at our disposal.

We have always been imbued with the spirit of power, which is one of the marks of evil in the Bible. It's called "pride" or "lust." Past theologians often erred in relegating these tendencies to individual psychological defects, whereas the Bible talks about much more fundamental powers. These are powers that overcome us and make us act; they are existential and collective impulses that have to be situated in relationship to the affirmation of Jesus as Lord or the reality of the kingdom of God. Pride and lust are not particularized sins, but rather the source and expression of our radical opposition to God.

In the past, however, the spirit of power existed vis-a-vis God and was only potentially concrete, for it did not have the means to express itself fully. It didn't have "the power." Now, this situation has changed. We have acquired the means to serve our spirit of power, particularly with the technology of energy. The development of atomic energy is closely linked to the spirit of domination, conquest, and human lust. People get all fired up about applying nuclear power not for the sake of its usefulness nor its profits (though, of course, that plays a role too), but because they are driven by the unrestrained search for power. This is what is dangerous. We are no longer capable of saying at any given moment, "Enough! We're stopping!" At any given moment, we have neither the criterion nor the motivation *not* to pursue to the nth degree everything that can satisfy our spirit of power.

In other words, the field of nuclear power, more than any other technical area, has seemingly unlimited development. Thus, when it comes to nuclear armaments, for instance, it is pointless to hope for a "non-proliferation" treaty or a serious enactment of arms limitation agreement. What I am saying is confirmed, in fact, by the very rapid proliferation of atomic weapons. We do not have to dwell on recent events in Iraq and Pakistan. Obviously, Iraq, thanks to France's delivery of enriched uranium, will soon have nuclear weapons, just as Israel has established a nuclear force thanks to France's delivery of a reactor. And Pakistan is even closer to this possibility with aid from Libya, which itself seems to be at least well on the way if not already in possession.

Non-proliferation is a pious ideology, a virtuous declaration that masks a reality that is quite the opposite (exactly as happens with the declaration of human rights). The root of this phenomenon is the unbridling of the spirit of power that can do nothing but will the means to its own satisfaction, no matter the cost. All other reasons are superficial. This is truly a question posed to Christians who, above all, must fight against all manifestations of this spirit of power. Here we stand on intrinsically theological grounds concerning nuclear energy, which has no other objective than the pursuit of power.

HUMAN SELF-SUFFICIENCY

When separated from God, we claim complete mastery over the world; we want to be independent and autonomous, reckoning that we can cope with everything. On entering the nuclear realm though, we face immense responsibilities.

First, we have entered a world of total uncertainty. If I object to *all* nuclear development, I do so because, when all is said and done, we don't know what we are doing. When you read expert and scientific reports—each as serious, as learned, as competent as the next one—you are struck by the mass of contradictions among them. What is the maximum radiation dose a person can be exposed to without danger? The answers vary from the straightforward to double talk. What are the results over a number of years? Impossible to say, as not enough time has elapsed. The point is, this lack of certainty dominates every aspect.

From the standpoint of economics, what is the cost price per

kilowatt hour for nuclear electricity? Once more, the answers vary from the straightforward to double talk, and there are even greater fluctuations in the estimates before and after the construction of a power plant. (In any case, the actual construction consumes a considerable amount of energy; for example, the French nuclear program involves an enormous increase in petroleum imports for 10 years.) What are the chances of an accident? Statistics show that they are quite small. Fair enough. At the same time, solid mathematical studies show that calculations of probability mean nothing when the risk verges on the absolute.

How to get rid of the wastes? There are no reliable and long-term solutions. Reprocessing? Most recent studies have demonstrated that reprocessing plants end up producing more plutonium than they process. How are we going "to deconstruct" the atomic piles in the core of the reactor once the plant has finished its cycle of production? Even experts favoring the atomic enterprise recognize that nobody knows. The only general answer is that they "hope" that technological progress will solve the problem 20 years from now.

I could go on listing the detailed questions that give rise to either total uncertainty or contradictions among the experts. This list is enough, though, to assert clearly that as long as we do not know the risks, as long as we do not know the meaning of what is being done, we must not do it. This prudent guideline, I maintain, is linked directly to faith in Jesus Christ. Faith cannot lead us to an irresponsible attitude under the guise of "confidence in God." We cannot take cover under the conviction that God, good and all-powerful, will set things straight. That is bad theology. We are called to act as responsible beings and the central question remains "What have you done to your sister and brother?" In this nuclear business, all we can answer is, "I don't know anything about it." This is precisely the answer that God cannot tolerate. It is the answer of the lukewarm, the flighty, the irresponsible person. This answer is fundamentally the inverse of the Word of God. If we do not know what we're doing, we must not do it.

A second aspect of self-sufficiency, equally unacceptable, is the irreversible nature of the trends brought about by nuclear development, irreversible trends that bring irreparable results. If there is an atomic catastrophe, it will be irreparable from every point of view—not just for the dead (in which case it wouldn't be different

from other catastrophes), but also for the genetic results and the natural environment. It could be possible to sterilize vast stretches, thousands of square miles which would no longer have any use at all. No material, medical, or even financial restitution would be possible. Soon no insurance company will cover atomic risk. We have here an ethical rule of thumb which, it seems to me, also stems from Revelation; namely, "When the risk generated becomes well nigh inevitable and totally irreparable, the action must not be undertaken." No argument can prevail against this maxim. This situation presents us with a modern, sociopolitical application of the commandment, "Thou shalt love thy neighbor as thyself." In other words our pursuit of the spirit of power was a matter of contempt and transgression against the first great commandment, a lack of respect for the limits God placed on our actions. Here it is a matter of a clear violation of the second great commandment given by Jesus Christ.

THE RIGIDITY OF THE SYSTEM

The growth of this atomic system brings about ever more impressive economic, political, and structural flexibility. The whole industrial process changes with the introduction of electricity from nuclear power plants. The operation of such a plant cannot be slowed down either by season or by night (contrary to all other energy-producing systems) because of the heat constraints that repeated variations would inflict on the metal casings enclosing the uranium rods. Nor can this electricity be put "on hold," so there must be continuous use at a level fixed by the plant.

In order to use up the nighttime "overload," the equipment and processes used in many establishments supplied by this electricity must be modified. At the same time, industry is forced to adopt new production procedures to use electricity instead of other energy sources (e.g., electric furnaces for melting metals and maintaining them in a molten state or drying at high frequency, a drying that has to be further accelerated for wood or reinforced concrete). In addition, non-stop use of this energy entails revisions in the norms of production, the expansion of units to manufacture the new equipment, etc. In short, "the all-electric factory" goes hand in hand with "the factory with permanent maximum operation."

This trend has two important consequences. First, the rigidity

makes adaptation difficult. The more precise and strained the system is, the less able it is to adapt. Techno-organizational integration leads to a certain paralysis in responses (whether technical or economic) or at least to a slowness in adaptation. This effect is made worse by the second one—the acceleration of events in the wake of technical innovation and the spread of disturbances (whether voluntary or involuntary). You could say that after a certain degree of integration (and the nuclear development is now the most powerful factor in integration), the "adaptation-event" relationship becomes an internal contradiction. Events mushroom while the technical-nuclear system is paralyzed.

We are faced, then, with one of those rigid situations that seem to me to be fundamentally anti-Christian. On the one hand, let's always remember that God is the liberator. No need to go further on that score. On the other hand, Jesus has shown us that all relationships should be established along the lines of flexibility, openness, in the concreteness of the here and now. The lesson is not only for interpersonal relationships: It is valid for any structure. Jesus reproached the Pharisees because they made God's law into an iron yoke for people, a total constraint; they made the commandment into an objective duty; they made detailed prescriptions so that there was no longer any room for initiative. They made the free Word of God into an inflexible, systematic code. Jesus came to bring flexibility, adaptability, openness, freedom back into it. In this way, the law of God (which, as James says, is "the Law of Freedom") is truly honored.

The law of God had become a social system. By analogy, it seems to me that any system that leads to inflexibility goes against the will of God. It is not just freedom in general either. Dictatorship, wherever it is found and whatever form it takes, is unacceptable to the Christian, because it is a rigid system leaving no "play" among the structures, no place for initiative. Institutional, economic, and social rigidity, in my opinion, are unacceptable Christian practice. And that is why nuclear development, in my opinion, is unacceptable. I have given above a single example of the inflexibility it breeds in the economic sphere, but I could show how, in many other sectors (e.g., the police administration, the recruitment of personnel, control), nuclear development always brings about the same result and increases the social rigidity in every sector.

WHAT ARE OUR LIMITS?
Questions for Thought and Discussion

1. How is the pursuit of nuclear armaments in conflict with the Christian affirmation of the sovereignty of God? What might penance mean for Christians aware of the evils present in nuclear technology?

2. Ellul argues that by trying to harness the power of the atom, we are trying to make ourselves the equals of God. Is there something inherently destructive in gaining such power? Is it safe to entrust such tremendous and potentially destructive power to the hands of human beings?

REDISCOVERING OUR HERITAGE:

The Pacifism of the Early Church

by Alan Kreider

"The early church was pacifist." "No it wasn't!" Both assertions are common ones; but both can't be right. Which is better? And why does it matter?

Many anti-pacifists admit that the early church appeared to be pacifist. In their attempts to explain this, they have made two points. First, they have claimed that the "pacifism" of the early Christians was limited to a few intellectuals—perverse men who were out of touch with the real world. Most Christians in the Roman empire had better sense and expressed their disdain for these theologians by serving in the legions.

Second, the anti-pacifists have asserted that these theologians were not actually anti-military. It was not killing to which they objected. Rather, they were offended by the idolatry that was an unavoidable part of army life in an empire whose emperors were divinized.

In his book *It Is Not Lawful for Me to Fight: Early Christian Attitudes Toward War, Violence and the State,* Jean-Michel Hornus responds to these claims. He does not assert that all early Christians were pacifists according to modern definitions of the term. He does not deny that some Christians were in the army. He admits that there were changes in the course of several centuries. And he bends over backwards to report individual cases which are hard to fit into his interpretation.

Nevertheless, in Hornus' careful study a pattern of early church thought and practice does emerge which is more in keeping with the pacifist than the anti-pacifist interpretation. One can summarize it in five statements:

• No Christian writer before Constantine's reign justified the participation of believers in warfare. Every writer who commented on this—and lots of them did—condemned it.

• The objection of these writers was based not just on their obvious revulsion to idolatry but also on their concern to be obedient to Jesus. His teachings had instilled in them a profound respect for life and a desire to love their enemies, even the "barbarians." He also had warned them of the impossibility of serving two masters; and this teaching applied in a special way to soldiers, who were in an authority structure which required absolute obedience. Furthermore, the believers were undergirded by an eschatological hope. In their worship and in their personal and communal life, they were experiencing a new reality which expressed God's will and would in the end be victorious. Until then they would be sojourners in conflict with an alien world.

• As early as A.D. 180 there were Christians in the army. And during the ensuing 130 years the number of these grew. Their total numbers, however, were never large, as the almost total absence of soldiers among the Christian grave inscriptions indicates. Most of the believers in the legions appear to have been either officers' sons, who were required to serve, or men who were converted while in the army. Some new converts submitted to martyrdom in their struggle to be released from the forces. Others stayed in. During the *Pax Romana,* the army was as much a civil service and police force as it was a military organization. It was therefore possible to spend a lifetime in the army without killing. And some Christians with a good conscience chose to remain in this non-combatant role.

• The early church's disciplinary measures, in agreement with the teaching of the theologians, disapproved of believers serving in the army. The *Apostolic Tradition,* for example, forbade converts to enter the forces. It permitted believers already in the army to remain there, but only under strict conditions: They were not allowed to be officers, and they were forbidden to kill. Anyone who disobeyed these regulations was to be excommunicated.

• In the fourth century, after the "conversion" of the emperor Constantine in 312 and the forcible "Christianization" of the Roman empire, the church's position changed. Theologians gradually abandoned their pacifism and adopted a new position: acceptance of "just war." Christians, who up to then had been non-conformist sojourners, made their peace with the world, settled down, and lost their distinctiveness. By the early years of the following century, one had to be a Christian to be in the army. Pacifism lived on, however, among professional non-conformists—the priests and

123

monks who continued to uphold the position which earlier had been that of all believers.

Why is this important to us, Christians seeking to be peacemakers in the 1980s? It is not that the early church was pure and to be copied without question. Hornus gives ample illustration of the compromise, self-seeking, and sin that were present among the early believers. And some of the positions which they adopted—for example, the willingness of many of them to wear military uniform in civil-service jobs—are not ones that would appeal to all of us.

But there are six ways in which I am convinced that we, both in our own lives and in our conversations with fellow Christians who are not yet pacifist, can profit from the early church.

• The early church is not normative for our belief or practice: Scripture is. But the attitudes of the early believers can shed important light on the original meaning of the New Testament. After all, the early Christians were close in time to Jesus Christ and the apostolic church. Their understandings of certain biblical passages may well be rooted in a tradition which accurately reflected the intentions of their authors. We therefore need to listen seriously to the early Christians. And when they say that Jesus' "love your enemies" meant *all* enemies (national and personal), and when the post-Constantinian theologians say that he meant only individual enemies, we will have some reason to prefer the former interpretation.

• We are often told that pacifism "doesn't work." We, on the basis of the early church's experience, can point to a lengthy period in which believers were convinced that it was working. For almost three centuries Christians lived lives of radical non-conformity, which included pacifism. Their social strategy was to seek a new society in the church which would be faithful to Christ; it was not to seize control in Rome in order to enforce a moral empire. During this period, the church grew in grace and numbers.

• Pacifism is an important part of the radical non-conformity of the early church; but it is only one part of a much larger package, each part of which was essential. Thus the Christians not only trusted God to protect them (pacifism); they also trusted God to provide for them (simplicity of life and economic sharing). Their trust was undergirded by their sense of God's presence in the Spirit, their common worship, and their sharing of their lives.

• Since the early church was pacifist, it provides us with a

common ground for discussing the Christian attitude toward war with friends from many Christian traditions. In the thinking of most Christians, the early church occupies a special place. Orthodox and Catholic Christians root their traditions in it; the Reformers and the Anabaptists in their differing ways sought to restore its lost purity; and modern charismatic Christians long to revive the dynamism of church life "as at the beginning." Thus we do not need to appeal to the historic peace churches for models of Christian pacifism. We can appeal to a common Christian heritage, which all of us share in the early church. Our pacifist appeal thus does not need to be sectarian; it can be genuinely ecumenical.

• Most traditions, of course, are also the product of the Constantinian centuries, during which Christians coerced belief and coupled the cross with the sword. But we are now living in a post-Constantinian world. With rare exceptions Christianity has once again become a voluntary, minority religion. It now makes sense, as it did for the early Christians, for *all* believers to live as sojourners—radically, communally, nonviolently.

• All of us can thus turn to the early church for encouragement. Many of the stories told by Hornus, and many of the passages from early Christian writings which he quotes, are inspiring. Let me close by citing one of these, from the early fourth-century apologist Lactantius:

> For when God forbids us to kill, he not only prohibits us from open violence, which is not even allowed by the public laws, but he warns us against the commission of those things which are esteemed lawful among men. Thus it will not be lawful for a just man to engage in warfare, since his warfare is justice itself. . . .

LIVING THE DISARMED LIFE:
Christ's Strategy for Peace
by John Howard Yoder

Following the example of Jesus himself, the first Christians and the writers of the New Testament were quick to see in the book of the prophet Isaiah a description of the innocent sufferings of Christ. They read there:

> He was counted among evildoers. . . .
> For our welfare he was chastised. . . .
>   Mistreated, he bore it humbly, without complaint,
> silent as a sheep led to the slaughter,
> silent as a ewe before the shearers. . . .
> They did away with him unjustly . . .
>   though He was guilty of no violence
>   and had not spoken one false word.
> (Isaiah 53:4–9)

In all ages these words concerning the one called the "servant of the Lord" have been beloved by Christians for the portrait they paint of our crucified master. We find these same words echoing in the New Testament, not only because they are beautiful words to describe Christ and his sacrifice on behalf of sinful humanity, but also because they constitute a call to the Christian to do likewise. There we read:

> If you have done right and suffer for it your endurance is worthwhile in the sight of God. To this you were called, because Christ suffered on your behalf, and left you an example; it is for you to follow in his steps. He committed no sin, he was guilty of no falsehood; when he suffered he uttered no threats. . . . (1 Peter 2:20–22)

The innocent, silently uncomplaining suffering of Christ is, in this teaching of Peter, not only an act of Christ on our behalf from which we benefit; it is also an example of Christ for our instruction which we are to follow. This portrait of Christ is to be painted again on the ordinary canvas of our lives. Had not Jesus himself said that those who would follow him must deny themselves and take up their cross? What then does it mean for the Christian to bear a cross?

We meet in this world some suffering which is our own fault; we bring accidents upon ourselves by our carelessness, or punishment by our offenses. This is not "bearing a cross"; as Peter wrote, there is no merit in taking punishment for having done wrong. "What credit is it," he asks, "if when you do wrong and are beaten for it, you take it patiently?"

We also sometimes suffer in ways we cannot understand, as from an unexpected or unexplained illness or catastrophe which strikes us. Such suffering the Christian can bear, trusting in God's supporting presence and learning to depend more fully and more joyfully on God's sustaining grace. Yet this is not what Jesus was talking about when he predicted suffering for his disciples.

The cross of Christ was the price of his obedience to God amid a rebellious world; it was suffering for having done right, for loving where others hated, for representing in the flesh the forgiveness and the righteousness of God among humanity, which was both less forgiving and less righteous. The cross of Christ was God's overcoming evil with good.

The cross of the Christian is then no different; it is the price of our obedience to God's love toward all others in a world ruled by hate. Such unflinching love for friend and foe alike will mean hostility and suffering for us, as it did for him.

Jesus instructed his disciples, simply and clearly, not to resist evil. He said, "Whoever slaps you on the right cheek, turn and offer him the left. If he sues you for your shirt, let him have your coat as well. . . . Love your enemies and pray for those who persecute you, only so can you be the children of your heavenly Father who sends his sun and rain to good and bad alike" (Matthew 5:39–45).

In saying this Jesus was not a foolish dreamer, spinning out futile hopes for a better world, thinking that if only we keep smiling everything will turn out all right, with our opponents turned into

friends and our sacrifices all repaid. He knew full well the cost of such unlimited love. He foresaw clearly the suffering it would mean, first for himself and then for his followers. But there was no other way for him to take, no other way worthy of God. Jesus' teaching here is not a collection of good human ideas; it is his divinely authoritative interpretation of the law of God.

In 2,000 years the world has not grown much more loving. The example of Cain, who killed his brother, still sets the basic pattern for dealing with conflicts, whether within the family or in the world of nations. Among nations it matters little whether they be religious or not in name; the choice of weapons and the readiness to retaliate are similar. How few are they, how few even within the Christian churches, who in this embattled world seek to be conformed only to Christ, to find in the suffering servant of the Lord, and not in some honored ruler, king, or warrior, the model for their lives!

"It is by this that we know what love is," says the apostle, "that Christ laid down his life for us. And we in turn are bound to lay down our lives for our brothers" (1 John 3:16).

Christians whose loyalty to the Prince of Peace puts them out of step with today's nationalistic world, because of a willingness to love their nation's friends but not to hate the nation's enemies, are not unrealistic dreamers who think that by their objections all wars will end. The unrealistic dreamers are rather the soldiers who think that they can put an end to wars by preparing for just one more.

Nor do Christians think that by refusal to help with the organized destruction of life and property they are uninvolved in the complications and conflicts of modern life. Nor are Christians reacting simply in emotional fear to the fantastic awfulness of the weapons created by the demonic ingenuity of modern humanity.

Christians love their enemies not because they think the enemies are wonderful people, nor because they believe that love is sure to conquer these enemies. They do not love their enemies because they fail to respect their native land or its rulers; nor because they are unconcerned for the safety of their neighbors; nor because another political or economic system may be favored. The Christian loves his or her enemies because God does, and God commands his followers to do so; that is the only reason, and that is enough.

Our God, who has been made known in Jesus Christ, is a

reconciling, forgiving, suffering God. If, to paraphrase what the apostle Paul said, it is no longer I who love, but Christ who loves in me, my life must bear the marks of that revelation (Galatians 2:20).

No individual created in God's image and for whom Christ died can be for me an enemy whose life I am willing to threaten or to take, unless I am more devoted to something else—a political theory, a nation, the defense of certain privileges, or my own personal welfare—than I am to God's cause and God's loving invasion of this world through the prophets, God's son, and the church.

One of the most difficult things to understand in the history of the Christian church is the haste with which preachers and others have labeled the selfish interest of their class, race, and nation with the name of Christ, making a holy cause of the subjection, or even the destruction, of those whom Christ came to save and bless with abundant life.

In any kind of conflict, from the fist fight to the labor dispute, from the family quarrel to the threat of international communism, the Christian sees the world and its wars from the viewpoint of the cross. "When we were God's enemies, we were reconciled to him through the death of his Son" (Romans 5:10).

The Christian has no choice. If the Lord's strategy for dealing with his enemies was to love them and give himself for them, it must be ours as well.

What does Christ say about the Christian and national loyalty? For centuries most professing Christians have believed that their faith made them not only more obedient citizens, but also more courageous soldiers; that God helped them not only to love their neighbors but also to hate and destroy their enemies. Since the Roman emperor Constantine allied his government with the church, priests and preachers have been crowning kings, blessing armies, and praying for the defeat of their nation's enemies, all in the name of the Prince of Peace.

Almost every theology and every denomination has explained how this had to be so. Today people of the church will argue that even nuclear weapons can be used by Christians against their fellow human beings if the nation so commands. But what does the gospel say?

The Bible does not ignore the existence of nations. But most

often when we read in Scripture of "the nations," it is to say that *out* of every tribe and tongue and people and *nation* persons have been redeemed to belong to God's people.

"You are a chosen race, a royal priesthood, a holy nation, God's own people," writes Peter of the Christian church (1 Peter 2:9). The nation to which the Christian belongs first is "God's own people," the fellowship of the saints, the church of Jesus Christ. This "people for God's special possession" is united not by a common language or territory or government but by one and the same divine call and a common response; reconciled to God, its members belong to each other. The unity thus created breaches every wall and rends every curtain, whether of bamboo or of iron.

This new nation, the people of God, is the Christian's first loyalty. No political nation, no geographical homeland to which an individual belongs by birth, can take precedence over the heavenly citizenship which is given a Christian in his or her new birth.

These pious phrases—citizenship in heaven, new birth, people of God—are nothing new. They are in fact *so* familiar, so well-worn, that it occurs to few Christians to stop and think what it would mean to take them seriously.

When God calls us to put first loyalties first, this means that Christians of different nations, even of enemy nations, belong more closely to each other, and have more in common with each other, than with their non-Christian fellow citizens. Not for nothing do Christians call one another brother and sister. How then could a Christian, for the sake of a country's prestige or possessions, seek to take the lives of spiritual brothers and sisters, when their sole offense was to have been born under another flag?

Not only in Abraham's time was it a testing of faith to be called by God to abandon all else out of loyalty to that "city, whose builder and maker is God." Even more so today, when nationalism has become a religion for millions, will the true depth and reality of the Christian profession of hosts of church people be tested when they must choose between their earthly and their eternal loyalties.

"What causes conflicts and quarrels among you? Do they not spring from the aggressiveness of your bodily desires? You want something which you cannot have, and so you are bent on murder; you are envious, and cannot attain your ambition, and so you quarrel and fight" (James 4:1,2).

130

These words of the apostle James have not been worn out. When there is conflict among people, whether within small groups or between nations, we try to dignify the clash with lofty principles. We may speak of truth and honor, of democracy and human rights, of great causes and noble goals. Yet the apostle is not deceived: "What is the cause of conflicts among you? . . . Your bodily desires . . . you are envious."

He has seen deeper than we care to admit. True enough, individuals—and even groups of people, and perhaps even, rarely, a nation—can seek sincerely some unselfish purpose; but only seldom and not for long. If great, noble, unselfish causes are constantly proclaimed to be the guides of a group's actions, even the most gullible of us have learned to check a second time to see the real reason.

In international affairs nations may show great concern, as they usually say, to "liberate" some poor people from "tyranny," when what they really care about is the price of sugar, the use of some mine or port, or the aggrandizement of their political influence. In the dealings between labor and management, each side speaks of the good of the national economy, when the real desire is for an immediate one-sided gain, even at the cost of a rise in prices for everyone. In a neighborhood or family disagreement, we hastily announce that serious moral principles are at stake—honesty or decency—where, as a matter of fact, it is our own pride that drives us.

If we thus understand the true root of conflict among people, this explains a number of things. It explains, first of all, why the Christian is and must be a person of peace. The Christian is not primarily someone who has joined a church, or has accepted certain teachings, or has had certain feelings, or has promised to live up to certain moral standards, though all these things are part of the picture. The Christian is a person who has been, in the words of Jesus, "born anew," who has started life over in a new way, who by the power of God working in him or her is a new person.

Conflict before was a normal, built-in part of one's nature; but now the person has been disarmed. The spring from which flowed enmity and strife has been clogged; the scrawny shrub of bitterness has been cut down to the stump. It may well spring up again; but the believer knows how to deal with it as with any other temptation—in repentance, confession, and spiritual victory.

131

The reason, therefore, for the Christian's being called to live above this world's battles is not that one of the Ten Commandments enjoins us not to kill, or not that Jesus as a new lawgiver orders us to love our enemies. The Christian has been disarmed by God. There is no need for *orders* to love one's neighbors, beginning in the smallest circle of daily relationships, or one's enemies; the Christian is driven to this by the love of Christ within his or her life.

The fact that selfish desire is a root of conflict explains furthermore why we cannot really expect whole nations and societies to build a peaceful world. Christian behavior flows from faith; we cannot impose it on entire nations. Many persons, when they hear of Christians whose conscience forbids their bearing arms, will argue that it is quite unrealistic to expect nations to follow this example. We do not wait, in our teachings about moral purity and holiness in any other realm, for the world to be ready to follow us before we follow Christ.

We know clearly that to be called by Christ means being different from the world. How then should our living the disarmed life depend on whether nations are ready to lay down their weapons? Jesus predicted that there would continue to be wars as long as this world lasts, just as he predicted that people's faith would grow cold and their morals loose. But this cannot be a reason for Christians to follow this world's ways, any more than the prevalence of theft or of waste is a model for Christians to follow.

When we say that we do not really expect nations to take the path of suffering and discipleship, this does not mean that it is wrong for Christians to desire and to work for peace among nations. The apostle Paul expressly instructs us to pray especially for rulers and for all those in authority, in order that we may lead a peaceful life. God's will is that people should be able to live quiet and godly lives; to permit this is the duty of government before God. We therefore can and should pray and testify concerning the folly of trusting in earthly arms, concerning the undermining of democratic government by peacetime military establishment, concerning the dangers of radioactive contamination and of "accidental war" which the great belligerent powers impose on the rest of the globe, and especially concerning the hideous immorality of the weapons now being devised.

It might even be that with more and more men and women

uneasy and disturbed about the menace of militarism, the example and the refusal of a few resolute Christians might sound out as an alarm and a rallying cry for intelligent citizens who were waiting for someone else to have the courage to speak first and to suffer for it. But the Christian does not renounce war because he or she expects intelligent citizens to rally around the cause; they usually won't. Rather, the Christian takes this stand because the defenseless death of the Messiah has for all time been revealed as the victory of faith that overcomes the world.

Someone will be asking, is this the whole picture? Is there not, after all, a moral difference between freedom and tyranny? Is it not our duty to care and even to sacrifice for the preservation of our civilization? Certainly not all such sacrifice can be accounted for as "selfish desires." Are we not socially responsible?

The Christian who has been disarmed by God would here have several things to say, but they may be gathered up into one question. Did not Jesus Christ face the same problem? Was not he, who was just as human as you and I, concerned for the victims of oppression? Was he not, with the thousands who gathered around to make him a king, a man before whom the path to political responsibility was opening? Did he not believe that it was God's prophetically announced will to glorify himself by establishing righteousness among the nations and to make Zion the center from which justice would go out to all peoples?

And yet, somehow, all of this did not swerve the Son of Man, in whom we see what God wants a person to be, from his certainty that to seek and to save the lost, his path must be one not of power, but of humility; not of enforcing justice, but of incarnating love. As Peter wrote, "He . . . committed his cause to One who judges justly" (1 Peter 2:23). And yet, has not the ministry of this one defenseless man—and of the line of disarmed martyrs in his train across the years—done more to unseat tyrants and to defend basic human rights than all the belligerent zeal of those who were seeking to defend God's people against the godless with the weapons of humanity? For the wrath of individuals does not accomplish the justice of God.

When the apostle Paul says that "the weapons we wield are not merely human" or "not those of the world" (2 Corinthians 10:4), most of us, accustomed to thinking on the "merely human" level, would have expected him to say, "not human but spiritual,"

or "not of this world but of another world." But he says, "not merely human, but divinely potent." This is the "almighty meekness" of our reigning Lord.

When the Christian whom God has disarmed lays aside carnal weapons, it is not, in the last analysis, because they are too dangerous, but because they are too weak. The believers in Jesus as Lord direct their lives toward the day when all creation will praise, not kings and chancellors, but the Lamb that was slain as worthy to receive blessing and honor and glory *and power.*

RECONCILING OUR ENEMIES:
A Biblical Study on Nonviolence
by Ronald Sider

For Christians, the cross is not some abstract symbol of nonviolence. The cross is the jagged slab of wood to which Roman soldiers spiked Jesus of Nazareth whom we follow and worship.

But why was he crucified? Was it merely because he came to die as a sacrifice for our sin? Or was it merely that he lived such an exemplary, loving life of concern for the poor and weak that he died a martyr to peace, justice, and love? Why did Jesus end up on the cross?

To answer that question, we must recall the historical context into which Jesus stepped and then reflect on what his life and message looked like in that historical setting.

Quite apart from the question of political freedom and independence for which the Jews eagerly yearned, Roman rule was hardly benign. Herod the Great, who ruled as a client king of Rome until 4 B.C., turned large portions of Palestine into personal estates worked by tenants—an oppressive arrangement depicted in Jesus' parables.

After A.D. 6, when Judea became a directly-governed Roman province, governors were often oppressive. Pilate, according to a contemporary, was "of hard disposition, brutal and pitiless." His administration was full of "corruption, violence, robbery, brutality, extortion, and execution without trial." Tax collectors exacted heavy taxation. And there was the ongoing danger that Jewish religious life would be violated—witness for instance Emperor Caligula's attempt to set up his statue in the temple in A.D. 41.

It is hardly surprising that apocalyptic, messianic expectation was widespread and intense in the first century A.D. Almost everyone longed for the dawning of the new age when the messiah would come to end the rule of the foreign oppressors.

Given the common assumption of all messianic expectation

that the messiah would end Roman rule, the Romans naturally took a dim view of messianic speculation. They viewed the succession of messianic pretenders who appeared in the first century A.D. as dangerous political enemies guilty of treason against Roman rule.

And they had good reason to be worried. When Herod the Great died, three different messianic pretenders provoked armed rebellion. The Roman governor of Syria came to Jerusalem and crucified two thousand rebels. Judas, who was probably a founder of the Zealots a few years later, attacked an arsenal of Herod three miles from Jesus' home town of Nazareth.

In A.D. 6, when Judea became a Roman province, an underground organization of violent revolutionaries emerged. Full of ardent zeal for the law and intense eschatological expectation, the deeply religious Zealots believed that God would intervene to usher in the new age if they could provoke a popular rebellion against Rome. According to the Zealots, slaying the godless was a religious duty.

To be sure, not all Jews of the time favored armed rebellion. The Sadducees and high priestly aristocracy preferred to collaborate with the foreign oppressors. The clan of Annas, which held the office of high priest almost all of the time between A.D. 6 and 41, used some of the vast sums earned from their monopoly on the sale of animals for temple sacrifices to offer huge bribes to the Roman governors. The moderate Pharisees also opposed rebellion, and the Essenes preferred to retreat into the Judean caves to wait quietly for the eschatological day of the Lord.

In the maelstrom of oppression, violence, and intense messianic expectation, the Jewish population apparently saw only three possibilities: armed, revolutionary resistance; more or less opportunistic accommodation to the establishment; and patient, passive endurance. Jesus of Nazareth began to proclaim and incarnate a fourth possibility—the way of suffering servanthood.

At the heart of Jesus' message was the announcement that the messianic age of eschatological expectation was beginning in his life and ministry ("Today this scripture has been fulfilled in your hearing"—Luke 4:21).

Not surprisingly, the good citizens of Nazareth took deep offense when Jesus insisted that the blessings of the messianic age would be available to everyone—even hated foreigners and enemies. Furthermore, at the center of Jesus' conception of the new messian-

136

ic age was the special concern for the poor, the release of captives, and liberation of the oppressed called for in the Jubilee. The new age which he saw himself inaugurating had specific economic and social content.

The eschatological Jubilee was central to Jesus' thought and work. In the sermon in Luke 6:20 ff., Jesus pronounced a blessing on the poor and hungry and promised that, in the new age, they would be satisfied. Conversely, the rich and full would experience a woeful reversal (Luke 6:24–25). Drawing on Deuteronomy 15, he commanded his followers to live by the standards of the dawning messianic age and make loans expecting nothing in return (Deuteronomy 15:35). This command is echoed in the Lord's Prayer where he taught his disciples to ask God to forgive their sins as they forgave everyone who had debts or loans owed to them (Luke 11:4).

Jesus' cleansing of the temple fits perfectly into this inauguration of the messianic Jubilee. Outraged that the wealthy, priestly aristocracy was collecting huge sums from their monopolistic sale of animals for sacrifice, Jesus called their economic practices robbery ("My house shall be a house of prayer, but you have made it a den of robbers"—Luke 19:46). And he drove them out.

This was not an armed attack on the temple but rather an exemplary demonstration against the misuse of the sanctuary to enrich the leading priestly families. It is hardly surprising that the Sadducees and priestly aristocracy considered a person who announced and acted out such a radical call for socio-economic change to be highly dangerous. Hence they moved promptly to destroy him (Luke 19:47).

Within a few days, they had him arrested and turned over to the Roman governor as a dangerous revolutionary. One reason Jesus got crucified, then, was that he began to live out the kind of radical socio-economic reordering expected when the messiah would inaugurate the Jubilee.

But it would be a gross distortion to suggest that Jesus was crucified *merely* because he offended the wealthy establishment with radical socio-economic proposals. He called people to live out the vision of the Jubilee precisely because the messianic age had begun in his own person and work.

Jesus also claimed the authority to forgive sins, which, as the Jewish bystanders immediately recognized, was a prerogative of God alone (Mark 2:6–7). And at his trial, when they asked him if

he was the messiah, the Son of God, he said "I am; and you will see the Son of Man sitting at the right hand of Power and coming in the clouds of heaven" (Mark 14:62). It is hardly surprising that monotheistic Jews charged him with blasphemy.

The Roman rulers, however, reserved for themselves the authority to mete out capital punishment. Hence the Jewish authorities could not execute Jesus, even though the Torah prescribed death for blasphemy. But since messianic pretenders were a clear political danger to Roman imperialism, Pilate was willing to crucify Jesus on the *political* charge that he claimed to be the king of the Jews.

Jesus of Nazareth was not the only messianic pretender crucified in the first century. But he differed from the others in at least two decisive ways. In the first place, something very unusual happened on the third day after his crucifixion. In the second place, his methods contrasted radically with all the others. He chose to implement his messianic kingdom with suffering servanthood rather than a violent sword.

Jesus' decision to use nonviolent means is visible at every crucial point in his career. At his temptation, when Satan offered him all the political and military power of the world (Luke 4:5–8), Jesus faced and decisively rejected the Zealot option of violent means to establish the messianic kingdom. At Caesarea Philippi, when Peter confessed that Jesus was the messiah, he quickly hastened to explain that as the messianic Son of Man, he would have to suffer and even die. And when Peter rejected that picture of a suffering messiah, Jesus harshly denounced him as an agent of that satanic one who had already tempted him with the Zealot option (Mark 8:27–34).

In the triumphal entry (Luke 19:28–40), Jesus consciously chose to fulfill the eschatological prophecy in Zechariah 9:9, precisely because it depicted a humble, peaceful messianic figure riding not on a war horse, but on an ass. The vision from Zechariah of a peaceful king who would "command peace to the nations" corresponded to Jesus' transformed picture of the messiah.

In the final crisis, he persisted in his rejection of the sword. He rebuked Peter for attacking those who came to arrest him (Luke 33:49–50). And he informed Pilate that his kingdom was not of the world in one specific regard—namely that his followers did not use violence (John 18:36). Obviously he did not mean that the

messianic kingdom he had inaugurated had nothing to do with the earth. That would have contradicted his central announcement of the eschatological Jubilee which he expected his followers to begin living. But he did mean that he would not establish his kingdom by the sword.

But Jesus not only lived the way of nonviolence. He also taught it. The Sermon on the Mount (Matthew 5:38–48 and parallel) contains the most important text.

To a people so oppressed by foreign conquerors that, repeatedly over the previous two centuries, they had resorted to violent rebellion, Jesus gave the unprecedented command: "Love your enemies." New Testament scholar Martin Hengel believes that Jesus probably formulated his command to love one's enemies in conscious contrast to the teaching and practice of the Zealots. Thus Jesus was pointedly rejecting one currently attractive political method in favor of a radically different approach.

Jesus' command to love one's enemies is in direct contrast to currently widespread views that Jesus summarizes in Matthew 5:43: "You have heard that it was said, 'You shall love your neighbor and hate your enemy.'" The first part of this verse is a direct quotation from Leviticus 19:18. As Leviticus 19:17 and the history of subsequent interpretation in the post-exilic period demonstrate, the neighbor that one was obligated to love was normally understood to be a fellow Israelite. Thus love for neighbor had clear ethnic and religious limitations.

A different attitude was permissible toward Gentiles. The Old Testament did not command or sanction hatred of the enemy. But Jewish contemporaries of Jesus did. The Zealots believed that "slaying of the godless enemy out of zeal for God's cause was a fundamental commandment, true to the rabbinic maxim: 'Whoever spills the blood of one of the godless is like one who offers a sacrifice.'" And the Qumran community's manual of discipline urged people to "love all the sons of light . . . and . . . hate all the sons of darkness."

Jesus' way is entirely different. For the followers of Jesus, neighbor love must extend beyond the limited circle of the people of Israel, beyond the limited circle of the new people of God. All people everywhere are neighbors to Jesus' followers and, therefore, are to be actively loved. And that love extends to enemies—even violent, oppressive foreign conquerors.

It is exegetically impossible to follow Luther's two kingdom analysis and restrict the application of these verses on love of enemies to some personal sphere, denying their application to violence in the public sphere. As Edward Schweitzer says in his commentary on Matthew, "There is not the slightest hint of any realm where the disciple is not bound by the words of Jesus."

In the preceding verses, Jesus had discussed issues that clearly pertained to the public sphere of the legal system and the authorized demands of the Roman rulers. Jesus rejected the basic, legal principle from the Torah that it was right to demand an eye for an eye and a tooth for a tooth (Matthew 5:38), thus placing his own personal authority above that of Moses. Jesus here was not dealing with some admonitions for private interpersonal relationships; he was dealing with a fundamental principle of Jewish and other Near Eastern legal systems.

Instead of retaliation to a corresponding degree against someone who had caused damage, Jesus commanded a loving response that would even submit to further damage and suffering rather than exact equal pain or loss from the unfair, guilty aggressor. Matthew 5:40 ("If anyone would sue you and take your coat, let him have your cloak as well") speaks of how one should respond in the public arena of the judicial system. And 5:44 ("If anyone force you to go one mile, go with him two miles") speaks of how to respond to Roman rulers who demand forced labor.

The verb translated as "force" is a technical term used to refer to the requisition of services by civil and military authorities. Josephus used the word to speak of compulsory carrying of military supplies. The Roman rulers could and did demand that civilians in conquered lands perform such services upon demand. Thus they were able to demand that Simon of Cyrene carry Jesus' cross (Matthew 27:32). Not surprisingly, the Zealots urged Jews to refuse this kind of forced labor. Jesus, however, rejects that angry, violent Zealot response to the oppressors' unjust demands.

But Jesus was not advocating a passive, resigned attitude toward oppressors. Certainly nothing in the text suggests that Jesus approved the unfair, insulting slap on the cheek or the demand for forced labor. But Jesus' response was to call on the oppressed to take command of their situation in a way that transcended the old age's normal categories of friends and enemies.

The members of Jesus' new messianic kingdom were to love

opponents, even oppressive, persecuting enemies, so deeply that they could wholeheartedly pray for their well-being and truly love them as persons.

The radical, costly character of Jesus' call for love toward enemies certainly tempts us to weaken decisively Jesus' message by labelling it an impossible ideal, relegating it to the millennium, or limiting its application to personal relationships. But that is to misread both the text and the concrete historical context in which Jesus lived and spoke.

In his original setting, Jesus advocated love toward enemies as his specific political response to centuries of violence and to the contemporary Zealots' call for violent revolution. And he spoke as one who claimed to be the messiah of Israel. His messianic kingdom was already breaking into the present; therefore his disciples should and could live out the values of the new age.

To be sure, he did not say that one should practice loving nonviolence because it would always instantly transform enemies into bosom friends. The cross stands as a harsh reminder that love for enemies does not always work—at least in the short run. Jesus grounds his call to love enemies in the very nature of God. God loves his enemies. Instead of promptly destroying sinners, he continues lovingly to shower the good gifts of creation upon them. Since that is the way God is, those who want to be his sons and daughters must do likewise.

Then Jesus died on a cross. He suffered the most despicable death possible. Paul's quotation from the Torah, "Cursed be every one who hangs on a tree" (Deuteronomy 21:23; Galatians 3:13), expressed the Jewish viewpoint. As for the brutally efficient Romans, they knew how to put down political threats. They regularly crucified political criminals, especially the constant stream of rebellious Jewish messianic pretenders.

It was the resurrection which convinced the discouraged disciples that, in spite of the cross, Jesus' claims and his announcement of the messianic kingdom were still valid. Jewish eschatological expectation looked for a general resurrection at the beginning of the new age. As the early Christians reflected on Jesus' resurrection, they realized that one instance of this eschatological resurrection had actually occurred in the old age.

Thus they referred to Jesus' resurrection as the first fruits (1 Corinthians 15:20–23) of that final, general resurrection. Jesus'

resurrection then was decisive evidence that the new age had truly invaded the old. Jesus of Nazareth was now called Jesus Christ (Jesus the messiah) because his resurrection was irrefutable evidence that his messianic claims were valid.

Not until we understand that Jesus Christ, the crucified one, is Lord, do we begin to penetrate to the full meaning of the cross. The crucified criminal hanging limp on the middle cross was the eternal Word who in the beginning was with God and indeed was God, but for our sakes became flesh and dwelt among us. The crucified one was he "who had always been God by nature [but] did not cling to his prerogatives as God's equal, but stripped himself of all privilege by consenting to be a slave" (Philippians 2:6-7). Only when we grasp that that is who the crucified one was do we begin to fathom the depth of Jesus' teaching that God's way of dealing with enemies is the way of suffering love.

The cross is the ultimate demonstration that God deals with his enemies through suffering love; Paul provides the clearest theological expression of this: "God shows his love for us in that while we were yet sinners, Christ died for us. . . . While we were enemies, we were reconciled to God by the death of his Son" (Romans 5:8, 10).

Jesus' vicarious cross for sinners is the foundation and deepest expression of Jesus' command to love one's enemies. We are enemies in the sense both that sinful persons are hostile to God and also that the just, holy Creator hates sin (Romans 1:18). For those who know the law, failure to obey it results in a divine curse. But Christ redeemed us from that curse by becoming a curse for us (Galatians 3:10-14). Jesus' blood on the cross was an expiation (Romans 5:18) for us sinful enemies of God, because the one who knew no sin was made sin for us on the cross (2 Corinthians 5:21).

Jesus' vicarious death for sinful enemies of God lies at the very heart of our commitment to nonviolence. Because the incarnate one knew that God was loving and merciful even toward the worst of sinners, he associated with sinners, forgave their sins, and completed his mission of dying for the sins of the world. And it was precisely the same understanding of God that prompted him to command his followers to love their enemies.

Because the one hanging limp on the cross was the Word who became flesh, we know for sure both that a just God mercifully accepts us sinful enemies and also that he wants us to go and treat

all our enemies in the same merciful, self-sacrificial way.

Since Jesus commanded his followers to love their enemies, and then died as the incarnate son to demonstrate that God reconciles his enemies by suffering love, any rejection of the nonviolent way in human relations involves a heretical doctrine of the atonement. If God in Christ reconciled his enemies by suffering servanthood, then those who want to follow Christ faithfully dare not treat their enemies in any other way.

It is a tragedy of our time that many of those who appropriate the biblical understanding of Christ's vicarious cross fail to see its direct implications for the problem of war and violence. And it is equally tragic that some of those who most emphasize pacifism and nonviolence fail to ground it in Christ's vicarious atonement. It is a serious heresy of the atonement to base one's nonviolence in the weak sentimentality of the lowly Nazarene viewed merely as a noble martyr to truth and peace rather than in the vicarious cross of the Word who became flesh.

The cross is much more than Christ's witness to the weakness and folly of the sword, although it certainly is that. In fact it is that precisely because the incarnate Word's vicarious death for our sins is the ultimate demonstration that the sovereign of the universe is a merciful father who reconciles his enemies through self-sacrificial love.

Given this understanding of Jesus as the unique Son of God, and his cross as the demonstration of God's method of dealing with enemies, it is hardly surprising that the New Testament writers regularly urged Christians to pattern their lives after Jesus' cross. Certainly the once-for-all sacrifice of Christ for the sins of the world was a unique element of his cross that could never be repeated. But that fact never prevented the New Testament authors from discerning in the cross a decisive ethical clue for the Christian's approach to opponents and enemies, indeed even friends, spouses, and fellow members of Christ's body.

In every strand of New Testament literature, and with reference to every kind of situation (whether family, church, state, or employment), the way of the cross applies. Jesus' cross, where he practiced what he had preached about love for one's enemies, becomes the Christian norm for every area of life. Only if one holds biblical authority so irrelevant that one can ignore explicit, regularly repeated, scriptural teaching; only if one so disregards Christ's

atonement that one rejects God's way of dealing with enemies; only then can we forsake the cross for the sword.

To be sure, church history is a sad story of Christians doing precisely that. After the first three centuries. when almost all Christians refused to participate in warfare, Christians repeatedly invented ways to justify violence.

And each of us, if we think honestly about the costly implications of suffering servanthood, will understand within ourselves how temptingly plausible it is to consider Jesus' nonviolent way an impossible ideal, a utopian vision practiced only in the millenium, or some idealistic teaching intended only for personal relationships.

But if one recalls Jesus' historical context, one simply cannot assert that that is what Jesus himself meant. Claiming to be their messiah, he came to an oppressed people ready to use violence to drive out their oppressors. But he advocated love for enemies as God's method for ushering in the coming kingdom. And he submitted to Roman crucifixion to reconcile his enemies.

If, as unbelievers of both past and present assert, the cross is the last word about Jesus of Nazareth, then his call to suffering servanthood was indeed a noble but ultimately utopian dream that responsible realists should ignore.

But if, as Christians claim, the grave could not hold him, then his messianic kingdom has truly begun and the way of the cross is the way of the risen sovereign of this whole glorious universe.

Lord, I believe; help thou my unbelief.

WILL CHRISTIANS PUSH THE NUCLEAR BUTTON?

Questions for Thought and Discussion

1. Kreider speaks of the early church discipline against serving in the military. Is that discipline possible in the church today? Why or why not?

2. How do you respond to Yoder's assertion that the Christian's first loyalty is to the new nation, the kingdom of God, before any nation of the world? How would Jesus respond to criticism that, in the face of the threat of tyranny, a standard of non-violence is impossible?

3. Sider makes the bold claim that Jesus' example of self-sacrifice, which led to the cross, is the way to deal with our enemies. What is the meaning and relevance of Jesus' example today? What would it mean for us to love our enemies sacrificially?

WHO SHALL SUFFER INJURY AT OUR HANDS?

Historical Christian Responses to War and Peace

by E. Glenn Hinson

Christians have taken three stances toward war and peace during their nearly 20 centuries of history. Only one of these, pacifism, originated with them. The other two, the just war theory and the crusade, were inherited; the former from the classical world, the latter from the Old Testament.

Circumstances have had much to do with shaping these positions. Though individual Christians have held varied view in every age, one or another of these three perspectives has emerged to a dominant place at one time or another. Prior to Constantine, when Christianity represented a harassed and persecuted minority, pacifism prevailed. After 313, however, as Christians began to enjoy the imperial favor and incorporated vast numbers of new converts, pacifism gave way to the just war view which ruled both Greek and Roman thinking. During the Middle Ages, a holy war or crusade fired the European Christian imagination. War was viewed as a means of wiping out infidelity, whether Turkish, Jewish, pagan, or heretical.

Since the Middle Ages, Christians have usually let national circumstances dictate attitudes. In times of peace they have listened to those who articulated the pacifist message, but in times of threat to the national security they have allowed themselves to become caught up with patriotic fervor. On such occasions the pacifists among them have suffered from suspicion and ostracism or even direct persecution.

The advent of the nuclear era casts a different light on the whole war/peace issue and especially the pacifist position. The development of gunpowder caused human beings only momentary

pause when they recognized how it had magnified human destructive capacities. After a little while, they got used to the effects and learned to cope with the devastation. Once more, there is cause to wonder whether human beings will make the same response to nuclear weaponry.

PEACEMAKING

We are apt to construe the word "pacifism" in a passive sense, unwillingness to fight, but that is a misinterpretation. The Latin means "peacemaking," and, as all should recognize, the early Christians, and may others since, understood its meaning in the light of Jesus' words in the Sermon on the Mount, "Blessed are the peacemakers, for they shall be called children of God" (Matthew 5:9).

Early Christian writers, as Roland Bainton has reported in his classic study *Christian Attitudes toward War and Peace,* repudiated participation in warfare for diverse reasons. Some objected to the affiliation of the military with pagan religious exercises. Worship of the emperor was common in the camps, for instance, and officers were expected to offer public sacrifices. Soldiers in the ranks, though, Tertullian observed *(On Idolatry),* could escape this obligation and might have been able to maintain a fairly strict Christian commitment.

The strongest reason for actively engaging in pacifism, however, was *agape*-love. "If we are enjoined, then, to love our enemies," Tertullian wanted to know, "whom have we to hate? If injured, forbidden to retaliate . . . who can suffer injury at our hands?" *(Apology).* In both West and East, the church fathers defended pacifism on the grounds that love and killing are incompatible with one another. Christians, Tertullian judged, counted it "better to be slain than to slay" *(Apology).*

Jesus himself, according to Origen, "did not consider it compatible with his inspired legislation to allow the taking of human life in any form at all" *(Against Celsus, III.7).* The *Canons of Hippolytus* directed that a "soldier of civil authority must be taught not to kill men and to refuse to do so if he is commanded." Aversion to shedding of blood continued even after Constantine. Emperors regularly deferred baptism until their deathbeds because, as commanders in chief of the army, they were guilty of murder.

It may seem surprising that in later centuries Christians chose any other path, but in the earliest attempts to understand Jesus we may discern already the source of confusion. Jesus apparently wrestled with his own identity and mission in the context of burgeoning Jewish nationalism. To be a militant messiah like David was one of his major options, and his intimate followers included Jewish nationalists.

Yet Jesus himself seems to have rejected the image of the Davidic messiah in favor of that of the Servant of Isaiah. That, at any rate, is how his early followers interpreted him. He came as a champion of peace and reconciliation, and he expected them to do the same.

Until about A.D. 170, there is no evidence for Christian service in the Roman army, though we must be careful not to argue too much from silence, for Christians were few in number and often went unnoticed. About 175, it is true, the pagan polemicist Celsus chided Christians for failure to exercise the proper responsibility of citizens. "If everyone were to do the same as you," he wrote, "there would be nothing to prevent [the emperor] from being abandoned, alone and deserted, while earthly things would come into the power of the most lawless and savage barbarians, and nothing more would be heard among men either of your worship or of the true wisdom" (Origen, *Against Celsus,* VIII. 68). But Celsus said this on the basis of limited acquaintance with Christianity, for, in the very period in which he wrote, Christians played a major role in the famous "thundering legion" under Marcus Aurelius.

From this time on, evidence for Christian participation in the army increases. The strongest objections to military service appeared in the East, especially among the monks, but so also did the most vigorous support, on the eastern frontier. Christians in northern Africa reacted in mixed fashions, some favoring and some strongly objecting to military service. Christians in Rome did not forbid epitaphs recording service in the army.

The pacifist approach has never prevailed in Christian thinking since Constantine, but it has had exponents, chiefly isolated individuals and small sects. After Constantine's conversion it was espoused still by monks. In the crusading era of the Middle Ages, it had a voice in Francis of Assisi and some Franciscans, the Waldensians, the heretical Cathari, and one branch of Hussites, led first by Peter Chelciky. It was the horrors of religious persecution and

wars, however, which gave birth to the peace churches, Anabaptists and Quakers.

THE JUST WAR

Constantine's conversion ended the dominance of pacifism as a Christian attitude toward war. To many Christians, such as Eusebius of Caesarea, it seemed that the millenium had arrived. Constantine, Eusebius said, was almost "another Christ," and Christians had to throw themselves fully behind him in his effort to place the whole empire under the Christian banner. By the early fifth century, the Emperor Theodosius II stipulated that Christians alone could serve in the army. Only a few monks dared to hold on to the pacifist position, and they could do so only by withdrawal from society.

Coming to terms with the state, Christians now settled for a revised version of the classical theory of war. The first to do so was Ambrose, Bishop of Milan, who seems never to have entertained scruples against military service. To the classical view he added two ingredients: that the war should be just and that monks and clergy should be exempted.

Augustine, Bishop of Hippo and the towering theologian in the West, framed the just war theory in its classical Christian form. Working from the code as set forth by Plato and Cicero, he laid down four conditions for a just war: (1) It is to be just in its intent, namely, to restore peace and to vindicate justice. Although Augustine recognized that perfect peace is not attainable on earth, he did not abandon hope for an approximate peace. (2) It is to be just in its disposition, that is, pursued with love. Unlike earlier Christians, Augustine saw no conflict between love and killing, for he differentiated inward attitudes from outward behavior. Actually love may command severity, "for in the trial of their patience, and the chastening of their spirit, and in bearing fatherly correction, [enemies] are rather benefited than injured" (*Against Faustus,* XXII. 75). (3) It is to be just in its auspices, waged only under authority of the ruler. The prince alone should decide when to use the sword. (4) It is to be just in its conduct. Drawing from classical sources, Augustine forbade wanton violence, profanation of temples, looting, massacre, conflagration, vengeance, atrocities, and reprisals. He believed Christianity had mitigated the harsher aspects of war. Like

Ambrose, he excluded monks and clergy from participation.

The just war theory yielded to a crusading spirit in the Middle Ages; apart from that, however, it has dominated Western thinking since Augustine's day. Yet practice has scarcely equalled theory, even in those periods when warring parties thought they abided by it. Medieval warriors and writers regularly adapted and accommodated the theory to suit circumstances, and it was only a short step from the just war, looked at one-sidedly, to the holy war or the crusade.

In the late 15th and early 16th centuries, conditions in Europe, particularly the rise of independent city-states such as Florence and Venice, favored a revival of the just war. This led naturally to its application by both Catholics and Protestants during the Reformation. Like Augustine, Luther viewed war as a police function of the state. He strongly opposed the crusade, which he considered a papal device; to his mind, popes were worse than the Turks whom they wanted to fight. Zwingli and Calvin both espoused the just war in theory, but the Reformed churches, caught up in the wars of religion, lapsed back into the crusading spirit. Their theocratic outlook, drawn from the Old Testament, lured them inevitably in that direction. Zwingli himself died on the battlefield during the second Kappel war in 1531.

Americans, shaped as they have been by the Puritan ethos, have tended to construe each of their wars, from battles with Indians to Vietnam, as crusades. World War II, however, so frightful in its all-engulfing character, forced many to take a new look at the just war theory.

THE CRUSADES

The just war theory, often twisted and distorted in application, gave way to the crusade during the 11th century. Proposed first as a way of imposing peace upon bellicose Europeans, it was soon directed toward the Turks, against whom the usual conditions applied to the just war were not thought to apply. Fighting them was a sacred cause: *Deus vult.* "God wills it." "Let all hatred depart from among you, all quarrels end, all wars cease," Pope Urban II urged at the Council of Clermont in 1095. "Start upon the road to the Holy Sepulchre to wrest that land from the wicked race and subject it to yourselves." Soon thereafter the same words roused the faithful to search out and destroy the heretical Cathari of southern

France and northern Italy. Heresy had no more rights than Islamic infidelity.

Medieval Christians drew this rationale from the Old Testament. Though it may never have been actually applied until the Maccabean period, crusaders of the Middle Ages found sanction for it in early Israelite conquests and efforts at reform as well as in Maccabean literature: God has entered into a special covenant with his people. As long as they remain faithful, God fights on their side. If they fail, that is evidence of their violation of the covenant and not of God's unfaithfulness.

According to the Deuteronomist, the Lord commanded Israel to expel the Hittites, Girgashites, Amorites, Canaanites, Perizzites, Hivites, and Jebusites from the promised land. Thus "when the Lord your God gives them over to you, and you defeat them; then you must utterly destroy them; you shall make no covenant with them, and show no mercy to them" (Deuteronomy 7:2, RSV).

The idea of a crusade emerged frequently by extension or by lapse from the just war concept among the descendants of Zwingli and Calvin. In France, especially after the massacre on St. Bartholomew's day, the Huguenots discarded the condition that a war has to be authorized by the prince.

Subsequently other conditions fell by the wayside. In England the Puritans first contended that they fought merely against the king's evil counselors, but later they argued that rebellion against a king is justifiable if he is a tyrant. They, too, carried on a holy war. In New England those who came to find freedom from persecution fought the aborigines with no less crusading fervor than the Spanish conquistadors employed in South America. During the American Revolution, colonists invoked the rationale that Puritans had used against the monarchs in England: God willed it. So have Americans talked about the War of 1812, the Mexican War in 1846, the Civil War (on both sides), the Spanish-American War, and World War I. World War I heightened crusading fervor to fever pitch with added dashes of patriotism. The American church was virtually of one mind on the rightness of the national cause.

CROSS AND CROSSROADS

World War II, however, forced serious reconsideration of the grounds for war, for the new military technology upped the level of violence and destructiveness many times. The dropping of the first

atomic bomb near the war's end not only wiped out the populations of two cities, but it also exploded the most optimistic hopes for pursuit of a just war and generated renewed interest in the active pursuit of pacifism. The question which cries for an answer is: Can any war, since any can now result in a nuclear holocaust which would obliterate all human life, be just in its intent, in its disposition, in its auspices, or in its conduct?

There is some talk today of "limited nuclear war." Conventional wars, it is argued, go on all the time. Nations regularly agree by treaty to outlaw this or that weapon, for instance, poison gases or bacteria. Could they not also limit the use of nuclear weapons?

History says this is unlikely. Contrary to the optimism of some conductors of war, once nations initiate hostilities, they seldom hold weapons in reserve, for the applicability of treaties in time of war is at best questionable. One belligerent act is met by a still grosser one. Little by little, as World War II illustrates all too vividly, war demolishes all inhibition. Just war becomes crusade. In a nuclear age, crusades may result in total destruction.

History shows, therefore, we are left with but one option: pacifism, the return to taking seriously Jesus' call to peacemaking. There can be no winners, maybe no survivors, in a war which calculates destructive force in terms of megatons of TNT. Peacemaking is not a passive role. Such a commitment may involve adoption of a lifestyle which lessens the risks of war, prayer for peace, searching of the issues which affect peace, participation in peacemaking groups, support of political candidates who work for peace, and zealous efforts at peacemaking. All of these we must do with the confidence that "in everything God works for good with those who love him, who are called according to his purpose" (Romans 8:28).

A BIBLICAL CALL TO NUCLEAR NON-COOPERATION:

Why the Church Must Say No to Nuclear Weapons

by Helmut Gollwitzer

In 1526 Martin Luther published his famous pamphlet, *Can Soldiers Be in a State of Grace?* This title expresses a question which the church cannot evade. It is an inevitable consequence of the Christian message that people who are influenced by it come to the church, which preaches this message to them, and ask: "If this message is true of God's reconciliation with the world, of his self-sacrifice on the cross for humanity whom he loved and had lost, and if his commandment is true that we are to love our neighbor and even our enemy, can we still participate in the use of force in the many forms customary in human society, and without which this society cannot subsist, because there is so much sin and evil in the world? Can we still continue to be judges, policemen, government officials, government ministers, statesmen, and soldiers?"

The church should not evade the duty of answering these questions, and it always has answered them. That is why it seems to me all the more surprising and shameful that it has taken us theologians and churchmen until 1957, 12 whole years since the first atom bomb was dropped, to make any clear statement about this question which is crucial for every Christian and for everyone who hears the Christian message, the question of whether people who participate in atomic warfare can be in a state of grace.

During these 12 years the church has, of course, not simply remained silent. Every group in Christendom, including the Evanston Assembly of 1954, the pope, and many others, has sent appeals admonishing the governments which possessed atomic weapons to come to an agreement on the abolition of nuclear weapons and the control of atomic energy and to stop their dangerous atomic experiments immediately.

But the weak point in all these appeals was that they gave no answer to the question: "What will you Christians actually *do* if, in spite of every effort, another war breaks out and has to be fought out with the new weapons? Will you then, as most of you did in the wars of the past, once more collaborate and encourage others to collaborate, reminding them of their duty to obey the authorities and to fight for their country? Or will you do something quite different?"

Martin Buber replied as follows to the question of why, hitherto, all the appeals against the use of atomic weapons had remained ineffective: "They were *not committed;* they only said what *other* people—those in the governments and the general staff of the armies—ought to do. They never stated what the authors of these appeals would do *themselves,* nor to what they committed themselves. There was no sentence in these appeals beginning with the word 'I'—in the case of war I will do this, not that! And it is only when one commits *oneself* that others really listen." That is why the protest of the 18 German nuclear physicists in March, 1957, had such a strong effect. It contained the following sentence: "We, at any rate, will not cooperate."

The statements so far made by the churches have not involved any self-commitment; that is why they have petered out like all the others, completely ineffective.

How can one obey the Christian message about loving God and one's neighbor, when one has to use force or even kill other people to maintain order and justice? This is where the conflict of conscience arises. Hitherto all the great Christian confessions have given the same answer (for different theological reasons but with the same result in practice).

The classic formulation of this answer is found in the Declaration made by the Confessing Church of Germany at Barmen in 1934: "In the world which is not yet redeemed in which the church exists, the State has been entrusted by God with the task of maintaining justice and peace, as far as is humanly possible, by using (or threatening to use) force." It is therefore the duty of every Christian to assist the state in this task. Just as the police are essential for the maintenance of justice and peace at home, so the army is essential to maintain justice and peace outside. As long as the state uses the army to defend justice, the Christian acts rightly in helping the state as a policeman, soldier, or munitions worker, even if this

involves having to kill those who threaten the country with armed force. Therefore a soldier *can* be in a state of grace.

But we must point out that this does not justify the use of violence unconditionally, nor participation in any war whatsoever. It related solely to certain definite cases, when the state was forced to have recourse to war in order to defend itself against unjust aggression and maintain justice. And even in such cases it was enjoined that the war must be conducted in accordance with the rules of honorable chivalrous combat: the civilian population must be protected, the destruction reduced to the minimum, the purpose being not to annihilate the enemy but to force the enemy to make peace. War had to a certain extent become humanized in Europe, thanks to recognition of the Red Cross, the protection of prisoners of war, and the prohibition of the use of gas and of dumdum bullets and the bombardment of open towns (as laid down in the Hague Conventions of 1907).

It was during World War II that a cleavage became apparent between the past efforts to humanize war and its future deterioration into complete brutality. It was clearly the last war in which the states involved still to some extent kept their pledge to fight in a civilized manner, but it had already shown signs of developing into an unrestricted war of annihilation.

The new factor in the situation due to the discovery of CBR (chemical, bacterial, and radiological, i.e., nuclear) weapons is that the government and military commanders are no longer in a position to decide whether they will wage war in accordance with international law. The new weapons have taken control of the situation. With such weapons it is impossible to conduct a war for the defense of justice, as in former times. They are suitable only for a war which tramples all justice and humanity underfoot.

It was only little by little that this truth became apparent to Christians. Theological ethics regarded the basic problem as solved: whether in certain cases a soldier can still be in a state of grace. They therefore did not ask themselves whether the development of modern technical weapons and military methods did not completely transform the nature of war to such an extent that it was high time for the church to protest. So we slid blindly into the age of total war, clinging to formulas which may have been applicable in earlier times. That is why people often ask us today whether the CBR weapons are really essentially different from the atrocities commit-

ted during World War II, and whether the church, which hitherto has never radically opposed participation in war, should do so now.

There is only one answer: the church ought probably to have refused to participate in war much sooner; at any rate, this is its very last chance to do so, because the new weapons of mass destruction have brutalized warfare so completely that participation in it is completely incompatible with the will of God.

The weapons which Paul, Augustine, and Luther had in mind could still be adapted to use in a war fought in defense of justice. Once the decision had been taken to apply force in the cause of justice, then the use of a rifle and a culverin was as justifiable as the use of a sword or a catapult. Although all lethal weapons are terrible in themselves, it could not be affirmed that such weapons "misused God's gifts, blasphemed against God's goodness, and betrayed man and woman who are made in God's image" any more than did the sword spoken of by Paul, in the face of the still more terrible reality of evil in the world and the need for adamant resistance to it.

The official reports and articles in the technical military periodicals today, describing the diabolical inventions of perverted science and strategy, give one the impression that they are written by lunatics. It suffices to read a few of them; they make it superfluous to give any lengthy explanations as to whether modern methods of mass destruction are different in quality from the weapons of earlier times.

By their very nature, these weapons eliminate all distinction between combatants and non-combatants. It is true that earlier types of weapons (from the axe to the bomb) could also be used against non-combatants; but that was an illegimate way of using them; it was not determined by their very nature. The new instruments of warfare completely abolish all distinction between combatants and civilians; in fact, their very purpose is to decimate the population of the enemy country. By their very nature these weapons are blind.

The suppression of the distinction between combatants and civilians, which characterized the wars of the past, by the existence of new weapons which aim at destroying not only the enemy's troops but the entire population, changes also the character of deterrence, which is the purpose of armament in peacetime. Hitherto

the purpose of armaments was to deter the enemy from aggression by threatening armed resistance.

The present methods of intimidation, on the other hand, are really threats to take reprisals on hostages. Intimidation by nuclear weapons is a threat to proceed to a terrible retribution: if millions of innocent citizens, adults and children, are wiped out indiscriminately, the same fate will be inflicted on the population of the enemy; it may even be undertaken as a preventive measure. This clearly means the end of that partial humanization of war which existed in the past, just as there can no longer be any mutually respected Red Cross and no code of ethics for the soldier. When soldiers are trained to massacre thousands of civilians at once, they cannot be expected to respect the life of an individual noncombatant.

These weapons destroy all connection between war and justice, on which the analogy between war and police work was formerly based. This analogy made it quite clear that a war undertaken in defense of justice could not resort to "any methods whatsoever," any more than murderers can be menaced by "any methods whatsoever" in order to deter them from crime. If a person has kidnapped a child and threatens to murder it, the police cannot kidnap the kidnapper's own child and threaten to murder it. When Hitler announced, in January, 1939, that he intended to "liquidate" all the Jews in Europe if war were declared, the Western powers could not retaliate by threatening to kill an expatriated German for every Jew.

Certain methods and certain threats destroy the very justice which they are trying to safeguard. For threats are effective only if one is prepared to carry them out. Hence the limitations on the police, who cannot have recourse to "any methods whatsoever" as the criminal does. But they accept these limitations in the name of justice, which they exist to defend, and endeavor to be stronger than the criminal while confining themselves to legitimate methods, i.e., methods which respect the difference between guilty and innocent persons. The same applies to international relations; war can no longer be said to safeguard justice when the methods which it employs, or threatens to employ, are in themselves crimes.

The Christian ethic concerning war was, moreover, based on the assumption that the purpose of the war was to conclude a just peace with the enemy who, through the use of force, had been

obliged to abandon unjust intentions and to accept a new phase of peaceful coexistence, just as the police use force not in order to kill but in order to disarm the offender. And the modern theory of the just war recognized the enemy's right to live and to exist as a sovereign state. The rules of warfare and the weapons used were in accordance with this theory; so were the hostilities which were always preceded by warnings and by a solemn declaration of war, and in which battles alternated with periods of respite so that diplomacy was never completely paralyzed and there was always opportunity for contacts, negotiations, and for the official intervention of neutrals.

The new weapons, on the other hand, have only one purpose: to take by surprise and annihilate the enemy. And they insist on nothing less than unconditional surrender. They correspond to a mentality which refuses to recognize the enemy's right to live and which is blind to any relationship except that of friend-and-foe. It refuses to recognize any *human* relation to or any responsibility toward the enemy and regards it as treason even to think that the antagonism may be relative. It is the mentality of those who think they are the only persons fit to live and who therefore want to destroy everything outside their own "world." It is the mentality of the "total war of extermination" waged by Hitler and Stalin against their political opponents within their own countries.

This mentality is now expressed in foreign policy through the new weapons. One can even say more: not only do these weapons correspond to this mentality; they condition it and impose it. They can be used (in fact or in threat) only if we are prepared to stop at nothing, to inflict every kind of disaster on those who touch our property, to stop at no injustice in order to defend our own rights, to destroy the lives and health of millions of people in town and country, including women and children and even the lives of future generations, in order to maintain our Western freedoms and privileges (or, on the other side, in order to maintain socialism).

These new weapons turn us all into murderers in our mentality; for that is the only mentality which can produce and use such weapons. The older weapons left the choice of how they should be used, so that there was still some purpose in urging people to use them rightly; the new weapons, on the other hand, cannot be used except for indiscriminate mass murder. Anyone who uses them is forced into the mentality of a murderer.

A Christian church which recognizes its fellow persons as bar-

riers appointed by God against our own sinful tendency to pride and self-glorification and which realizes that it is the body of Christ extending over all frontiers, a Christian church which recognizes that in the enemy camp there are also those whom God loves and who are members of the body of Christ, might still consider it possible to participate in the former struggles between combatants, owning to its own existence within the secular orders. But if the church were to participate in an atomic war of annihilation it would destroy itself spiritually, even more than externally. It must therefore make it quite clear in advance that it will refuse to take part in such a war.

Unlike any of the weapons of warfare used in the past, even including the biological and chemical weapons, atomic weapons affect future generations and vegetation of the earth. They are particularly horrible because they cause disastrous mutations in the reproductive genes. They thus perpetuate the destruction that they cause for an indefinite period: peace is rendered impossible. They are, therefore, completely unsuitable as means of achieving peace. The total destruction which they cause and their unforeseeable consequences exclude all possibility of forgiveness between nations. In the case of mass destruction, they would affect the very nature of humanity, and the biological changes wrought would be signs of a far deeper change: the fact that humankind had already lost all sense of right and wrong.

In contrast to all past weapons, which did no harm to anyone in peacetime, the very fabrication of these new weapons takes a heavy toll of human lives, the number being still under dispute. For reasons of home policy, therefore, when carrying out atomic experiments the governments concerned select sites which will affect their own people as little as possible. The victims of the experiments are therefore the people of small, defenseless states. No moralist can possibly explain how all this is compatible with the Christian ethic concerning the duties of governmental authorities.

Once all the illusions about the CBR weapons have been destroyed, the tremendous difference will become apparent between these weapons and methods of warfare used in previous centuries; and it will be obvious that they exceed the limits within which the church has hitherto been able to regard military service as compatible with the will of God.

Christians must face the question of what they will do when

they have to make their ultimate decisions; they must say quite openly that in such a case they cannot participate, that if an atomic war should break out they would take up arms only for police purposes, i.e., to protect human life from violence and oppression in the resulting chaos. In this way they will not allow themselves to be led astray by political interests and arguments. They will hold firm to the conviction that a policy which does not break God's commandments is bound to be the better policy in the long run.

Fear of Bolshevism must not drive us to resort to methods which do us more harm (both spiritually and physically) than any dictatorship could. They are the methods of a desperate practical godlessness. No one who has heard of the reality of God through the Gospel can compromise with them. Survival at all costs is a wickedly pagan policy. A Christian church which refuses to participate in it, and which remembers its own mission of peace in the world, will inspire fresh confidence and be a healing influence in a sick world menaced with disaster.

Our analysis of the transformation of warfare brought about by the new weapons can lead us to only one conclusion: there must never be an atomic war, and there never *will* be an atomic war as far as it depends on us Christians, on Christian politicians, on you and me. "You and I will not have anything to do with these inventions of the devil." That is the Christian message which the pastor must pass on to the congregation: "We shall not participate, even in case of reprisals."

Christians cannot participate because the only condition under which it ever was permissible for them to think of taking up arms was in order to defend justice. But when the authorities urge a Christian to participate in these preparations for universal massacre, there is only one answer to be given: "*Si omnes, ego non.*" If all consent, I refuse.

WHO MUST TAKE RESPONSIBILITY?
Questions for Thought and Discussion

1. With Augustine's standards in mind, do you think nuclear war meets the requirements for a "just war"? What was your reaction on reading that, in a nuclear age, pacifism is the only response left to Christians?

2. Gollwitzer argues that, due to the injustice inherent in nuclear war, Christians should refuse to participate in it. What do you think of his contention that the witness of Christians against nuclear war and the arms race is completely ineffective as long as we express our objection but do nothing? What would noncooperation with nuclear war mean in our daily lives?

THE CENTRAL MURDER:
Jesus' Crucifixion and the Nuclear Holocaust
by Dale Aukerman

If it is our death that Christ died on the cross, there is in the cross the constraint of an infinite love.

James Denney

From the teaching of Jesus and from his crucifixion we learn that murder is the central negative motif in human history. There is murder at the beginning, at the middle, at the close: the righteous son is killed; God's righteous Son is executed; followers of the Son are slain. Jesus, crying out to the doctors of the Law and the Pharisees (Matthew 23), could summarize the history of Israel, negatively seen, as the ever-repeated rejection and killing of the men of God, from Abel in the first book of the Hebrew Scripture to Zechariah in the last (2 Chronicles). Jesus saw that the sequence was about to reach its culmination in what would be done to him. This summary was given still more vivid expression in the parable of the wicked husbandmen who mistreat or kill one representative after another sent by the owner of the vineyard and finally kill the owner's son (Mark 12:1–9 and parallels).

Jesus stressed that his followers should expect treatment comparable to that given him. Stephen confronted his antagonists with a similar survey of Israel's history, now including its culmination in Jesus' crucifixion. In Stephen's death by stoning, the murder sequence was continued. In the gospel apocalypses and Revelation, the close of history is depicted as a time filled with catastrophe and mass slaying, especially of the people of God.

In the two great commandments Jesus called his followers to love God and their fellow human beings. John later emphasized the inseparable unity of the two commandments, from the negative side: "If any one says, 'I love God,' and hates his brother, he is a liar; for he who does not love his brother whom he has seen, cannot love God whom he has not seen" (1 John 4:20). The dual drives to

be rid of God and the countering brother—the opposite of the dual loves to which we are called—coincided completely in the drama of the murder of Jesus. Malice toward the visible brother formed a continuum with rejection of the unseen God; the judicial murder of the brother was at the same time an attempt to do away with God. "As it is, you want to kill me when I tell you the truth as I have learned it from God" (John 8:40, JB). All their sin entered into the murder, which came as the supreme expression of the totality of their sinning. Behind the desire to murder any human being looms that most terrible possibility: "blasphemy against the Holy Spirit, in other words, the murder of God in us" (Max Thurian, *Marriage and Celibacy*).

Still as Christians we can at times discern in ourselves the dual drives to be rid of God and our enemy. The desire to be rid of God lies behind all my sinning; the desire to do away with an enemy is the identifiable extreme of what is wrong within me. This means that any manifestation of the drive to be rid of a fellow human being—the hostility-hatred-murder continuum—carries with it inseparably the drive to be rid of God and veers back across the centuries into that crucifixion of the Christ.

Paul wrote: "We are convinced that one has died for all; therefore all have died" (2 Corinthians 5:14). James Denney, pointing to the second half of the statement, explained: "This clause puts as plainly as it can be put the idea that His death was equivalent to the death of all. In other words, it was the death of all men which was died by Him" *(The Death of Christ)*.

Taken into his dying was the death of Abel and Stephen and Martin Luther King, Jr. Taken in also was the death of Cain and Caiaphas and Adolf Hitler. Comprehended in the death of that Victim was the death of every victim of the hostility-hatred-murder continuum. When one person kills another, he inflicts a death which entered into Jesus' dying. When anyone, in hatred or apathy, hands over another into dying, the result was present already in that betrayal long ago. Massacre of multitudes in war was component in the one death. The words of the Son of Man on the judgment throne apply also to evil inflicted: "As you did it to one of the least of these my brethren, you did it to me" (Matthew 25:40).

Pragmatic readiness to sacrifice other human beings pervades history. This was given most cogent expression in the words of Caiaphas to his fellow oligarchs: "it is better for one man to die for the

people, than for the whole nation to be destroyed (John 11:50, JB). The dire alternative was envisioned: "If we let him go on in this way everybody will believe in him, and the Romans will come and destroy the Holy Place and our nation" (John 11:48, JB). This necessity, so obvious to common sense, requiring in certain situations that some (and from an adversary group unlimited numbers) be given over to death for the survival and well-being of the many, would seem here to be supremely persuasive: the death of only one is required to save the whole nation from being destroyed. The danger pointed to was an actual possibility, not something imaginary or fabricated. The oligarchs were chiefly concerned not about the many but about their own position and power with its base in the many. But still, whether for the many or for the privileged few, what could be a more reasonable and natural recourse than the sacrifice of just one person?

Most of the subtleties and persuasiveness of all arguments throughout history (the theological ones also) for the sacrifice of some on behalf of the collectivity are compacted in that formulation by Caiaphas. Such arguments reckon that the numbers of victims (from within the collectivity) will be acceptably limited when viewed in comparison with the supremely important good at stake. Nuclear gamesmen too proceed in a most outrageous stretching of Caiaphas' point.

The pragmatic readiness to sacrifice human life, which found superlative expression through Caiaphas, took as focal Victim Jesus of Nazareth. But there was something that outweighed that readiness, even the totality of it within all of history: the willingness of Jesus to become Victim of that pragmatism and thus "*identify Himself* with the countless victims of wars, with all those who have been deliberately sacrificed to the Political Necessities and Social Duty, to [with] the millions of human beings who have been slaughtered and constrained to slaughter each other by being more or less persuaded that their deaths would be serving Justice and Law. By His readiness to become the victim of such a belief, Jesus unmasked its monstrous falsity, and showed His disciples in advance that they could never adopt it themselves" (Jean Lasserre, *War and the Gospel*).

On a ruined wall in Hiroshima is dimly etched the figure of a human being who was standing next to it when the flash came. The body, though instantaneously vaporized, stopped enough of the

awful light to leave that abiding epitaph. When German theologian Heinrich Vogel gazed at the dim silhouette, the thought gripped him: Jesus Christ was there in the inferno with that person; what was done to him was done to Christ; the horror he had no time to experience, Jesus felt. The Light of the world stood uncomprehended, comprehending, and undone by the hideous splendor of man's stolen fire.

We can envision the Risen Jesus there in the foot of that cross of cloud, the Victor as Victim. But the death of the person next to the wall, the death of those Japanese multitudes, weighed upon Jesus already at Skull Hill. What the Crucified One took to himself at the Midpoint of history, the Risen One, drawing near, takes to himself hour after hour, disease by disease, enmity by enmity, war by war in the sequence of history.

We can recite numbers or call up mental images of Auschwitz or Dresden, the Black Death or the slave trade, Julius Caesar's massacres or Tamerlane's, Stalin's or the Pentagon's in Indochina. But the awesome magnitude of such horrors remains a mystery impenetrable unless we approach it through the Man of Gethsemane and Golgotha. I can meditate on the vaporization of a few in Hiroshima and Nagasaki; but my mind cannot visualize the snuffing out of 250,000 human beings. There is, though, the slain One, whose mind, heart, body in A.D. 30 and A.D. 1945 took all that in. Because the fullness of God dwelt in him, he could take to himself and know the full magnitude of human hate, killing, and death. We can know more of Jesus' agony when we begin to see that the slaughters, the hate and guilt of multitudes throughout all history converged on him. And reciprocally, by contemplating his agony, we can better grasp the magnitude of what has been inflicted on others.

What is currently being prepared for and what would be fought, would come as war against all human beings, not just against those in "enemy" countries. Everyone would be to some extent a casualty of such a war, and quite possibly everyone would die, over a period of time, as its victim. In Hebrew thought a single murder cast an imperiling shadow over the entire faith community; the gravity of the disorder it constituted touched upon all within that corporateness. In that perspective, how ominous and vast is the shadow over the U.S., resulting from innumerable murders, from media violence, from past military slaughters. But that shadow in its greater breadth looms over all humanity in its corporateness—

165

looms, as a dreadful dynamism, which has taken embodiment in the nuclear arsenals. It is as the central Person of all humanity that Jesus Christ is presently threatened by this guilt and doom.

God, in order that we might meet Him, made Himself small in Jesus. But Jesus also, in his smallness as one human being, represented the totality of humankind. He was formed that our vision might rest not only on this focal expression of the invisible God but also on this singular image of the neighbors we have been too nearsighted to see and of the myriads of human beings we have had no sight to see. This latter dimension is indicated by Jesus' words in the judgment scene pictured in Matthew 25:31–46. Though we cannot envision all who should be within our view, we are to see him who is focus and head of that vast throng.

That 300,000,000 persons or a billion or four billion might be killed in a nuclear world war is beyond the imagination of any mortal. My nearest approach to the magnitude of that horror comes when I realize that Jesus would be the central Victim in the midst of the annihilation. Each victim he would know; each passion, each death he would feel. He in whom God has drawn near would be there with the least of all who are his in a thousand infernos. The slain Brother would be there with every brother and sister, with every terrified child, as the slower ghastliness of radiation sickness spreads across the continents. A darkness more enduring than that on long ago Passover would cross the world. From innumerable parched lips would come some echo of the cry, "My God, my God, why hast thou forsaken me?" (Matthew 27:46); for that elimination of intolerable neighbors would bring with it an apparent doing away with God. But the One who gave utterance to that cry, the Neighbor-Brother-God, who was done away with, would be there in the midst.

This means that all the nuclear weapons delivery systems of this world point toward a target that comprehends all human targets: Jesus. The cold warriors of West and East, with no eyes to glimpse the "enemy" multitudes, see the One least of all. But Christians must understand that no nuclear weapon is aimed which does not point toward him: "As you did it to one of the least of these my brethren, you did it to me."

It is not given us to know whether a nuclear world war, if this comes, will constitute the engulfing terminal murder of all human beings. We can know that it would come as the greatest crucifixion

of humankind and as such the worst recrucifixion of Christ. Therefore the awesome magnitude of the guilt in nuclear terrorism (even apart from holocaust) is second only to that of the guilt in the Crucifixion of Jesus.

BEING WITH THE LAMB:

A Sermon

by Richard Mouw

> [*The kings*] *will make war on the Lamb, and the Lamb will conquer them, for he is Lord of Lords and King of Kings, and those with him are called and chosen and faithful.* (Revelation 17:14)

The book of Revelation is a series of visions; visions which portray the forces of righteousness and unrighteousness clashing in history. It is not necessarily a blow-by-blow description of that sequence of events, but it does depict in various ways the kinds of struggles that take place in history. I find it helpful to read the book as a symphony which has many subthemes and excursions and detours, but which comes back repeatedly to a very basic theme: The victory of history belongs to Jesus Christ, no matter what forces attempt to confront his power.

The book of Revelation depicts history as a scenario in which superhuman powers are at work. This emphasis is, I think, a necessary corrective to the individualistic thinking we Christians often engage in as we reflect on the historical process.

It is nothing new to say that there are powers at work in history which are more than human powers. We see that already in the Garden as our first parents were encountered by the serpent. We learn throughout the Scriptures that the evil in the world is more than the sum total of human choices, even human evil choices; there are superhuman forces which present themselves to us in mindsets and attitudes. Rebellion is in the air. A perversity that is not so much our own invention as it is a presence which lures and diverts us both as individuals and as nations draws us in the direction of evil.

Paul said, "We wrestle not against flesh and blood but against principalities and powers." The theme is picked up in the hymn:

Christian dost thou see them
on the holy ground
how the powers of darkness
compass thee around?
Christian dost thou feel them
how they work within
striving, tempting, luring
goading into sin?

This seductive power of evil was present in the creation from the beginning and preys upon human beings in the political, economic, and military arenas. What the book of Revelation highlights is that these powers of darkness can lure, goad, and tempt nations; they can tempt the human bearers of political and military power. A very real possibility is that in our history the kings of the earth will give their honor, power, and authority over to the beast who embodies the spirit of Antichrist.

That rebellion is the context of the Revelation text, for the political and military power described there as belonging to the kings is given over to the beast for satanic purposes. The message is clear: The actual flesh-and-blood governments which we encounter in history can become on occasion the very forces of Satan.

This teaching would not have surprised Christians in biblical times. They were well aware of Jezebel and Ahab, of Herod and Nero. John himself was a political prisoner on the isle of Patmos, condemned to be there by powers and authorities who were bent on silencing the gospel. Nor should it surprise us, in the light of more recent history, for we too know the likes of Hitler and Stalin and Idi Amin. And even in the course of our own nation's recent history, we know that governments can become captivated by the desire for deception, secrecy, and perversion.

Of course, governments are not always so easily categorized. Very often they are themselves pulled in different directions, are subject to a variety of forces, and on occasion are even allured successfully by the forces of righteousness. But, nonetheless, even though it may be difficult to categorize a given government or policy in the absolute terms common in apocalyptic writings, we must learn from these scriptures that a spiritual battle is taking place in history, a battle from which the political, military, and economic authorities of our day are not immune.

We must learn how to discern these tendencies of government when we see them moving in the direction of idolatry and arrogance; when we see them becoming wantonly destructive and hardening hearts against the cries of the poor, the oppressed, and the disenfranchised. We must be wary of governments who boast of being number one; who insist that they are "the greatest nation on the face of the earth"; who boast that they will not back down before any force or power; who take pride in their military might; who are dedicated to the domination of other nations.

Let me be even more specific. I think that we as Christians should be very concerned about the United States' role in the arms race. We now have the nuclear capacity to destroy the entire population of the world 12 times over, and during the past week we once again manufactured the materials for about 20 more nuclear bombs, each hundreds of times more destructive than those dropped on Hiroshima and Nagasaki.

At the very least, on a purely common sense level, in the light of the recent empirical facts of history, we should be suspicious of this concentration of destructive power in the hands of any human beings, at the disposal of any government—especially governments which, as we know, are capable of bungling stupidity. And, as Christians, we must be sensitive to an even more desperate possibility: that the flesh-and-blood governments of this world, including the government of the United States of America, can give their power and authority over to the beast.

The Revelation text also describes the outcome of the struggle that takes place when those kings who give their authority and power over to the beast engage in a war against the Lamb. It does so in marvelously simple and concise terms. It says, "and the Lamb will conquer them." Here, indeed, is a summation of the whole gospel: Jesus is the victor. Throughout his earthly ministry, Jesus confronted the powers of evil which are at work in the creation; powers which cause disease, poverty, injustice, insanity, and death. And on the cross he confronted these powers decisively.

At the cross, the powers of organized religion, big business, government, and the forces of racial discrimination, male domination, and economic exploitation united in their attempt to destroy the Lamb of God, to erase him from the historical record once and for all. They dismissed Jesus as a misfit, a joke, a misguided zealot. But on the third day, after having made himself completely vulner-

able to all the abuse and ammunition that they could throw at him, he came forth from the tomb, breaking the seal of Pilate in that first great act of Christian civil disobedience, an event which Paul describes in Colossians 2 this way: "He disarmed the principalities and powers and made a public example of them, triumphing over them."

The Lamb has already conquered the kings of the earth, and some day that victory will be publicly manifested. Jesus is the victor; it is as simple as that, and it is our only hope.

That fact requires a response. Those who are with the Lamb are called and chosen and faithful. Christians are called to make a very basic choice to identify consciously, unambiguously, and publicly with the cause of Jesus Christ.

Those of us who are Calvinists have a very nice way of putting this commitment: "My only comfort in life and in death is that I am not my own, but belong to a faithful savior, Jesus Christ." But we haven't often thought very deeply about what it means to spell out that covenantal confession in economic, political, and even military terms. I suggest that we have much thinking to do about the meaning of our confession, whether we are Christian Reformed or Methodist or Catholic or Presbyterian or Mennonite.

A teacher of mine who was a Christian pacifist was once confronted by a few of us from his class as we argued with him about his views. Finally, one of my fellow students cried out in utter frustration, "But if we did what you suggest the Russians would destroy us!" I will never forget his response, which deeply troubled me at the time and continues to stick with me. He said, "That is not the worst thing that could happen to me." One of us asked, "Well, what is?" He replied, "The worst thing that could happen to me would be for the Russians to separate me from the love of God which is in Jesus Christ. But I know that they can't do that."

Even though I don't think I ever quite became the pacifist that he would have wanted me to be, I learned a profound lesson. As we form our political, economic, and military attitudes we have to always ask ourselves as Christians, as biblically informed followers of the Lamb: What is the worst thing that could happen to us? And then we must act in the light of our answer. And of course, the worst thing that could happen to us is that we fail to be with the Lamb, that we fail to be called and chosen and faithful.

This is the question that we must face today. What does it

mean to be faithful to the Lamb in the midst of the arms race? How can we be with the Lamb today as the nations are building weapons of mass destruction?

If we are to be with the Lamb, it seems to me that we must be absolutely certain of and secure in our identify as the people of the Lamb.

Belonging to Jesus Christ means that we must bring all other relationships and commitments into subjection to his lordship. We can't submit our sex lives to the lordship of Christ, while allowing Exxon to decide our energy practices. We can't let Jesus decide what we will do with our nickels and dimes, while leaving it up to Wall Street to decide what we will do with our dollars. We can't let Jesus decide our family policy, but the State Department our foreign policy. Abraham Kuyper put it well: There is not one square inch of the whole creation that does not belong to Jesus Christ.

We can pray for peace. We must pray, if for no other reason, simply because we are commanded to do so in God's Word. But there is more to it than that: Prayer is political action. It is, among other things, petitioning the king of the universe, and thereby proclaiming our true citizenship as members of a holy nation, the church, over which Jesus reigns as Lord.

We must witness fearlessly and publicly on behalf of peace. It is time for all Christians, whatever our confessional traditions, to say that under no proper understanding of the use of violence, from the Christian perspective, is it ever justifiable to employ nuclear weapons. We must say that boldly and loudly and publicly and prophetically: "No more bombs! For God's sake stop the madness! No more bombs!"

We are called to be peacemakers. We must explain to the nation in which God has placed us that we don't want to be protected or defended by nuclear weapons, that we refuse to give our loyalty to a nation which defines its worth in terms of its ability to destroy.

And finally, in all of this we must be "realistic." Now that sounds like I am going to take everything back and qualify my strong remarks in a manner that will render them impotent. But to be realistic is to act in accordance with our view of what reality is.

A realistic expression from a Christian point of view is this: "Christ is risen." Another realistic statement is: "Blessed are the peacemakers for they shall be called the daughters and sons of

God." Another: "'Tis not with swords loud clashing nor roll of stirring drums, but deeds of love and mercy the heavenly kingdom comes." And another: "They will make war on the Lamb, and the Lamb will conquer them, and those who are with him are called and chosen and faithful." I pray to God that we will all be "realistic" in the midst of the arms race.

CHRIST AS VICTIM AND VICTOR:
Questions for Thought and Discussion

1. Aukerman states that what overcomes all of humanity's "pragmatic readiness to sacrifice human life" is Jesus' willingness to become its victim. What is the significance for our lives and actions today of Jesus' willingness to suffer?

2. Mouw talks of separation from the love of Jesus as the worst possibility for the Christian. What do you think is the worst thing that could happen to you? Do you believe that Jesus would be with you even if that were to happen? What is the difference between Christian realism and the "realism" of the world?

MY PEOPLE, I AM YOUR SECURITY:
A Nuclear Prophecy

In the summer of 1978, David H. Janzen, a member of the New Creation Fellowship in Newton, Kansas, fasted and prayed about a Christian witness against the arms race. He was given what he felt to be a prophecy from the Lord, and shared it with his fellowship, who confirmed it. It was then shared with a group meeting at the Mennonite World Conference held in Wichita, Kansas, in July of that year; that group felt led to share it with the whole general assembly. Following is the prophecy.

My people, proclaim to your government and your neighbors that you do not need armaments for your security.
I am your security. I will give the peacemakers glory as I defended and glorified my own defenseless son, Jesus.

My kingdom is international.
I am pleased that my children gather all around the globe to give allegiance to one kingdom. My kingdom is coming in power.
No powers, not even the powers of nuclear warfare can destroy my kingdom.
My kingdom is from beyond this earth.
The world thought it had killed Jesus, Jesus through whom I have overcome the world. Therefore, be not afraid.

You are a gathering of my kingdom;
My kingdom will last forever.
Taste the first fruits now;
Embrace the international fellowship in Christ and praise me together.

Do not fear the nuclear holocaust.

Do not panic or take unloving short cuts to fight the armaments monster.
I go before you to do battle.

This is a spiritual battle, the battle to destroy war.
Do not attempt to fight this battle on your own.
Fear, guilt, and anger will make you spiritual prisoners of the
enemy if you fight on your own authority.
Learn to hear my voice. Learn to be at unity with those who
love me.
I will lead and protect my army.
I will coordinate the battle in many nations.

I want to show you where the idols of this age are hidden.
Learn where are the missile silos, the bomb factories, the cen-
ters of military command, the prisons for dissenters.
Understand that those who bow down to fear trust in these
idols for salvation.
Stand beside their idols and proclaim my liberating kingdom.
Invite them to share your life in me. Perfect love must be
your weapon, for perfect love casts out fear.

If you obey my call, you will be persecuted, misunderstood, powerless.
You will share in my suffering for the world,
but I will never abandon you. You belong to my international,
eternal kingdom.

Do not say time is running out. Do not threaten or despair.
I am the Lord of time. There is no time to seek the world's
approval,
but there is time to do what I will lay before you.

By my mercy I have extended time.
I extended time for a perverse human race when I called
Noah.
I lengthened the time of repentance by sending my prophets.
I have averted nuclear disaster many times for you.
Jesus offers you all time, time to repent and come to me.

Obey my call and there will be time to do what I am laying
before you.
Now is the time.

I want you to learn who around the world has refused to bow down
to the god of fear or worship weapons of terror.
Hold hands around the world with my soldiers, my prisoners.
Pray for each other and share my strength with them.
I love those who put their trust in me and will put joy in their
hearts.

There is time to build my kingdom.
There is time to protest armaments and to build a spiritual
community for those who turn from the idols of fear.
Call them to join you in the security that flows from Father,
Son, and Spirit,
my community, given for you.

My seed is planted in every one of my children;
It is waiting to break the husks of fear that it may grow
toward my son's light.
I did not plant my spirit in Russians or Americans, Arabs or
Israelis, capitalists or communists that they might destroy
each other,
but that they might recognize my image in each other and
come together in praise of their creator's name.

My beloved children,
Share the burden of my heart,
know my love so that you may learn to die for one another.
There is time to do this.
Trust me and I will sustain you within my kingdom forever.

RESTING ON GOLGOTHA'S CROSS:
Security in a Nuclear World
by Gordon Cosby

The only ultimate question is, where do we finally place our security? At the place of our deepest inner being, where do we let down our full weight?

Biblical faith guides me to the answer. It says that the gospel is the power of God. God's supreme act of love was the sending of his son, Jesus Christ, who was among us in weakness.

Many do not see the ultimate revelation of God in Christ. I do. Being surrendered to him has fundamentally changed me. My old self, which was in opposition to God, is dead, and I am in union with his son. In this reality I'm safe. Jesus said, "Fear not those who kill the body and after that have nothing that they can do." Nothing can fundamentally harm me.

I'm now in a new realm of grace. I trust myself forever to that stupendous love which has acted for me in the weakness and folly of Golgotha's cross. My ultimate security is in that folly.

All of this, in a very insecure world, is for me the bottom line, as it is for all Christians. Any other course is to be at war with God and his way of righting wrong. No other way has any reality. Any other way produces insecurity.

Any form of compartmentalization, any area in which we do not trust God, is doubting him and questioning his integrity. This trust in the Father's care must exist both in the personal and the public domain, for my personal life is never separate from my life in society; my faith affects how I want society to be organized.

The assumption is often made that God cannot look after me unless society is organized in its present form, with its special advantages for my nation, my business group, my income group. So we Christians hold on with a death grip to the present way of ordering society.

Of course, every church structure and every political structure

is provisional. We should always be moving toward a more equitable and just structure which will spread the benefits to everybody. To be unwilling to entertain radical changes in political structures is to say that we really trust the structures that ensure us privilege rather than believing that God will provide our needs.

There is a particular idolatry which makes a mockery of the so-called faith of millions of Christians: our dependence on military expenditures for "national defense." This state of affairs is a negation of biblical faith.

Abraham, our father, was just a wandering Aramean. God protected him and kept his promise to him. Moses, our liberator, went stuttering into the presence of Pharaoh with a rod in his hand. It was God who acted, who brought his people safely across on dry land.

The new Moses, the new liberator, defeated the powers of darkness. He defeated the principalities and powers. He did it not by might. He did it by a lonely death on a cross.

Is God now working in an entirely different way? It would seem that the world thinks so. And, of all the nations, the United States most thinks so. From 1960 to 1975, the U.S. spent $1,090 billion on military expenditures.

We do not trust God. We trust our technology and skill to kill more devastatingly and completely than our brother and sister nations.

Let us not be too quick to scapegoat the military. The people who serve the military are not more evil than people who form other combinations of power in our society. If we are to assess culpability, a passive, silent church bears by far the heavier responsibility. I, who understand something of the realities of power because God has grasped me, and you, who have been redeemed by Christ, should have taught the world better. The judgment of faithlessness is first of all upon us, the people of God.

One thing history confirms: The nation who trusts in anything other than God is abandoned by God. Every attempt at security fails because God abandons that people. We feel that the danger of extinction is being held back by 9,500 missiles. They are not holding anything back. God in his mercy is holding it back. The missiles are the vials of his wrath waiting to be overturned. We would be safer without them.

To take the major share of the world's resources from the

179

daily needs of people and use them to make credible our threat to commit mass murder is wrong. Such an action lets others live in abject squalor so that we may *possibly* survive a nuclear nightmare. If that is not wrong, then there is nothing wrong.

The God of biblical revelation is against this. Jesus Christ, now the sovereign Lord of all human history, is against this. The accumulation of nuclear arms is contrary to what it means to trust God and to believe that he will act in our behalf as he acted again and again in Israel's history.

Do we trust Israel's God or not? I say we are mocking Israel's God. We are mocking Jesus who died for us, and there is no alternative except for him to abandon us to our fate, unless we repent. Under the circumstances he cannot provide the supernatural protection that could bring us safely through.

But our good news is that repentance is a gift of God's grace that is available to us. That gift produces a profound inward change that then expresses itself in action.

For many of us, the cost of repentance will be high. Our jobs will in some way be affected, jeopardizing our financial security. We must bring our fears to consciousness and pray for the gift of boldness and freedom to follow Christ, the moving center of our lives.

Still others of us are already overextended. We question how it is possible to give energy to yet another cause. We must fundamentally rearrange our priorities. The issue of national security is not just one among many: It is the overriding idolatry of our age.

My final word is one of hope. One thing we know: God is ceaselessly active in our world. He loves our planet, its environment, and all of his children on it. He loves his church, the body of his dear son. We are his church. It is my faith that God is even now giving us the gift of repentance, and that the world's present desperate crisis will be the occasion of the church's finest hour.

ASTONISHING HOPE:
Good News in a Time of Despair
by James Forest

Jesus stood before the congregation in Nazareth, Luke tells us, and read the text from Isaiah which begins, "The spirit of the Lord is upon me, because he has anointed me to preach good news to the poor."

Those present knew a great deal about bad news and about poverty. The news to which they were accustomed was news of hunger, of the abusive activities of occupation soldiers and the immense problems of being tenant farmers subject to absentee landlords and their local agents; news of the growing burden of taxes which paid the cost of their own subjection, of fresh acts of collaboration by religious and political leaders with the Romans, of beatings and executions. Jesus' hearers were people systematically humiliated. Many must have painfully felt the silence and even absence of God, and sensed the abandonment of creation, the abandonment of God's own faithful people, to the power of death.

The context in which the good news was announced was a situation of despair. Jews could readily experience their lives as being in the end time. Jesus, in his teaching, did not challenge that sensibility but rather taught how to live in an end time, how to become faithful in an end time.

We also live in an end time. The utopian expectations celebrated at this century's beginning seem to us far more distant and unimaginable than pharaohs and sphinxes. The century has become a habitat of nightmares, a time of despair.

Some of the words and phrases that reveal the reasons for the widespread sense of dread include:

World War I, World War II, Verdun, the Holocaust, Pearl Harbor, the Siege of Leningrad, Hitler, Stalin, Auschwitz, Babi Yar, Dresden, Hiroshima, Nagasaki, and the Berlin Wall; tiger cages, My Lai, the Christmas Bombing, and the Plain of Jars; the

SS-20, the cruise missile, the MX, the Minuteman II, the neutron bomb, and the Trident submarine; thalidomide, cancer, and plutonium.

To pronounce such words is to pronounce a litany of unbearable sorrows. The words fall on consciousness the way industrial acid rains fall on the limestone surfaces of old cathedrals, eating away those surfaces that celebrated human hope. The words strip us of those optimisms that have falsely been called "hope": humanistic visions of reason overcoming ignorance, distances, hunger, war, squalor, all our inventions and traditions of institutionalized suffering.

How does the acid rain of bad news affect us? Let me share three brief stories:

• An American Roman Catholic bishop told me of an encounter with a group of students 15 and 16 years old. He asked how many were hoping to be parents one day. Only a few raised their hands. In the conversation that followed, several of the students explained rather dispassionately that nuclear war seemed inevitable before the end of the century. It seemed unfair to bring children into a world in which there was so little hope that they could grow up.

• I met a woman who had been a counselor at a New York City abortion center; she has since become a pacifist and is part of a project encouraging women to continue with pregnancies despite economic or other difficulties. Among various reasons she encountered for abortion from those she counseled was their expectation of nuclear war.

• Earlier this year a visitor to my office described a demonstration against nuclear weapons in the United States, during which an account of the horrors suffered by the people of Hiroshima when the atomic bomb exploded was read aloud. Our visitor noticed a young father fall on his knees, holding a small child in his arms. The father wept. Afterward, when our guest went over to talk with him, the man explained, "I was weeping over the dead body of my own child. I was weeping because I live in a world in which the leaders are preparing to burn our children."

Religious people, even religious peacemakers, often keep silent about such signs of the time. Perhaps we fear to speak of despair because we see a danger that our words will make our lack of hope only more contagious. Perhaps we are silent because we too

are so vulnerable; we feel trapped and powerless, and we think God is as powerless as we are.

Significant exceptions to the silence are persons who see peacemaking as a process of healing in which response to fear is crucial. One of these is Henri Nouwen, who wrote in *Clowning in Rome* about the situation in which we are living:

[It is a world] clouded with an all-pervading fear, a growing sense of despair, and the paralyzing awareness that humanity has come to the verge of suicide. We no longer have to ask ourselves if we are approaching a state of emergency. We are in the midst of it here and now.

You do not have to be a great prophet to say that coming decades will likely see not only more wars, more hunger, and more oppression, but also desperate attempts to escape them all. We have to be prepared for a period in which suicide will be as widespread as drugs are now, in which new types of flagellants will roam the country frightening the people with the announcement of the end of all things, and in which new exotic cults with intricate rituals will try to ward off a final catastrophe. We have to be prepared for an outburst of new religious movements using Christ's name for the most un-Christian practices. In short, we have to be prepared to live in a world in which fear, suspicion, mutual hatred, physical and mental torture, and an increasing confusion will darken the hearts of millions of people.

Fear can have a genuine and even creative function. There are realities which appropriately awaken fear. And fear, like an alarm clock, awakens us; it arouses conscience and response, revives and reshapes our vocations.

But alarms clocks are useful for only a few moments; they are not meant to ring throughout the day. When fear becomes a constant howling, instead of awakening us, it paralyzes and deadens us. Imagination and conscience, rather than being stirred to life, are stunted. The expectation of unparalleled catastrophe can take root in us in such a way that what we dread becomes more certain in our psychological and spiritual surrender to fear.

It is fear which initiates our dependence on weapons and pro-

vokes us to develop systems of manipulation and greed, creating occasions for war. It is fear that constantly animates the arms race and fuels lusts for power. Beneath layers of economics and ideology lies the bedrock of fear.

It is the fear that events have gone too far, that it is now "too late," that so often imprisons a response. We too may be among the prisoners Jesus spoke of that day in Nazareth. To the extent that fear is at the center of our lives, we too are blinded and chained.

Fear, always infectious, becomes more so in our present context. There is not a soul alive who is not imprisoned by war and the massive preparations for war. The world itself has become the target of war. Everyone lives upon the target.

The shadow of the possibility of a final, human-authored holocaust erodes even the normal and ancient joys. The face of a child, the petals of a flower, the most breathtaking works of art— everywhere there is the gray shadow. Everything, everyone is condemned to burn. Daniel Berrigan, in a poem, comments, "They have taken away our joy."

It was Leon Bloy who observed, "Joy is the most infallible sign of the presence of God."

The good news Jesus announced in Nazareth is the news that gives us back our joy, our hope, our ability to discern the presence of God. It gives us the courage to see, to liberate, to share our lives, to share the land and its fruit with the generosity of God.

The good news is an experience of healing. As fear retreats to a more useful location, away from the center of our lives, hope and courage take its place. This is the normal activity of grace. It is a healing event which, though rooted in ourselves, has its branches in the community.

It is not unimportant that Jesus so often taught in parables. Through the parables one could more easily see the ordinary miracle of God's involvement in our lives.

In trying to talk about a spiritual transformation in ourselves which could lead us toward an authentic hope, I cannot help but think of parables—experiences of the activity of God in my life and the life of friends.

One parable concerns Mel Hollander, who in the late 1960s was in Vietnam as an American civilian social worker. Doctors discovered that Mel was suffering from a cancer of the lymph system

and estimated that he had, at most, six months to live. Mel, a promising writer in his early 20s, had already been dispirited by the climate of death in Vietnam and was deeply depressed by its sudden invasion of his own body.

He went to New York in hopes of a medical cure. His doctors found no hope.

He heard of a course at Union Theological Seminary for those who would be working with the dying. Mel went to the seminary to register for it. While there, he heard that another course—this one on the seemingly more esoteric subject of John's Book of Revelation—was being offered by Daniel Berrigan. As self-pitying as Mel was at the time, there was still in him some of the curiosity that had led him to Vietnam.

Mel arrived at the appointed classroom for the Berrigan lecture. Other students arrived. Dan Berrigan arrived. The hour for the class to start arrived. And it passed. The room was silent and still. Mel didn't realize that it was Dan's custom to begin his classes with a brief period of meditative silence. The silence made Mel terribly nervous. When Dan's eyes settled on him—Mel was by now a very pale, rather woeful looking figure in the late stages of his cancer—Mel became still more nervous. He thought perhaps the class was silent because they were waiting for this uninvited guest to leave. But Mel held his seat—when you are going to die, it can be rather freeing; you needn't be so polite.

At last the silence was broken. Dan Berrigan spoke directly to Mel with the simplest of questions: "What's the matter?"

Mel briefly considered various responses, including "It's none of your business." But the responses seemed both useless and truthless. So he said to the rather rude Jesuit, "I'm dying. I'm dying of cancer."

There wasn't a pause in Berrigan's response. Nor was there a sudden convulsion of sorrow or pity in his face.

"That must be very exciting."

Confrontation with death, with the awful power of death made present in a young life, normally brings shock and horror. The pious promise their prayer. Others swallow in silence. Most flee. Few can imagine thinking, much less announcing, "That must be very exciting."

For Mel this brief, impossible sentence fell into his life like a

stroke of lightning, an instant of zen enlightenment, a transfiguration: "Yes! How true! It is the most extraordinary event of my life! I have never before faced death."

As it happened, Mel was not, in fact, so quick about getting to the cemetery. The cancer evaporated from his body nearly as fast as water boils out of a teakettle.

Mel continued with the Berrigan class and began others. He became a Quaker and worked full time in the anti-war movement after leaving the seminary. When the Vietnam War ended in 1975, he was one of the first to respond to its refugees, and one of the rare ones to reckon with the problem of postwar repression in Vietnam. Mel not only outlived the first death sentence but, until his death last year in a fire, lived quite extraordinarily on behalf of other survivors.

I described this event as a parable. I see in Dan Berrigan's response the role of the ministering church in the world and the role of the peacemaker. I see in Mel with his terminal cancer and his hopelessness a vivid image of all of us in this world who have been consigned to a future nuclear holocaust, and those many dying already of its consequences in the disruption of attention to human life and its requirements.

Mel is ourselves with all our secret fears, the unconfessed dreads that imprison our lives and which cripple our response to suffering. Mel is us feeling sorry for ourselves that we belong to what might be the last human generation, the generation which harvests the work of so many generations of weapons designers. Mel is our self-pity.

The response of a faithful church, a faithful community, is to find a way of saying the good news and releasing us from captivity; a way of saying, "Isn't it exciting?"

Such a sentence is soaked with the resurrection—a profound confidence in the power of God and God's unshakeable commitment to us, both in our suffering and on both sides of death. The statement of good news is soaked with heaven, that same wisdom which once led Theresa of Avila to say, "All the way to heaven is heaven, because Jesus said, 'I am the way.'" It is a declaration that vividly communicates a sense of the presence of God, that hurls the mind into a wakefulness to that presence.

Perhaps we Christian peacemakers are too silent about these realities, too slow to express our complete dependence on the grace

of God, the power of the resurrection. Do we fear—among our other fears—to seem too foolish, too pious, perhaps a little traditional, even old-fashioned? Such fears can be as awesome as those generated by the presence of nuclear weapons. Nearly 2,000 years have passed since Jesus spoke of good news to the people in Nazareth, and much longer since Isaiah spoke of the Spirit's anointing. Our end time is so much more rational and scientific. Talk of prayer and God and such things can seem an awful embarrassment, a public confession of irrelevancy.

But I wonder where else we can hope to find a way of overcoming those legion fears that have so long been leading humanity toward the situation of the last generation? How else to find the resources of hope when there is no longer a basis for optimism?

The "acceptable year" of which Jesus spoke that day in Nazareth was the Jubilee Year—the year in which rest and justice and forgiveness were at the very center of life for an entire people. As Jesus gave expression to this text from Isaiah in his own life, he was taking an ancient hope and giving it a new definition. Instead of Jubilee Year, a period of forgiveness and restoration of community every 49 years, he announced a way of life that was centered on forgiveness and reconciliation, with an end to fear and violence. This marked an end to blindness as well—the blindness through which we dehumanize others and perceive others as enemies, a prerequisite for war.

The proclamation of Jubilee, in that occupied country rapidly moving toward a disastrous war of liberation, is analogous to the exclamation, "That must be very exciting." In a situation of bad news, Jesus speaks of good news. In a situation of oppression, liberation. Of blindness, sight. Of captivity, freedom. He not only recites an ancient text, he says, "Today this scripture has been fulfilled in your hearing." The excitement that followed is not surprising; neither is the fact that Jesus narrowly escaped being murdered by a crowd angered by his statements following the Jubilee text.

The world *excitement* comes from the Latin word *exitare:* "to move rapidly away." Some in Jesus' audience in Nazareth were inclined to move Joseph's son rapidly away from the synagogue and toward death. Jesus, on the other hand, was inviting his listeners rapidly away from participation in or subjection to the bad news all around.

Jesus' word was an excitement to create community in a situ-

ation of radical breakup. It was an excitement to do justice in the midst of injustice. It was an excitement to see in a situation in which blindness might seem more comforting. It was an excitement to refuse weapons in a situation that was driving many toward greater reliance on weapons. It was an excitement to the activation of faith in a situation of despair. It was an excitement to forgiveness where forgiveness seemed not only impossible but horribly inappropriate.

The Jubilee, with its root in the Sabbath, has to do with the exciting adventure of living with the belief that the Messiah is already with us. Thus we have the possibility of forgiveness, of seeing even in a hardened enemy a potential neighbor and friend, and in a war criminal an unhardened pacifist. In the grace of God, such transformation is possible. It has already happened. We have known bits of that transformation in our own lives. When sight is given the dimension of grace, we see ourselves not only in an unspeakably marvelous world and universe, but we see possibilities of transformation everywhere. Eyesight without grace, no matter how acute, is blind to the essentials, is trapped in the divisions and violence of the past.

The Jubilee message announced by Jesus of Nazareth, like Berrigan's pronouncement to Mel, revives a sense of wonder and astonishment. An essential quality of religious life and peacemaking is an ability to perceive the miracle of existence, the beauty of created things, the confession of God that is in all beauty. It is through this sense of wonder that we find ourselves drawn to become guardians of life and opponents of those forces which are contemptuous of life. It is this wonder which nourishes love and which helps us awaken in others a similar wonder. We can say with G. K. Chesterton, "I am astonished that people are *not* astonished."

The Jubilee announcement, like Berrigan's manner toward the pale stranger in his classroom, is blunt, and even rude. Perhaps there is a place for holy rudeness. It may be rude to speak of forgiveness and reconciliation in situations of death caused by cancer or of life under ruthless landlords and violent soldiers.

There has been steady motion toward a military apocalypse for many centuries, and its weight was felt painfully by the Jews of Nazareth who first heard Jesus' announcement of Jubilee. We live today in a situation of possible world-embracing catastrophe, which for many is inevitably a time of despair. It is a despair which often

occurs very quietly. We can be its victims as easily as anyone. Against the weight of such nuclearized bad news, it becomes difficult to imagine good news.

A main task of religious life and peacemaking is to free ourselves from subjection to the huge fears that our situation can bring upon us, which can either paralyze life-supporting responses or produce a resistance which is so embittered that it only deepens human entrapment in violence. The experience of faith reveals the presence and power of God in such a way that a resistance to destruction that is in its nature reconciling becomes possible. We cannot simply refuse collaboration in destruction and offer resistance to it; we must become for others channels of hope. It is, after all, not we who hope, but God who hopes in us; and because it is God who has the hope, that hope is sure.

The hope that is sure is that, despite ourselves, despite our weapons, despite the arms race, despite all the injustice and division, God intends to save us, and has already done so. We can live and act with a confidence that is entirely absent for those imprisoned in dependence on weapons. Far from pitying ourselves, far from refusing to bring a new generation of children into the world, far from resigning the human species to extinction, we can embrace our times, live the Jubilee, and surprise the gloomy with the words, "Isn't it exciting?"

WHAT DO WE HAVE TO GIVE
OUR CHILDREN?

Questions for Thought and Discussion

1. How do you respond to the prophecy? How does the fact that time is the Lord's affect your reaction to the world's situation?

2. Cosby asserts that God in his mercy is holding back the wrath of nuclear war and that the U.S. would be safer without its nuclear arsenal. What does your faith say is the position of most security? If we really placed our security in God, what difference would it make in our response to the nuclear arms race?

3. Do you feel burdened by the fear of nuclear war as Forest describes? When has your fear of something caused you to "wake up" and act in the past? Where do you find hope in a nuclear age?

PART III.

FAITH AT WORK:
Christians Rise to the Nuclear Challenge

What can Christians in the U.S. do to respond to the nuclear crisis? This is both a political and an internal church issue. What steps can we take toward public policy change and economic conversion? What must we do to put our own houses in order and make a visible witness to what we believe? Many churches and individual Christians are already taking action. What have they done and envisioned that may prompt additional creative and faithful responses? Articles in this section evaluate the past, suggest guidelines for the present, and dream dreams for the future.

THE WORK OF PRAYER:
The Heart of Christian Witness
by Jim Wallis

Prayer. That is the word that kept coming back to me while attending a conference of antinuclear activists several years ago. The word seemed a little incongruous at first. There I was, in the midst of a meeting to plan scenarios for political action, and my strongest sense was the need for prayer. But that word was soon confirmed. Other Christians at the conference approached me individually and expressed their need to pray.

These initial feelings soon deepened and developed into a specific sense of being called to prayer as an active response to the present nuclear danger. That call has now been strongly confirmed in Sojourners community. It has created among us a heightened expectation of God's leading, and a clearer sense of our own direction in peacemaking.

At a time when the forces of destruction at work in the world appear so overwhelming, and when we often feel so hopeless and helpless, there is nothing more important for Christians than to be moved to and moved by prayer. The beginning of our response to so great an evil is to go to our knees. The nuclear threat now hanging over the world should drive Christians to a new depth and intensity of prayer. In the Bible, prayer is not the passive, general, and abstract sort of ritual common in many of our churches. Biblical prayer is more active, concrete, historically specific, and politically informed. Prayer in the Bible is offered *for* some things and *against* other things. Prayer is for salvation, healing, peace, righteousness, justice, deliverance, and protection. Prayer is against sin, unrighteousness, injustice, idolatry, destruction, calamity. Prayer is directed against kings and rulers when their behavior is evil and contrary to the welfare of the people.

In the sixth chapter of Ephesians, Paul says we are engaged in

spiritual warfare with the principalities and powers, and he lists prayer as a weapon to be used against those powers.

What does it mean?

The nuclear powers have us in their grip. By nuclear powers I mean the assorted institutions, technologies, habits, and assumptions that have brought us to the brink of total destruction. It is increasingly clear that the politicians, generals, bureaucrats, and corporation executives who are the visible perpetrators of the arms race are not fully in control but, in fact, are under the control of forces beyond themselves.

The nuclear powers have taken control and possessed us like demons. They exercise their dominion through the illusion of their absolute authority and the offering of false security. Their rule is based upon a lie: a lie about their ultimate power and a lie about what they can provide us.

The lie, however, is very effective. Whole populations are held captive by fear and by the frenzied pursuit of false security.

What can explain the church's long and dreadful silence and accommodation in the face of the nuclear threat? It can only be that we are guilty of forgetting and of falling into idolatry. We have forgotten who we are and who our God is.

We have succumbed, along with the rest of the public, to the myths, the fears, and the false worship perpetuated by the nuclear powers.

We are on the road to nuclear disaster because we are worshiping at the altars of false gods. We have forgotten the Lord. We have forsaken God's authority and the true security God offers.

We have instead believed the lie.

When Paul speaks of Christ's "disarming" the powers, he simply means that he exposed their lie, showed them for what they were, unmasked the illusion of their power, and stood free of their rewards and punishments. Jesus' freedom from the fear and control of the powers was rooted in the deep knowledge of who he was and to whom he belonged. His communion with his father was his constant source of strength and power.

Prayer is the act of reclaiming our identity as the children of God; it declares who we are and to whom we belong. The action of prayer places us outside the realm of the powers and principalities. As prayer declares our true identity, it destroys our false identities. In prayer we act upon who we really are, and thus prayer has the

effect of diminishing the illusions that have controlled us. It is therefore an act of revealing the truth and unmasking the lie. Prayer allows us to step out of our traps and find ourselves again in God.

We can regain ourselves from the control of the powers only by placing ourselves totally in God's hands. Prayer, therefore, not only declares our true identity but also declares where our true security is. As prayer roots our security in God, it roots out the false securities that enslave us and lead us to war.

Henri Nouwen once shared with our community how the desert fathers regarded prayer as an act of "unhooking" from the harness of the world's securities. Such prayer may be the only action powerful enough to free us from our spiritual bondage to property, money, power, ideas, and causes that have made us willing to destroy everything in the desperate and futile effort to protect them. Only those who have truly found their security in God can resist the violent tugs and pulls of the false securities offered by the nuclear powers. By re-establishing our security in God, prayer becomes an effective weapon in combating those powers.

Historically, prayer and worship have always been at the heart of the most powerful expressions of Christian witness against tyranny and violence. Prayer, while offered for the sake of the world, will change those who pray. Motivated by a great evil in the world, prayer first raises the question of our own complicity in the evil. Prayer humbles us. It starts in confession and repentance and recalls our identity as God's people. To pray is to recognize that, before the evil can be overcome, we must be transformed. Prayer, therefore, is central to conversion.

Rather than merely criticizing the idolatrous authorities responsible for the evil, prayer radically asserts what our higher authority is. In recognizing God's authority over the evil powers, prayer moves us beyond opposition to affirmation, beyond resistance to celebration.

Thus prayer and the results of prayer are the most revolutionary of acts. The powers and principalities of this world are aware of this; that is why they consider those who pray in this way to be a threat.

Prayer changes our frame of reference; it is not merely a preparation for action. Prayer must be understood as an action in itself, a potent political weapon to be used in spiritual warfare

against the most powerful forces of the world. Prayer is not undertaken in place of other actions; it is the foundation for all the other actions we take.

We must learn to pray with the expectation that God will act in us and in the world. The nations are moving toward nuclear war. That terrible fact puts the world in unprecedented danger. In the face of so grave a crisis, let the church be the church. Given the enormity of the nuclear danger, let us give ourselves to a renewal of prayer and of faith.

Prayer is a necessity. Without it we see only our point of view, our own righteousness, and ignore the perspective of our enemies. Prayer breaks down those distinctions. To do violence to others, you must make them into enemies. Prayer, on the other hand, makes enemies into friends. When we have brought our enemies into our hearts in prayer, it becomes most difficult to maintain the hostility necessary for violence. In bringing them close to us, prayer serves to protect our enemies. Thus prayer undermines the propaganda and policies of governments designed to make us hate and fear our enemies. By softening our hearts toward our adversaries, prayer can become treasonous. Fervent prayer for our enemies is a great obstacle to war and the feelings that lead to it.

Consider what might happen if the churches made prayer for our enemies a regular part of the eucharist. If, when we prayed for unity, we included a prayer for our enemies, if every time we gathered for worship, we paused to remember and pray for the particular people our government has termed "enemies"—how differently might we begin to regard our adversaries? Our whole posture toward them would change. In a world on the brink of nuclear war, no change could be more welcome or urgent. Particularly in a nuclear age, prayers for our enemies should be incorporated into the eucharistic liturgy. Such a practice would have the effect of confronting every Christian with the humanity of those who we feel oppose us, and it would do so right at the heart of our worship of Christ. Such a proposal should be offered in every church and denomination.

Prayer for our enemies takes them into our hearts. It would bring the Russian people and other potential adversaries into our daily consciousness, serving as a regular reminder of their existence. As we pray, we begin to see people as God sees them. With continuing prayer, our anger subsides, our hurts are gradually

healed, and we begin to understand the others' anger and hurt. It is exceedingly difficult to hate people while we are praying for them. Prayer undermines hostility and enables us to identify with another person. We bring them to mind in the presence of God, and our minds are changed toward them. We begin to understand things from their perspective; their feelings, fears, pains, struggles, joys, and hopes. To identify with an enemy is to turn an enemy into a friend.

At present, however, our enemies remain faceless to us. Facelessness is, in fact, their prime characteristic. We assure ourselves that they are nothing like us. We are good and they are bad. Our cause is noble, but their purpose is evil. We can be trusted but they are completely untrustworthy. They know neither reason nor love, only irrationality and hate. It is almost impossible to imagine our enemies showing kindness, gentleness, or compassion. Have you ever wondered why we almost never picture our adversaries with their children? To do so would be to see the intimacy we know in ourselves but cannot accept in our enemies.

Necessary to the preparation for war is the dehumanization of our enemies. They become sinister and disgusting. Our enemy's way of life is depicted as inhuman. They are seen bearing nothing but ill intentions toward us. We tag them with derogatory names that further hide the human faces of those we are making ready to destroy. Japanese become "Japs" or "Nips," Germans become "Krauts" or "Jerrys," Vietnamese become "gooks," "slopes," or "slant eyes," and, of course, Russians are simply "Communists." That particular word is enough to spark images of red devils anxious to kill our families and torture our children en route to world domination. Lt. William Calley, on trial for the murder of Vietnamese villagers at My Lai, said in his own defense, "In all my years in the Army, I was never taught that communists are human beings."

Since our enemies are incapable of normal human feelings and values, they are feared. Their very existence threatens our way of life. Since they are less than human, they must be treated as such. They are different, so they must be dealt with differently. Force is the only thing that people like these understand. It is the only choice we have—war.

The root cause of war is our lack of conversion, our utter lack of love. Conversion, including the renewal of compassion for our

neighbor, is the only enduring road to peace. Understanding and defending the humanity of enemy populations becomes increasingly important as pressures for war mount. Reviving our capacity to love has become an urgent political necessity as the superpowers come to regard millions of their neighbors as nothing more than expendable enemy populations in a nuclear exchange. We face unimaginable destruction unless our hearts are enlarged to recognize a neighbor in the face of our enemy.

This kind of conversion is not likely to happen overnight. We know how difficult it is for affluent Americans to see the face of poverty. But if it is hard for us to establish proximity to the poor who are all around us, it is even harder to touch the human faces of nuclear victims who, for the most part, are not victims yet. Just as conversion in a hungry world means coming face to face with the poor, conversion in a nuclear age means coming face to face with the human reality of nuclear annihilation. In each case, the converted person is one who can see and feel the human suffering. In other words, to be converted is to have compassion for the victims. It means to carry, in your own heart, the human suffering of others. During the Vietnam War, the peace efforts that were most enduring usually came from those who deeply felt the agony of Vietnamese people. Those whose actions were most ideologically motivated failed to produce the same quality of peace activity. The same is true today in people's response to the pain of El Salvador, South Africa, Cambodia, or South Korea. In every case, it is the human face of suffering that begins to melt our hardness of heart.

One of the most difficult problems in confronting the nuclear arms race is its lack of visible victims. We have a very hard time seeing the human consequences of nuclear war. Hiroshima and Nagasaki are too long ago and too far away for many of us to comprehend fully. The Japanese victims of those two atomic blasts have courageously attempted to alert the world to the horror of their own experience, but most people have yet to be touched by their testimony. More recently, there have been revelations of U.S. soldiers and civilians victimized by nuclear testing, but once again the effect on most of us has been small.

I know of few persons who have been deeply converted on the matter of nuclear war. It is still very distant to us and far removed from our hearts. Even antinuclear activists often display more anger and fear than the compassion born out of deep identification

with the victims. I was recently with one nuclear resister, though, who demonstrated to me what conversion means in the face of nuclear war. We spoke of the problem of the invisible victims of the arms race. He became very emotional. We simply must see it," he said. "The faces of the people of Hiroshima and Nagasaki must be ever before us. I can see those faces now in the faces of my own wife and children, of my friends, and even of the people on the street." The nuclear arms race had become a personal thing to this man. He carries the vivid picture of nuclear war with him always and sees it painted on the smiling faces of those he loves most. The question for him is no longer a debate over political policy, military strategy, or national security; it has become a test of love. The eyes of the people of Hiroshima are deep wells of pain; the bodies of the nuclear victims have been twisted, their visages marred. They cry out to us that we might see the future of the world in their pain. Only if we can look into their eyes and see the eyes of our children and our neighbors, our enemies and ourselves, will we be converted.

When nuclear war comes, we will all see and be horrified. But then it will be too late, and we will wonder, in our agony, why we did not see earlier. Conversion is to see the human face of nuclear war *now*, before it occurs. Conversion means to enter into anticipatory suffering with every potential victim. To see is to act. We cannot hide our faces from the poor; neither can we turn away from the faces of the nuclear victims. In both cases, to turn away from them is to turn away from our own flesh. In a hungry world, we suffer the loss of what children might have otherwise become. In a nuclear world, we suffer the loss of any future for children at all. Our blindness must be removed and our hearts opened to the nuclear reality. This too is a radical surgery for which we must also turn to the Lord. Conversion always means two things: seeing Jesus and seeing our neighbor. Perhaps when we see Jesus in the faces of the nuclear victims, our hearts will be opened.

LETTING GO OF ALL THINGS:

Prayer as Action

by Henri Nouwen

The call to prayer is not an invitation to retreat to a familiar piety, but a challenge to make a radical move toward prayer as "the only necessary thing" (Luke 10:42). In praying about the nuclear crisis, we discover a dimension of prayer not seen before, a dimension that becomes visible precisely in the confrontation with the powers and principalities.

What I see happening is the discovery of prayer as the act: the most radical and most revolutionary act, they act by which everything is turned around and made new, the act by which the barriers of fear are broken down, the act by which we can enter into a world which is not of this world—the act, therefore, that is the basis for all other actions.

We cannot know fully on what we are embarking. It is a very courageous direction, but also a direction which is more demanding than any earlier call. It is a call to martyrdom, a call to die with Christ so as to live with him. Are we ready for that? I doubt it.

In a recently published book about his experiences in the German concentration camps, Floris B. Bakels witnesses to the power of prayer as an act. Bakels, a highly sophisticated and richly educated Dutch lawyer, simply states that prayer saved him not only physically, but also mentally and spiritually. Why? Because prayer meant for him a process of death and rebirth that enabled him to live as a hopeful man while hundreds of people around him died daily from hunger, torture, and execution.

In the midst of the most horrifying circumstances, Bakels, who never considered himself a religious man, unexpectedly found himself responding to his dying friends by speaking to them about "God, Jesus and the gospel" and discovered a new peace in himself and others that was not of this world. It was hard for Bakels to

grasp fully what was happening to him. But now, 34 years later, he writes:

> I had an idea . . . hard to articulate. . . . Being born again presupposes also for me a dying, a dying however of the old man, the birth of a new man. . . . But this departure of the old man . . . was an ultimate sorrow, a "sorrow towards God," a worldsorrow, a sorrow for what is passing, for the vanishing world, for the letting go of all things. . . . I started to realize my strong attachment to this world, but to the degree that this process of detachment developed itself, my adoration of the . . . beauty of this world increased. It was heartrending, it was one great birth pang. What to do? . . . What about love, the love for a woman, my wife, my family, the butterflies, the waters and the forests? . . . All the attractiveness of that great rich life on earth . . . was I too attached to it? Under the shimmering of eternity I started a new process, a laying down of the old man, a saying farewell, a departing, even an attempt to be no longer so attached to life itself . . . and then . . . a wanting to take up the new man, to be a quiet flame, a reaching upwards, forgetting my own miserable body, a wanting to come home to the Power out of which I was created. . . . I couldn't articulate it well. . . . I only knew one thing to do: to surrender everything to Him. (*Nacht und Nebel: Mijn verhaal uit Duitse gerangenissen and concentratiekampen*)

This process of dying and being born again, experienced by Floris Bakels during World War II, belongs to the core of prayer as an act. Today, as our world is slowly becoming an enormous concentration camp threatened by a new and even greater holocaust, I wonder if this act of prayer is not the most important response. It is the response in which fear is overcome by breaking through the barrier between life and death. I want therefore to better understand Floris Bakel's profound prayer experience and to seek that experience in our own days of nuclear threat.

In a situation in which the world is threatened by annihilation, prayer does not mean much when we undertake it only as an attempt to influence God, or as a search for a spiritual fallout shelter, or as an offering of comfort in stress-filled times. Prayer in the

face of a nuclear holocaust only makes sense when it is an act of stripping ourselves of everything, yes, even of life itself. Prayer is the act by which we divest ourselves of all false belongings and become free to belong to God and God alone.

This explains why, although we often feel a real desire to pray, we experience at the same time a strong resistance. We want to move closer to God, the source and goal of our existence, but at the same time we realize that the closer we come to God the stronger will be his demand to let go of the many "safe" structures we have built around ourselves. Prayer is such a radical act because it requires us to criticize our whole way of being in the world, to lay down our old selves and accept our new self, which is Christ.

This is what Paul has in mind when he calls us to die with Christ so that we can live with Christ. It is to this experience of death and rebirth that Paul witnesses when he writes: "I live now not with my own life, but with the life of Christ who lives in me" (Galatians 2:20).

What has all this to do with actions to end the arms race? I think that the most powerful protest against destruction is the laying bare of the basis of all destructiveness: the illusion of control. In the final analysis, isn't the nuclear arms race built upon the conviction that we have to defend—at all cost—what we have, what we do, and what we think? Isn't the possibility of destroying the earth, its civilizations, and its peoples a result of the conviction that we have to stay in control—at all cost—of our own destiny?

In the act of prayer, we undermine this illusion of control by divesting ourselves of all false belongings and by directing ourselves totally to the God who is the only one to whom we belong. Prayer therefore is the act of dying to all that we consider to be our own and of being born to a new existence which is not of this world.

Prayer is indeed a death to the world so that we can live for God. The great mystery of prayer is that even now it leads us into a new heaven and a new earth and thus is an anticipation of life in the divine kingdom. God is timeless, immortal, eternal, and prayer lifts us up into this divine life.

Here the meaning of the act of prayer in the midst of a world threatened by extinction becomes visible. By the act of prayer we do not first of all protest against those whose growing fears make them construct nuclear warheads and build nuclear missiles and

submarines. By the act of prayer we do not primarily attempt to stop nuclear escalation and proliferation. By the act of prayer we do not even try to change people's minds and attitudes. All this is very important and much needed, but prayer is not primarily a way to get something done.

No, prayer is the act by which we let ourselves know the truth that we do not belong to this world with its warheads, missiles, and submarines; we have already died to it so that not even a nuclear holocaust will be able to destroy us. Prayer is the act in which we willingly live through in our own intimate being the ultimate consequences of nuclear destruction and affirm in the midst of them that God is the God of the living and that no human power will ever be able to "unmake" God. In prayer we anticipate both our individual death and our collective death and proclaim that in God there is no death but only life. In prayer we undo the fear of death and therefore the basis of all human destruction.

Is this an escape? Are we running away from the very concrete issues that confront us? Are we spiritualizing the enormous problems facing us and thus betraying our time, so full of emergencies? It would be so if the act of prayer would become a substitute for all actions. But if prayer is a real act of death and rebirth, then it leads us right into the midst of the world where we must take action.

To the degree that we are dead to the world, we can live creatively in it. To the degree that we have divested ourselves of false belongings, we can live in the midst of turmoil and chaos. And to the degree that we are free of fear, we can move into the heart of the danger.

Thus the act of prayer is the basis and source of all action. We need to affirm this over and over again because when our actions against the arms race are not based on the act of prayer, they easily become fearful, fanatical, bitter, and more an expression of our survival instincts than of our faith in God as the God of the living.

When, however, our act of prayer remains the act from which all actions flow, we can be joyful even when our times are depressing, peaceful even when the threat of war is all around us, hopeful even when we are constantly tempted to despair. Then we can indeed say in the face of the overwhelming nuclear threat: "We are

not afraid, because we have already died and the world no longer has power over us." Then we can fearlessly protest against all forms of human destruction and freely proclaim that the eternal, loving God is not "the God of the dead but of the living" (Matthew 22:32).

TO WHOM DO WE BELONG?
Questions for Thought and Discussion

1. Wallis says that prayer in the face of the nuclear threat is an active and historically specific act. He says that the act of prayer "declares who we are and to whom we belong." How do you respond both to the simplicity and the power in that claim? What changes have you experienced in your life as a result of prayer?

2. According to Nouwen, the basis of the arms race is the illusion of control. How does Nouwen see our prayer as undoing that illusion? How has that been true in your own experience?

LIKE STREET PREACHING IN DOWNTOWN ROME:
Witnessing at Nuclear Weapons Facilities

by Mernie King

The arms race has become such an integral and pervasive part of our national life that most U.S. residents now live in the vicinity of a nuclear weapons facility. While it is true that every person on the earth is threatened by the dark cloud of impending nuclear horror, we in the United States are in a distinct position to know first-hand both its danger and its physical reality. This is the case because of the wide geographical diversity and multifaceted nature of the nuclear weapons process.

The nuclear tentacles reach into every possible aspect of our business, labor, science, and religion as well as the military. Each of the government, scientific, industrial, and military facilities that are a part of the nuclear weapons process is a deadly link in a chain of events and a way of life that undermine life itself.

Some of us in the United States live near the scientific installations where the horrendous but intellectually captivating ideas are hatched. These laboratories and research institutes, sometimes on university campuses, design and develop the nuclear weapons systems.

Then there are the places where the political ideas and ideologies are constructed to justify and legitimate the never-ending flow of new weapons technologies: the think tanks and university departments of strategic studies.

Perhaps the most visible and culpable elements of the arms race are the institutions and locations of political decision-making, where official policy is set and money is appropriated to pay for nuclear weapons. Included in this list are the Congress, the White House, federal buildings, local congressional offices, and political party headquarters. The political decisions are executed by govern-

ment agencies like the Department of Defense (Army, Navy, and Air Force) and the Department of Energy, which have countless branches and installations.

The nuclear fuel cycle entails numerous steps, including uranium mining and milling, fuel processing, fabrication, reprocessing, waste management and storage, and transportation. It involves many different plants and locations spread all over the country.

The production of the nuclear weapons themselves is a gigantic and tremendously profitable enterprise that involves many companies. They contract with the government to provide materials and services that make the construction of nuclear bombs and their delivery systems possible. Their profits often furnish the incentive for new steps in the arms race. Both corporate offices and production sites should be regarded as primary nuclear facilities.

The most obvious points of the nuclear weapons cycle are the actual installations where the warheads are deployed or stored. These include missile sites, bomber bases, and submarine ports as well as various arsenals around the country. At such places the missiles actually stand poised ready to unleash almost instantaneous death.

There are a number of nuclear weapons testing facilities currently in operation without which new weapons systems could not be deployed. And not to be forgotten are the places where nuclear weapons are displayed and promoted, such as arms bazaars, air shows, and museums.

Churches and Christian groups are taking a stand against nuclear weapons in increasing numbers. A ministry of witness at nuclear weapons facilities could be one very important way for Christians to express that conviction.

Already people around the country are witnessing at nuclear facilities. Some of the most notable actions have been at Rocky Flats, Trident installations, and the Pentagon. But demonstrations of Christian concern are springing up with increasing frequency at many other places as well.

A Georgia newspaper, the *Augusta Chronicle,* recently reported, "For the third time this year members of a Columbia, South Carolina–based religious group gave out leaflets to workers at the Savannah River plant asking them to think about the destruction caused by nuclear weapons." The Savannah River plant is

located in a rural area near Aiken, South Carolina. It makes the plutonium buttons that trigger hydrogen bombs and is operated by the Department of Energy.

The group mentioned is a fellowship of Christians from South Carolina and Georgia, made up of Roman Catholics, Episcopalians, Presbyterians, Baptists, and Quakers. John Brown, one of its members, explained, "We often go to the plant on special days like Good Friday and the anniversary of Hiroshima to witness to the reconciling nature of the gospel."

Public demonstrations at the Savannah River nuclear site have included marches, liturgies, prayer vigils, an "Easter drama," and civil disobedience. The group has made special efforts to communicate with plant employees. Some workers have resigned, saying that the Christian witness had focused for them the moral issues involved in making nuclear weapons.

In Pittsburgh a group called Christian Peacemakers has been witnessing at the international headquarters of the Rockwell Corporation for almost five years. Rockwell, one of this country's best known military contractors, produces major components for both the MX and Trident systems and operates the plutonium reprocessing plant in Rocky Flats, Colorado.

Christian Peacemakers has consistently done leafletting, vigiling, drama, and other symbolic actions, including civil disobedience, on the sidewalk in front of the office entrance. The group observes many of the events on the liturgical calendar by going to Rockwell.

For 40 consecutive days in October and November of 1980, a prayer vigil was held during the lunch hour at the federal building in Salt Lake City. The witness was sponsored by Utah Clergy and Laity Concerned About the MX. The group's purposes for gathering were to pray for peace, make a Christian call for a nuclear arms moratorium, call for economic conversion, and help stop the MX from being deployed in Utah and Nevada.

Pastor Stephen Sidorak, formerly of the Centenary United Methodist Church in Salt Lake City and organizer of the vigil, stated that there was ample biblical precedent for using the "40-days" imagery, including the temptation of Jesus in the desert and Noah's 40 days in the ark while the flood destroyed all life from the earth. Pastor Sidorak said that by being in front of the federal

building, Christians were able to remind passers-by that the world is only 30 minutes away from destruction in the event of a nuclear war and that there is no security in nuclear weapons.

Our own church's practical experience with public witness has confirmed our theological and political understanding of it. A recent incident illustrates this point. Members of our congregation had gathered at the Pentagon in Washington. There were about 60 of us standing two and three abreast in a semicircle around a small table which held a loaf of bread and a cup of wine. Above our heads was a large banner that asked, "What does it mean to follow Christ?" We held a dozen signs that quoted scripture verses like "Love your enemies" and "Be not conformed to this world." Two additional signs read "Nuclear weapons betray Christ" and "Stop the arms race."

A crowd soon gathered, curious to see what we were up to. We sang and read Scripture. We took time to focus on remembering the death of Jesus in the breaking of the bread and sharing the cup and invited all who would follow Jesus and seek his way of peace to join us. After the worship we remained standing for a silent vigil.

During our witness a man from the crowd approached us, intently reading each of our signs. Finally he walked up to one of our members and declared that he agreed with all the signs that quoted Scripture but not with the two that referred to nuclear weapons and the arms race. Those, he said, were untrue and had no business being held by people who preach the gospel.

This incident emphasizes the importance of witnessing to our faith in public situations. The man's comment reminded us that, for many, Jesus is acceptable as long as he is separated from history. His life and teachings in abstraction are palatable to most people. But Jesus in the midst of history is still an offense. The man who approached us apparently agreed with Jesus that we should love our enemies but rejected the application of that commandment to the particulars of our historical situation.

To many the admonition to love our enemies is believable only as long as the enemies are general and unspecified. But when the enemies are identified as Russians, Iranians, Cubans, or whomever the government names as its adversaries, the statement becomes outrageous. "Love your enemies" is admired as the word of the

Lord until it is suggested that it means you can't simultaneously love your enemies and plot their annihilation with nuclear weapons.

Witnessing at a nuclear facility is one way of insisting that the gospel is neither an abstraction nor historically irrelevant.

Whether at the gate of a bomber base, at a submarine station, or in front of a congressional office, being at a nuclear facility can provide Christians with the occasion to share the power and meaning of early apostolic faith. It is rather like the street preaching of the first century in downtown Rome. We can once again see that the routine proclamation of faith in Jesus, the simple theological affirmation of his lordship, is pregnant with political meaning.

The early Christians were keenly aware of the way Jesus died. Many of them had experienced firsthand the suspicious and hostile environment that surrounded his death. They were well aware of the public perception that he was killed as a result of conflict with the ruling authorities. So when these early followers made a commitment to share in the Lord's life, they knew that the conflict between the way of Jesus and the way of the world would become their struggle too.

Going to nuclear weapons facilities is one important way for our churches to break out of their comfortable social and political environment to know firsthand the struggle of faith that engages the world.

Jesus was attacked and persecuted because he was viewed as a threat to the very heart of political and economic power. By calling on people to transfer their primary loyalty to his kingdom, Jesus was competing with Rome and Jerusalem for the hearts and minds of the people. He was challenging normal political authority by calling into question the most basic of its assumptions.

The affirmation that Jesus is Lord will always take place in the context of rival lords and competing saviors, who contend for our loyalty by offering what appear to be attractive arrangements to guarantee security and well-being. In the present environment of disintegrating political patterns and personal anxiety, no offer seems more persuasive or enticing that the "protection" of nuclear weapons. Thus, lordship and idolatry can be seen to be parallel subjects that by nature must be addressed simultaneously. We need to push these twin issues beyond seminary classrooms and church discussion groups into the public arena.

By worshiping Christ at nuclear installations, Christians can

assert their faith in the Lord Christ in the presence of his most seductive rival. We clearly say whom we will worship and whom we will not worship. We declare that the false god's claim of nuclear protection is a cruel hoax, both politically and spiritually. Nuclear weapons, exposed by the light of the Word of God and the lessons of history, can be seen to offer only impinging death. In public worship Christians can dethrone the major pretender to Jesus' position as both Lord and Savior. The visible display of faith under the very shadow of nuclear weapons is a witness to the presence of God in the specifics of our history.

The gospel is a testimony of God's bodily intervention in history. God in Christ offered his life into the concrete reality of human life and events. By being physically present wherever nuclear weapons are represented, we can continue and count on God's intervention in even the worst of human situations. God placed Jesus in the very midst of humanity's broken and sinful places. Today we can carry on that Christian tradition of intervention by symbolically and physically placing ourselves between the bombs and their intended victims.

These nuclear facilities are our Auschwitz and our Dachau. While millions of innocent people were murdered at Auschwitz and Dachau, the death of many millions more is being prepared for by the production and deployment of U.S. nuclear weapons. If we had lived in Hitler's Germany, how would we have responded to the extermination policies and the ovens of Auschwitz? The contemporary counterpart to that faith question is how we will respond to the present nuclear crisis. Would we have intervened at Auschwitz crying, "No, this can't go on!"? Will we interrupt business as usual at Rocky Flats, missile sites, or federal buildings crying, "In the name of God, stop!"?

Christians should go to nuclear weapons facilities simply because it is right and follows from our faith. But politically and economically the effect could also be cumulatively substantial. What if all over the country groups began to show up at places associated in any way with the bomb—each week a few more until the nation really began to notice?

Such visible and mounting opposition could add potent fuel to a vibrant social movement that demands disarmament and economic conversion. For disarmament will begin only if a substantial segment of the population makes clear its active support for it and

brings the necessary pressure to bear on the political process. Acts of public witness could be a sign of this beginning and a call to involvement by increasing numbers of people.

Courageous people must lead the country to withdraw its support from the arms race and thus undermine the whole nuclear weapons system. By adding a strong dose of biblical peace, justice, and social vision to the political environment, Christians can make a vital contribution.

TAKE THE MESSAGE TO JERUSALEM:
Declaring the Gospel of Peace in the Churches
by John Stoner

At that very hour some Pharisees came, and said to him, "Get away from here, for Herod wants to kill you." And he said to them, "Go and tell that fox, 'Behold, I cast out demons and perform cures today and tomorrow, and the third day I finish my course. Nevertheless I must go on my way today and tomorrow and the day following; for it cannot be that a prophet should perish away from Jerusalem.' O Jerusalem, Jerusalem, killing the prophets and stoning those who are sent to you! How often would I have gathered your children together as a hen gathers her brood under her wings, and you would not! Behold, your house is forsaken." (Luke 13:31–35)

Christians are always tempted to accept the Pharisees' belief that Herod is the chief threat to their mission and then change their course to combat his villainy. But instead of focusing on Herod, Jesus insisted that all needed to repent, and journeyed toward Jerusalem where the action was controlled by those who made the greatest claims to represent God.

In the United States today discerning Christians are asking what they can do about the monstrous evil of the nuclear arms race. They struggle with where to direct their efforts, conscious of their limitations. Time, money, and energy must be concentrated. What should be the strategy of the Christian nuclear resistance witness? Are there signs of the times which may give us a clue?

It would be hard to think of a place where support for nuclear armaments is more entrenched, insidious, or determined than in U.S. churches: Opposition to nuclear disarmament in the churches is entrenched in the God-and-country mentality which has characterized American Christianity for two centuries. It is insidiously

213

wrapped in an aura of piety and Bible-believing religiosity. It is determined to prove that America's cause is God's cause and that America, like God, can be Number One.

Given this, it is time for the Christian anti-nuclear movement to change its focus to include the religious establishment as well as the military establishment. To go to Wheaton, 475 Riverside Drive, and Notre Dame in addition to Rocky Flats, Seattle, and the Pentagon. To challenge apostasy as well as atheism. To go to the religious conventions and not only the arms bazaars. To strike at military recruiting in the churches as it does in the schools.

Why hasn't the Christian nuclear resistance movement directed its campaigns more pointedly toward the church and the religious establishment? Two reasons come to mind.

On the one hand, some Christians have bypassed the church in their peace advocacy because they consider the church too weak to bother with, so devoid of power that it can be ignored at no loss by those who want to see God's will done on earth as it is done in heaven.

In this view the church (local congregation, TV evangelist, denominational structure, Christian neighbor, etc.) is so hopelessly compromised with militarism and nationalism that God has long since lost interest in its fate and has turned to other instruments to accomplish his will. Christians holding this view tend to have a very spiritualized doctrine of the church, believing (if they believe in the church at all) in some type of invisible church, a communion of like-minded but widely dispersed souls. It is a view of the church that has little in common with the New Testament, not to mention its contradiction with the historical and sociological evidence that the church is a very real, concrete community of influence in human affairs.

On the other hand, there are Christians who despair at addressing the Christian establishment about nuclear madness because they see the church as nearly all-powerful, virtually impregnable to any truth which contradicts its chosen direction.

These earnest Christ-followers view the local congregation as a ponderous glacier, undeterred by the rantings of maladjusted pacifist members. They see the TV evangelists as magicians who hypnotize their audiences, with no openness whatsoever to new truth which would affect the content of their message. In this view there is no faith that God could convert the believers, no hope that the

awesome power of the Christian community could be harnessed for the goals of life and sanity.

As one who was born in a Christian home and has lived for nearly four decades in a denomination which seems not even to have heard of August 6, 1945, I know that it is not easy over the long haul to take the church as seriously as it says it should be taken. The resistance to truths which should be obvious from the most cursory reading of the gospel is unbelievable. The tenacity with which the most deplorable myths of a militarized society are believed is frightening. The determination with which minor issues are scrutinized and important issues ignored is appalling. And yet, the church must be addressed for several reasons, all of them related to the fact that Jesus journeyed toward Jerusalem, the heart of the religious establishment.

THE ACCOUNTABILITY OF THE CHURCH

The church should be a primary focus of the Christian antinuclear witness because it is accountable for the truth which it has received. Viewed in this light, the church's support of the nuclear deterrence doctrine is more reprehensible than that of any other segment of society. There is a scriptural principle which says, "To all whom much is given, of them will much be required" (Luke 12:48).

The church has been given enough truth in Scripture and through Spirit-led prophets today that its default in the matter of the nuclear threat is culpable in the extreme. The failure of the church to lead in the right direction on the nuclear issue, and its commitment all too often to the opposite direction, requires repentance. The church must be told that it's not good enough to abhor the idea of nuclear *war*. Rather, the church is required to abhor the idea of nuclear *deterrence,* unless it can be morally right to threaten to do an immoral thing.

Jesus looked behind the act of adultery to the thought, behind the act of murder to the intention. Nuclear deterrence is to nuclear holocaust what lust is to adultery, and whoever condemns the latter cannot condone the former. Nevertheless, it is done all the time. Indeed, belief in nuclear deterrence prevails in the church. This signals a great apostasy, and the church must be called to account.

If lust were endorsed as widely and as publicly in the church

215

as nuclear deterrence is, there would be an outcry of massive proportions, and rightly so. But the abomination of nuclear deterrence, the threat to destroy whole continents of people, the righteous and the wicked together, is accepted as if it were a proposal to mow the parsonage lawn on Monday instead of Friday.

The efforts of the Christian witness for nuclear resistance must be focused on the church because the church knows that God abhors evil intentions as well as evil deeds. If nuclear holocaust ever destroys this beautiful world it will only be because millions of people first condoned the preparations for it. And the church will be held accountable for its members who paid for it without protest, or even planned for it in their business, political, and military positions.

THE REPENTANCE OF THE CHURCH

The church should be a primary focus of the Christian antinuclear witness because the church believes in repentance. To repent is to change one's way of thinking and acting, to have one's mind turned around. This is precisely what is needed in the matter of the arms race. The thought that security, peace, and freedom come from violence and the threat of violence is wrong and must be replaced with a right thought. The mindset which believes that the threat of nuclear war prevents nuclear war is false. This mind must be turned around to see that love, justice, and the power of the Spirit of God prevent nuclear war.

It is obvious enough that the movement for nuclear moratorium and disarmament has as its goal to change people's minds. It is not considered good manners to state it so bluntly in an age of "I'm OK, you're OK," but the church didn't get its start on the premise of good manners. So it should come as no surprise to evangelicals, humanists, Republicans, or Democrats when the Christian peace movement comes on with a call to repentance.

This is not to say that we should expect the call to be welcomed, and particularly not by those who specialize in calling others to repentance for other sins. The prophets of God spent most of their time, and encountered most of their opposition, calling God's people to repentance. In light of this it is a bit surprising how quickly the prophets today turn their message and energy away from the church toward other audiences. One wonders, has the

word of the Lord been giving the generals more discomfort than the bishops? Should it? Many are calling Ronald Reagan to account. Who is calling Jerry Falwell to account? And Word Books? And Fuller Seminary?

Some of the prophets of our time are like Jonah in reverse. They are running away from God's command to call the church to repentance, spending all of their time in Nineveh addressing the pagans. Is this, as it was for Jonah, out of anger at the thought that the church might repent if it heard the Word?

There is another dynamic which may divert us from focusing the call to repentance on the church. We all seek ways to absolve ourselves of responsibility for our most obvious failures, which tend to be those in our closest relationships. Sometimes we do this by turning our attention away from the failing relationship, as if to suggest that other, wiser persons will be more responsive to our efforts. Thus if our marriage is troubled we devote ourselves to the peace movement. If our children are wild we coach Little League to show that we are good with children. And if we are not succeeding in calling the church to accept Christ's way to peace and security we try to persuade the government to accept it.

The Christian nuclear resistance movement should be calling evangelists, bishops, pastors, deacons, and Sunday School teachers to repentance from believing the doctrine of nuclear deterrence. If success is its goal, it must succeed in this or it will not succeed at all. If truth is its goal, it cannot bypass those who claim to have the truth. If faithfulness to Christ is its goal, it must go with Jesus to the synagogue week after week to challenge the interpretation of the Scribes and finally to Jerusalem to confront the power of the high priest.

THE MISSION OF THE CHURCH

The Christian peacemaker's witness should be aimed toward the church because God's mission in the world is hindered by an unfaithful church. The early church did not evangelize the ancient world by endorsing the militarism of the Roman Empire. If you can imagine the early Christian deacon Stephen calling on Roman soldiers to fall upon his persecutors with spears and swords for his defense, then you can imagine a TV evangelist saying that America's military power protects the church from godless communism.

217

If you can imagine Isaiah describing a Servant of the Lord who kills rather than suffers, then you can imagine Christian pastors blessing war in Memorial Day sermons. If you can imagine Jesus taking a sword and joining in the fight which Peter started in the Garden of Gethsemane, then you can imagine a born-again Christian as commander in chief of the armed forces.

For 300 years the Christian movement repudiated the use of the sword, declaring that its power resided in prayer, faith, and the Spirit of God. Those were years of miraculous growth for the church. The blood of the martyrs was indeed the seed of the church. The cross of Jesus defined the life of the disciples, and the power of the resurrection was turned loose all around. "The Way" is what they called Christianity in those days. But today The Way has been turned into The Experience, and the Christian life has been changed from a journey into a psychological state. The Bible's preoccupation with the direction of our lives and the use of our energies has been replaced with the American dream of peace of mind and material success.

When the Jesus of this new Christianity enters the synagogue at Nazareth and reads from the Scriptures, he does not proclaim release to the captives or liberty for the oppressed. Instead, his words are: "I'm OK, you're OK. I preach the gospel, you make nuclear bombs, she oppresses the poor, he destroys the balance of nature. I'm OK, you're OK."

There is no wrong and there is no right. The world ignores such a vapid message, as it should; or it joins it in large numbers and nothing is changed. Everything is as it was before. The Christians in the U.S. aim their nuclear bombs at the Christians in the USSR, who aim theirs back. The Christians in France do the same, and the Christians in a score of other countries vie for a piece of the action.

Jesus weeps.

And the world goes to hell without even a decent guess of what the gospel is really about.

THE SPIRITUAL POWER OF THE CHURCH

The energies of the Christian nuclear resistance movement should be channeled toward the release of the spiritual power which is latent in the church through the indwelling Holy Spirit. The pow-

er which must replace bombs and missiles is spiritual power, the power of the Holy Spirit.

God has chosen to bestow his Holy Spirit in a special way upon the church. History and experience attest to this fact. This is not to claim that the Spirit of God is not at work elsewhere than in the church, for God's Spirit certainly is. But the awareness of the freedom and universality of the Spirit's work in the world should not obscure the fact of God's choice to give his Spirit freely and specially to the church.

The constituency for the way of peace will not be drawn together by talk alone. The focus of evil will not be overcome by barrages of pamphlets or itinerations of speakers. The message we have is that of the prophet: "Not by might, nor by power, but by my Spirit, says the Lord of hosts" (Zechariah 4:7).

An empty soul is no match for a loaded gun, as much as we might wish it were. We shall have to be filled with the Spirit of the living God to confront the dead works of a church compromised by militarism. Life in the Spirit is nurtured in the fellowship of a caring community. We must function as the church in order to speak to the church. The message we take to the church has come to us through the church. We play back what the church has canonized in Holy Writ. The Spirit, the Word, and prayer are our weapons.

The same Spirit who enables the prophet to speak to the church will empower the church to speak to the world. Let no one underestimate the power of a Spirit-filled church.

Imagine people from every tongue, tribe, and nation standing together saying that the way of the Lamb that was slain is their way; that they will have no truck with weapons of destruction. Imagine them going before presidents and generals, bishops and evangelists, bureaucrats and technicians to say that death holds no fear for them and that they will take no life to save their own.

Imagine them joining hands in China, India, South Africa, Venezuela, Mexico, the United States, and Canada declaring that God is their defense and that they renounce all violence, from nuclear deterrence to revolutionary war.

Imagine yourself going to visit your pastor to talk about the way of peace. Imagine yourself walking with Jesus toward Jerusalem, because that, in the end, is where you have to go.

The cross is near Jerusalem. But so, too, is the resurrection.

FREEZING THE ARMS RACE:
The First Step Toward Disarmament
by Danny Collum

The nuclear arms race between the U.S. and USSR is like two cars racing across a desert, heading toward a cliff. They have been racing for days on parallel tracks, covering hundreds of miles, and gaining in speed. In the course of the competition, they have made certain rules.

One regulation sets speed limits, but those limits are always faster than the cars are going. They accelerate to reach them. Another rule sets boundaries to the raceway so each car can see where the other is as they speed along. But the course still leads to the cliff. And every hour, they are getting closer.

The cars have now reached the point where they must immediately slam on their brakes and stop before they go over the cliff. If those cars can simply brake to a halt soon enough, it may be possible for the drivers to get out, look ahead over the cliff, and look back at the hundreds of miles they have come. Then they could agree that the race was never worth winning anyway; they could admit that each had sped along largely because each didn't want the other to be ahead.

If sense prevailed, both drivers could then get back into their cars, turn them around, and begin driving—perhaps slowly at first, then gaining speed—back over the hundreds of miles they had covered. With patience, persistence, and momentum in that direction, they could eventually reach their original starting point.

That would be nuclear disarmament. It is a very distant goal. Today, in the middle of the arms race, it seems nearly irrelevant. But it is the road to survival. And all that is asked of us first is that we stop before plunging over the cliff. This is what a freeze on nuclear arms would do. It is the point at which to begin.

In the first months of 1981, the prospects for nuclear disar-

mament were as bleak as they had ever been. The SALT II treaty was dead in the Senate. Dialogue between the U.S. and the Soviet Union had broken down completely, while tensions between the two superpowers mounted over crises in the Middle East, Central America, and southern Africa. Ronald Reagan had begun his administration by intensifying the new Cold War and promising a military buildup three times bigger than the one during the peak years of the Vietnam War. Reagan administration officials vowed there would be no new arms control talks until the U.S. arms buildup was complete and the Soviet Union changed its foreign policy in the Third World and Eastern Europe. And some administration officials were talking openly about the possibility of the U.S. fighting, winning, and surviving a nuclear war.

In this grim political environment the campaign for a nuclear freeze was initiated. The freeze coalition gathered around the simple notion that the only way to stop the arms race would be to stop. It formulated a call for the U.S. and the USSR to stop all further production, testing, and deployment of new nuclear weapons or weapons delivery systems as a first step toward complete nuclear disarmament.

The people who conceived the freeze campaign hoped that in the vacuum created by the death of SALT II and the Reagan administration's total disinterest in arms control, a popular initiative backed by solid local organizing could emerge that would change the whole framework of the nuclear weapons debate. Years of arms control talks had only served to perpetuate the arms race. A fresh approach like the freeze initiative seemed to be the only thing that could bring a break in the cycle of nuclear competition.

The freeze organizers also saw that the SALT II treaty had primarily failed not because of the Soviet invasion of Afghanistan, but because there was no popular constituency for it that could counter the heavy lobbying of the cold warriors of the Committee on the Present Danger. It was hoped that a simple, concrete, attainable, but substantive objective like the freeze could serve to focus the growing public unease about nuclear war.

The freeze proposal also had the advantage of being particularly timely. For several years the U.S. and Soviet arsenals have been at a rough parity. But the U.S. is poised to begin the next escalation, which will be the move into counterforce weapons like the MX, Trident II, and cruise missiles. These weapons are de-

signed to be accurate enough to destroy enemy missiles while they are still in their silos. They are not designed to deter a nuclear war but to fight and win one. They represent the most dangerous step yet in the arms race, making nuclear war more likely than ever. If the U.S. goes through with the development of counterforce weapons, the Soviets will surely follow in a few years. The freeze proposal would stop the further production, testing, and deployment of new systems before these new weapons are in place.

The freeze initiative first demonstrated its potential public appeal in November 1980, when three western Massachusetts state senatorial districts passed a freeze referendum with 60 percent of the vote, despite the fact that the same districts voted for Ronald Reagan for president. Building on that early success, the freeze campaign adopted a strategy of building a grassroots constituency for disarmament, planning to go to Congress only after hometown support had been organized and national momentum generated.

As the headlines of the last several months attest, the strategy is working. The nuclear freeze campaign has changed the terms of the nuclear debate, and the freeze initiative has been adopted by hundreds of town meetings, city councils, churches, and professional and civic groups. The momentum for a freeze is bound to multiply if, as is expected, freeze initiatives are passed by voters in California, Michigan, Delaware, New Jersey, and the District of Columbia in November 1982.

Instead of the freeze campaign going to Congress, Congress has come to the freeze campaign. During the February 1982 holiday recess, congresspeople found themselves bombarded with questions from their constituents about nuclear arms control and the freeze. In Massachusetts, the pressure was so great that Edward Kennedy saw a bandwagon in the making and jumped on board by introducing, with Mark Hatfield of Oregon, a nonbinding resolution that incorporated the language of the freeze campaign's "Call to Halt the Nuclear Arms Race." That resolution and an identical one in the House have drawn 170 cosponsors so far.

The freeze campaign has also forced President Reagan to show an uncharacteristic interest in nuclear disarmament. Only two months after the introduction of the Kennedy-Hatfield resolution, Reagan hurriedly unveiled his plans for Strategic Arms Reduction Talks (START) with the USSR. Reagan's proposal calls for those negotiations to lead to a reduction of the U.S. and Soviet strategic

missile arsenals by about one-third. The timing of the START announcement was clearly intended to offset and dilute the impact of the freeze movement, and the content of his plan is designed to outflank the freeze campaign by claiming that he is going beyond a freeze on new weapons to seek drastic cuts in existing arsenals. But the specifics of the START plan raise questions about the seriousness of the president's new-found desire to control the arms race.

The plan calls for a reduction by both sides to 850 land- or sea-based ballistic missiles, to be armed with no more than 5,000 total warheads. And only 2,500 of those warheads could be deployed on land-based missiles. The subceiling on land-based warheads would require massive one-sided reductions by the Soviet Union. More than 72 percent of the Soviets' warheads are landbased, compared to 22 percent for the U.S.

The Soviets have always counted on their edge in land-based missiles to make up for their inferiority in submarine and bomber technology. The reductions Reagan seeks would require the Soviets to begin a long and extremely expensive program of upgrading their submarine-based missile capability if they hope to regain a position of parity. The ceiling of 850 on total launchers would also require disproportionate Soviet reductions. They have more total missiles than the U.S. because they are not as far along in "MIRVing," putting several independently targeted warheads on each missile.

The second phase of Reagan's plan would seek an equal ceiling on the "throw-weight" or total explosive capacity of each arsenal, another area in which the Soviets lead. But the throw-weight yardstick is considered irrelevant by most strategic experts. The Soviets have built bigger weapons to make up for the fact that they are not as accurate as ours. The Reagan administration is bringing in throw-weight only because it would enhance U.S. superiority by requiring one-sided Soviet cuts.

The Reagan plan does not deal at all with what kind of systems could be deployed, only with numbers of weapons. So it would be possible for the U.S. to replace its existing Polaris and Minuteman missiles with the Trident II and MX systems, launching us directly into the dangerous new world of counterforce.

Any treaty that might result from the START talks will take years to negotiate. The SALT II treaty was in the works for seven years. During that time there will be no limits on the weapons both superpowers can build. Both are likely to take advantage of that

interim to build as much as possible before a treaty takes effect.

While the Soviets have stated their willingness to begin arms reduction talks, they have made it clear that they do not consider Reagan's plan a serious proposal. Former U.S. Secretary of State Edmund Muskie has expressed the fear that Reagan's plan could be "a secret agenda for sidetracking disarmament" while the U.S. builds toward a greater and more dangerous strategic superiority.

Far from eliminating the need for a freeze on nuclear weapons, Reagan's START plan is further evidence that a freeze is necessary. Though Reagan's proposal calls for reductions, it is still based on the idea that there is a Soviet advantage that has to be overcome and that it is possible for the U.S. to attain a position of superiority that would allow us to be able to fight and win a nuclear war. In fact, the multiple overkill capacity on both sides makes all the quantitative and qualitative distinctions between the two arsenals irrelevant and the prospect of war an unthinkable horror. It would seem that only a dramatic step like a total and immediate freeze could possibly break the bizarre circular logic of the arms race that has captivated our leaders for 37 years.

There are varying scenarios for how a freeze could come about. It might be agreed to by both sides as a prelude to disarmament negotiations. Or it might become the subject of negotiations itself, in which case all the old suspicions and angling for advantage would surface in a process that could take years. The simplest way to begin a freeze would be for one side to declare it unilaterally and invite the other to reciprocate as a sign of good faith to begin the disarmament process. As the only nation to have used nuclear weapons and as the initiator of each succeeding stage of the arms competition, the U.S. has a special responsibility for stopping the race. And in the present situation any risk involved in stopping the arms race pales to insignificance before the risk of continuing it.

However it might finally be implemented, the proposal for a nuclear weapons freeze deserves support as the most workable option available for reversing the drift toward total war. But we should be clear that the freeze is not a panacea. It is only a minimal first step toward real disarmament. As Reagan has already illustrated, it could be very easy for a clever politician to co-opt the freeze movement's language while subverting its goal of abolishing nuclear weapons. There is also a danger that the freeze proposal could lose its impact as a break with the psychology of the arms

race if it becomes too bogged down in technical questions like verification.

Though the freeze initiative has its own limitations, its greatest potential lies in the direction it suggests of taking the nuclear arms race out of the hands of the Pentagon experts and corporate technicians and placing the initiative and responsibility with the people who pay the bills and would become the victims. If the history of the nuclear arms race should teach us anything, it is that disarmament will only become possible when there is a mass movement that demands it. The freeze campaign has only begun to tap its potential for building such a movement. The freeze proposal is simple, direct, and in everyone's interest; and the effects of Reagan's military budget are rapidly turning the freeze into a bread-and-butter economic issue.

We are already seeing that the involvement of the churches is crucial to the building of a disarmament movement. In the abolitionist, suffragist, civil rights, and antiwar movements of the past, Christians have provided vital moral leadership, commitment, and vision. The need for those qualities is even greater in a movement audacious enough to take on the nuclear arms race. So far, however, freeze activity in the churches has been cast mostly in terms of what the government should do. The integrity of a Christian witness against the arms race requires that we tell the government what we intend to do as well.

For Christians, unilateral steps toward disarmament have to begin in our own lives with concrete acts of noncooperation with the arms race. Movement is taking place in this direction with the increasing practice of war-tax resistance, with church people raising the issue of employment in nuclear facilities with their parishioners, and with Christians becoming involved in direct action at those facilities. But courageous as these beginnings are, much more will be required of us.

Legal segregation and the disenfranchisement of blacks in the U.S. was finally ended by acts of Congress. But the politicians were forced to act by a movement that had at its heart thousands of black Christians in the South who put their lives on the line. In the same way, today's widespread outcry for disarmament in large part had its seeds in small groups of committed, mostly Christian, people who kept raising the issue of nuclear weapons, often at great risk, for years before it was front-page news. Without such a faith-

ful core, a broad and diverse movement like the one growing around a nuclear freeze could easily become diffused and compromised. People of faith can make a special contribution to such a movement by keeping it true to its own best goals and ideals and by bringing to it the spiritual force that springs from lives of sacrificial peacemaking.

When viewed up close, the course of history often seems like a roller coaster. When Ronald Reagan came into office, many peace activists were convinced that all was lost and nearly fell into despair. Now that the freeze campaign is having some impact, it would be easy to fall into an excessive optimism about the task of disarmament. The struggle to abolish nuclear weapons is, and will continue to be, a difficult one. There are very powerful interests in both the U.S. and the Soviet Union who have a stake, whether financial, political, or psychological, in the present state of affairs.

Jesus' call for his people to be peacemakers requires that we intervene in the politics of our time to stop the arms race. The freeze campaign is an appropriate tool for such action, and its growth is certainly encouraging. But perhaps the greatest contribution that Christians can bring to their work for peace is to remain undeterred by the ebb and flow of the political tides and to stand firmly on our faith in God, which gives us hope for this world that is beyond optimism.

PEACE BY PEACE:
A Model for Peace Ministry in the Local Churches
by Mernie King

In recent years, the initial stages of what could become a strong and vibrant peace movement have emerged within the churches of this country. This new-found attachment to peace is due to the convergence of a renewal of faith and an awakened perception of the unprecedented danger of nuclear war.

In a time when the nations are courting political and military disaster, there are signs of hope in the church. With increasing frequency, the call to peace is being heard from pulpits, seminary classrooms, and Christian publications. In many places, Christians are reaching a critical turning point. They see the nuclear threat as having everything to do with their faith in Jesus Christ.

As with any fresh and untested conviction that is spreading in the lives of Christians, the peace concern requires discernment, direction, and leadership. The churches need to construct an appropriate focus and method to incarnate the peace of Christ. Most importantly, the emerging peace mission requires committed people who will pursue it in costly ways.

Strong and active peace and justice organizations are already available to Christians. The Fellowship of Reconciliation, with a large membership and many local chapters, is deeply rooted in the religious pacifist tradition. In recent years, Pax Christi—for Roman Catholics—and New Call to Peacemaking—for the historic peace churches—are involving growing numbers of people. The Atlantic and Pacific Life Communities network has long offered persistent resistance to the arms race. World Peacemakers, an outgrowth of Washington's Church of the Saviour, gives important help in starting and maintaining peace groups both within and across congregational lines. Many denominations have "peace fellowships."

But some local churches are sensing a need to develop indigenous peace ministries or peace mission groups within their congregations. The church is the primary social context of Christians' lives, the place where we gain and maintain our identity. It is only natural that our principal concerns and our calling be grounded and worked out there.

The feeling of many Christians that they need to look beyond their congregations for ways to witness Christ's peace is a telling indictment of the church's life. The church's very purpose is to be evidence of Christ's peace to the world.

Peace is Christ's gift to those who participate in his kingdom. It is a mark of the reconciling love that exists between brothers and sisters. The church has no greater peace to give to the world than the quality of peace it experiences in its own fellowship. A peace ministry should emerge naturally from the church as its members experience solidarity with Christ and one another.

In the Community of Communities, a network of church communities of which Sojourners Fellowship is a part, peace ministry is becoming accepted as a normal part of the church's life. It is not seen as special or somehow dissimilar from the church's other work. It is supported as are the church's other ministries of preaching, counseling, pastoral care, and work with the poor.

In our experience, ministry develops as church members are made aware of a need and make decisions together about gifts and calling. Ministries are given the authority of the local church so that they may act on its behalf. The peace ministry, like any other, is only as strong as the support it receives from the members of the congregation.

In a recent Community of Communities combined peace ministries meeting, several of the churches shared their stories of how they had reached consensus on active opposition to war. In each case the process was long, slow, and painful. Yet the fruit of those struggles is already significantly aiding the cause of peace.

Since the members of so many U.S. churches still accept the assumption of the need for nuclear strength, this gradual and painstaking process will of necessity be repeated. The church desperately needs the small pockets of people who are willing to stay home and do the difficult work of evangelizing, educating, and leading it into peacemaking. The hope that the local churches can become building blocks in a new peace movement is grounded in our belief that

faith is already present in the churches and in our experience of the Spirit bringing change in our own hearts.

Most of us who are now committed to peace and disarmament can look back to a time when we weren't. Somehow, somewhere, we began to change, usually with the help, understanding, and encouragement of a brother or sister. Peace ministries will be built on the conviction that the Spirit is active, making repentance and change realities.

At Sojourners our peace ministry has a threefold purpose: to serve our own congregation, to put our commitment to peace into public witness, and to raise peace as a call of faith among brother and sister congregations. Any peace ministry will have a crucial role to play in the church's internal or common life. Its initial and ongoing task is to lead members of the congregation to strengthen their identities as peacemakers. A peace ministry's first job should be to encourage church members to explore deeply the foundations of their faith in Jesus, where peace is found. Prayer, biblical reflection, and study will begin and facilitate this process.

While peace work has always been a part of Sojourners, we inaugurated our own specifically full-time peace ministry with a special Lenten series on prayer and the arms race in 1979. The series was a time to make our desire for peace an integral part of our prayer life and to reflect theologically on the role of the church in resistance to nuclear war. It included a study of military and political analysis to inform our prayer and to direct our action.

Essential to a peace ministry is a reliance on worship. In worship the church claims and exhibits its loyalty to Christ. Worship is the primary place where Christians cast off their need for protection from the nation's nuclear arsenal. Through worship the churches undermine the idolatry of the arms race.

As with every work of the church, the peace ministry's focus is deeply pastoral. The church's approach to peacemaking has too often been top-heavy with efforts to pass resolutions applauding peace and condemning nuclear weapons at regional and national church levels. These documents are usually directed toward the federal administration or Congress and never get back to local churches. Often the church has asked more of the government than it has been willing to ask of its own people.

In the U.S., very often it is the Christians who have their fingers on the nuclear button. If the church would get its own house

in order, the threat of nuclear weapons could be powerfully confronted. Congregations must together make decisions to support and encourage one another in their opposition to the arms race. For the members of the churches who build, finance, maintain, and threaten to use nuclear weapons, a call to self-examination is sorely needed. Perhaps the most important contribution many churches could make to disarmament would be for their members to simply repent of their participation in the arms race and give up their warmaking vocations.

When church members do take up the challenge of changing their lives, the peace ministry will need to respond with support and counsel. The internal congregational issues of war taxes, military-related jobs, and military service need sensitive and honest pastoral guidance by the peace ministry.

The peace ministry also has an external function. It must lead the congregation in public witness. Christian peace ministry is built on the belief that the church's witness can reduce the level of violence in the world, can help bring a halt to the arms race and show forth the possibilities of new life based in faith and hope in God. The peace that Jesus freely bestows upon his people can never be contained. As it is nurtured in Christian fellowship, it is to be simultaneously shared with a world obsessed with war.

The peace ministry can begin serving the church by helping to identify the particular issues the church should engage and places where the church should be present. A local church may often find itself unclear about where it should give its attention and energy. The peace ministry can help facilitate a process of discernment.

A church with little or no experience in active peacemaking and public witness may need to seek outside help for orientation, education, and training. One of the first tasks of a peace ministry may be to set up workshops and training sessions led by experienced and trusted people from other Christian and peace organizations. Church members should also be encouraged to participate in regional and national disarmament conferences. It is also helpful for new people to receive training in nonviolence to help them feel more comfortable in an unfamiliar role.

The style and content of the church's witness is of critical importance. The peace ministry should help in the selection of the forms of witness and symbols which will communicate the church's message.

Public peacemaking needs to be seen as an opportunity to witness to faith in Jesus and to make evident its fruits—peace and justice. Increasingly, many Christians are finding worship to be a powerful form of public protest. In worship we can not only say no to false lords and competing saviors, but Christians can also offer to the world the alternative values of faith in God and hope that new life can overcome death.

Almost every church in the U.S. will find itself in geographical proximity to an installation where nuclear weapons are being built, deployed, promoted, or displayed. Military bases, construction and production sites, weapons exhibitions, defense contractors, and federal buildings are literally everywhere in this country. With growing frequency, churches are taking on ministries of presence at these facilities as a protest to their existence and as a call to spiritual, political, and economic conversion. Peace ministries can coordinate these activities.

Already many Christians are leafletting, vigiling, worshiping, and often simply praying at these places. In the past year, Christians in cities like Detroit and New York have sponsored Good Friday stations of the cross marches, stopping to remember the passion of Jesus at sites connected to the arms race, such as corporate headquarters and senatorial offices. In September 1979 and 1980, hundreds of Christians gathered in front of the Sheraton Hotel in Washington, D.C., for worship and protest of nuclear weapons being promoted and displayed inside at an arms bazaar. On Memorial Day in Tucson, Arizona, an Episcopal church celebrated the Eucharist in front of the federal building on behalf of those who will die in nuclear war if the arms race is not reversed. It is this kind of public demonstration accompanied by persistent educational efforts that can build a favorable political climate that will lead to change in public policy.

Another possible pursuit for a local church's peace ministry may be to take its church's peace concern before a neighbor congregation. A cross-congregational evangelization and education process is crucial if the church's peace witness is to grow. This means establishing relationships of integrity and understanding which raise the question of the arms race as a matter of faith. A local peace ministry may also want to carry its commitment to denominational gatherings and judicatory meetings.

Who makes up a church's peace ministry? It begins at the

point of church members' interest, commitment, and gifts. Some churches will find it helpful to commission full-time people for the peace ministry just as it does for the pastoral or educational ministries. These full-time people need to be supported by a mission group or committee. Other churches have appointed a task force of part-time people to oversee and carry out their peace ministry.

Indigenous church peace ministries are already serving a vital function in some congregations and are an important goal for others. These ministries can be a significant force in congregational and parish renewal by helping people understand that authentic faith must be rooted in real historical events. Peace ministries can foster renewal by presenting the nuclear threat not simply as a call to political action or merely as an historical crisis, but as an occasion for the renewal of faith in the churches. The churches will never make a costly commitment to peace until there is a renewal of the Spirit in the church's life. The reawakening of faith and peacemaking will go hand in hand.

The church's peace witness will only be theologically and politically viable as the church regains a sense of its vocation as the people of God. The church's life and its ministry are dependent on its prayer, fellowship, pastoral accountability, and nurture. The church's action and witness are intrinsically related to its renewal of authentic worship. A vital part of the peace ministry's task is to serve the local church in bringing about a whole and healthy congregational life.

Renewal does not occur in a vacuum but rather in the midst of the historical issues that impinge on the church's life. No other event or situation can compare with the nuclear arms race in calling for a response of faith. Perhaps it is set before us as a test.

MAKING PEACE:
Questions for Thought and Discussion

1. King speaks of Christian actions at nuclear facilities. Where are the nuclear facilities near you? What kinds of witnesses could you imagine making at one or more of them? How could you involve your church and other Christians in such actions?

2. According to Stoner, why is it both difficult and necessary to speak the truth to the churches about nuclear weapons? What relevance do you see in the experience of Jesus and the prophets in speaking hard words to the religious people and authorities of their times?

3. Collum emphasizes the importance of a citizens' movement to stop the arms race. Why is our action called for, and what are some of the things we can do, as Christians and church members, to participate in an effective freeze movement?

4. In what ways would you affirm or challenge King's statement that "the church's very purpose is to be evidence of Christ's peace to the world"? What are the characteristics of a church that is evidencing Christ's peace? What is your vision for the peace work of the church, and how would you see such a ministry being established and nurtured in your own church?

THE MORAL EQUIVALENT
OF DISARMAMENT:
A Call for Church War Tax Resistance

by John Stoner

Seventy years ago William James wrote that "the war against war is going to be no holiday excursion or camping party." War, said James, has been given the function of "preserving our ideals of hardihood." War is seen as society's most demanding enterprise, and hence its most rewarding effort. Strong character emerges out of struggle, and war institutionalizes the most strenuous form of human struggle.

These arguments, says James, "cannot be met effectively by mere counter-insistency on war's expensiveness and horror. The horror makes the thrill; and when the question is of getting the extremest and supremest out of human nature, talk of expense sounds ignominious."

What is needed, declared James, is a moral equivalent of war. "So long as anti-militarists propose no substitute for war's disciplinary function . . . they fail to realize the full inwardness of the situation."

James proceeded to advocate "a conscription of the whole youthful population for a certain number of years" to go off "to coal and iron mines, to freight trains, to fishing fleets in December, to dishwashing, clothes-washing, and window-washing, to road-building and tunnel-making, to foundries and stoke-holes, and to the frames of skyscrapers." There they would "have paid their blood-tax, done their own part in the immemorial human warfare against nature; they would tread the earth more proudly. . . ."

The idea of the government *conscripting* young people to do necessary work, is, I believe, a fatal flaw in James' proposal in "The Moral Equivalent of War." Such universal conscription would give the government an inordinate amount of control over the fundamental choices of all young people, vastly increase the power of the

THE MORAL EQUIVALENT OF DISARMAMENT

bureaucracy, and undoubtedly provide at the same time a back-handed method of feeding the ranks of the military.

But James has done us an enduring service by raising the issue of moral equivalency. Today the church is called upon to consider a new application of this basic principle.

For some decades now we have been hearing the church call on governments to take steps toward disarmament. And it would be difficult to think of a thing more urgent or more appropriate for churches to say to governments. It is hardly necessary here to give another recitation of the monstrous and unconscionable dimension of the world arms race, culminating in the ever-growing stockpiles of nuclear weapons and the refinement of systems to deliver their carnage.

The church has done part of its duty when it has said that this is wrong. But the time has come to say that the good words of the church have not been, and are not, enough. The risks, the disciplines, the sacrifices, and the steps in good faith which the church has asked of governments in the task of disarmament must now be asked of the church in the obligation of war tax resistance.

It is, at the root, a simple question of integrity. We are praying for peace and paying for war. Setting euphemisms aside, the billions of dollars conscripted by governments for military spending are war taxes, and Christians are paying these taxes. Our bluff has been called.

In all candor it must be suggested that the storm of objection which arises in the church at this idea borrows its thunder and lightning from the premiers, the presidents, the ambassadors, and the generals who make their arguments against disarmament. War tax resistance will be called irresponsible, anarchistic, unrealistic, suicidal, masochistic, naive, futile, negative, and crazy. But when the dust has settled, it will stand as the deceptively simple and painfully obvious Christian response to the world arms race. A score or a hundred other good responses may be added to it. We in the church may rightly be called upon to do more than war tax resistance, but we should not be expected to do less.

Let the church take upon itself the risks of war tax resistance.

For church councils to take the position that the arms race is wrong for governments—and not to commit themselves and call

upon their members to cease paying for the arms race—is patently inconsistent. This is probably a fundamental reason why the church's pleas for disarmament have met with so little positive response. Not even governments can have high regard for people who say one thing and do another.

If governments today are confronted with the question whether they will continue the arms race, churches are confronted with the question whether they will continue to pay for it. As specialists in the matter of stewardship of earth's resources, they have contributed precious little to the most urgent stewardship issue of the 20th century if they go on paying for the arms race. How much longer can the church continue quoting to the government its carefully researched figures on military expenditures and social needs and then, apparently without embarrassment, go on serving up the dollars that fund the berserk priorities?

The arms race would fall flat on its face tomorrow if all of the Christians who lament it would stop paying for it.

It is not simple to stop paying for the arms race as a citizen of the United States, or anywhere else for that matter. If you refuse to pay the portion of your income tax attributable to military spending, the government levies your bank account or wages and extracts the money that way. If your income tax is withheld by your employer, you must devise some means to reduce that withholding, such as claiming a war tax deduction or extra dependents. If, as an employer, you do not withhold an employee's war taxes, you will find yourself in court, as has happened to the Central Committee for Conscientious Objectors.

All of these actions are at some point punishable by fines or imprisonment, and none, in the final analysis, actually prevents the government from getting the money. Nevertheless, it must be said that the church has not tried tax resistance and found it ineffective; it has rather found it difficult and left it untried.

It has considered the risk too great. Individuals fear social pressure, business losses, and government reprisals. Congregations, synods, and church agencies equivocate over their role in collecting war taxes. There is the risk of an undesirable response—contributions may drop off, tax-exempt status may be lost, officers may go to jail. To oppose the vast power of the state by a deliberate act of civil disobedience is not a decision to be made lightly.

It would be inaccurate to give the impression that Christians individually and the church corporately in the U.S. have done nothing in war tax resistance. There have been notable, even heroic, exceptions to the general lethargy. The war tax resistance case of an individual Quaker was recently appealed to the Supreme Court on First Amendment grounds, but the court refused to consider it. A North American conference of the Mennonite Church is grappling with the question of its role in withholding war taxes from the wages of employees.

Among Brethren, Friends, and Mennonites, sometimes called the historic peace churches, there is a rising tide of concern about war taxes. The Catholic Worker movement and other prophetic voices in various denominations have long advocated war tax resistance, but have truly been voices crying in the wilderness. For all our concern about the arms race, we in the churches have done very little to resist paying for it. That has seemed too risky.

But then, of course, disarmament also involves risks. Could there be a moral equivalent of disarmament that did not involve risk? In this matter of the world arms race it is not a question of who can guarantee the desired result, but of who will take the risk for peace.

Let the church take upon itself the discipline of war tax resistance.

Discipline is not a popular word today, but it should be amenable to rehabilitation at least among Christians, who call themselves disciples of Jesus. How quickly does the search for a way turn into the search for an easy way! And how readily do we lay upon others tasks whose disciplines we are not prepared to accept ourselves!

War tax resistance will involve the discipline of interpreting the Scripture and listening to the Spirit. In a day when the Bible is most noteworthy for the extent to which it is ignored in the church, it is an anomaly to see the pious rush to Scripture and join ranks behind Romans 13 when the question of tax resistance is raised. In a day when the authority of the church is disobeyed everywhere with impunity, it is a curiosity to see Christians zealous for the authority of the state. In a day when giving to the church is the last

consideration in family budgeting and impulse rules over law, it is a shock to observe the fanaticism with which Christians insist that Caesar must be given every cent he wants.

As the church has grown in its discernment of what the Bible teaches about slavery and the role of women, so it must grow in its discernment of what the Bible teaches about the place and authority of governments and the payment of taxes.

War tax resistance means accepting the discipline of submission to the lordship of Jesus Christ in the nitty-gritty of history. Call it civil disobedience if you wish, but recognize that in reality it is divine obedience. It is a matter of yielding to a higher sovereignty. Those who speak for a global world order to promote justice in today's world invite nations to yield some of their sovereignty to the higher interests of the whole, and those persons know the obstinacy of nations toward that idea.

It may be that the greatest service the church can do the world today is to raise a clear sign to nation-states that they are not sovereign. War tax resistance might just be a cloud the size of a man's hand announcing to the nations that the reign of God is coming near. It is clear that Christians will not rise to this challenge without accepting difficult and largely unfamiliar disciplines.

But then disarmament also involves disciplines. The idea that one nation can take initiatives to limit its war-making capacities is shocking. To do so would represent a radical break with conventional wisdom. How is it possible to do that without first convincing all the nations that it is a good idea?

Let the church take upon itself the sacrifices of war tax resistance.

It is never altogether clear to me whether Christians who oppose war tax resistance find it too easy a course of action, or too difficult. It is said that refusing to send the tax to the IRS and allowing it to be collected by a bank levy is too easy—a convenient way of deceiving oneself into thinking that one has done something about the arms race.

And it is said that to refuse to pay the tax is too difficult. It is to disobey the government and thereby to bring down upon one's head the whole wrath of the state, society, family, business asso-

ciates, and probably God himself. Moreover, the same person will say both things. Which does he/she believe? In most cases, I think, the second.

The sacrifices involved in war tax resistance are fairly obvious. They may be as small as accepting the scorn which is heaped upon one for using the term "war tax" when the government doesn't identify any tax as a war tax, or as great as serving time in prison. It may be the sacrifice of income or another method of removing oneself from income tax liability. It can be said with some certainty that the sacrifices will increase as the number of war tax resisters increases, because the government will take reprisals against those who challenge its rush to Armageddon.

Yet there is the possibility that the government will get the message and change its spending priorities, or provide a legislative alternative for war tax objectors, or both. In any case, for the foreseeable future war tax resistance will be an action that is taken at some cost to the individual or the church institution with no assured compensation except the knowledge that it is the right thing to do.

But then disarmament also involves sacrifices. The temporary loss of jobs, the fear of weakened defenses, and the scorn of the mighty are not easy hurdles to cross. A moral equivalent will have to involve some sacrifices.

Let the church take upon itself the action of war tax resistance.

The call of Christ is a call to action. It is plain enough that the world cannot afford $400 billion per year for military expenditures even if this were somehow morally defensible. It is plain enough that the dollars which Christians give to the arms race are not available to do Christ's work of peace and justice.

In these circumstances, the first step in a positive direction is to withhold money from the military. If we say that we must wait for this until everybody (and particularly the government) thinks it is a good idea, then we shall wait forever.

Having withheld the money, the church must apply it to the works of peace. What this means is not altogether obvious, but there is reason to believe that a faithful church can steward these resources as wisely as generals and presidents. The dynamic inter-

action between individual Christians and the church in its local and ecumenical forms will help to guide the use of resources withheld from the arms race.

This is a call to individual Christians and the church corporately to make war tax resistance the fundamental expression of their condemnation of the world arms race. Neither the individual nor the corporate body dares hide any longer behind the inaction of the other. The stakes are too high and the choice is too clear for that. We can have no illusions that this call will be readily embraced or easily implemented by the church.

But then we did not think that disarmament would be an easy step for governments to take. The church has an obligation to act upon what it advocates, to deliver a moral equivalent of the disarmament it proposes. If effectiveness is the criterion, it is certainly not obvious that talking about the macro accomplishes more than acting upon the micro.

A single action taken is worth more than a hundred merely discussed. When it comes to heating your home in winter, you will get more help from one friend who saws up a log than from a whole school of mathematicians who calculate the BTUs in a forest. To talk about a worthy goal is no more laudable than to take the first step toward it, and might be less so.

The reasons generally offered for not taking such radical action as tax resistance are distressingly reminiscent of the justifications offered for not resisting Nazism in Germany. It was always a matter of waiting for some new, more obvious proof that the regime was evil, of believing explanations of what was happening when such explanations were couched in religious or semi-religious language, of expecting some person in a position of authority to make the break first, and of hoping that right would ultimately prevail without requiring any personal sacrifice beyond the ordinary.

Few Christians in Germany ever saw these conditions for their own involvement in prophetic resistance fulfilled, and the population drifted slowly into holocaust.

It is not easy to learn from history. We expect more of others that we do of ourselves.

OBLIGATION OF CONSCIENCE
by Raymond Hunthausen

In January, 1982, Hunthausen became the first U.S. bishop to publicly resist paying federal income taxes in response to the government's military practices. He explained the reasons for his action in the following pastoral letter to his people.

As you all know, I have spoken out against the participation of our country in the nuclear arms race because I believe that such participation leads to incalculable harm. Not only does it take us along the path toward nuclear destruction, but it also diverts immense resources from helping the needy. As Vatican II put it, "The arms race is one of the greatest curses on the human race and the harm it inflicts on the poor is more than can be endured."

I believe that as Christians imbued with the spirit of peace-making expressed by the Lord in the Sermon on the Mount, we must find ways to make known our objections to the present concentration on further nuclear arms buildup. Accordingly, after much prayer, thought, and personal struggle, I have decided to withhold 50 percent of my income taxes as a means of protesting our nation's continuing involvement in the race for nuclear arms supremacy.

I am aware that this action will provoke a variety of responses. Many will agree with me and support me as they have done in the past. Other conscientious people will be puzzled, uncomprehending, resentful, and even angry. For the sake of all, I shall clarify what I am attempting and not attempting to do by my tax-withholding action. I do so in the prayerful hope that all continue to discuss this nuclear arms issue in a spirit of mutual openness and charity. How ironic if we as Christians were to discuss this issue of disarmament for peace in a warlike fashion.

I am not attempting to say that there is but one way of dealing with the problem of the arms race and the nuclear holocaust toward which it leads. I recognize the need for a number of different strategies for the promotion of arms reduction. Accordingly, I welcome the diverse efforts of many individuals and groups, including the efforts of some of my fellow bishops, to call attention to the seriousness of this matter and to suggest practical ways of acting with regard to it.

I am not attempting to divide the Christian community. I pray that because of our openness and respect for one another, we can grow together by our concentration on the goal of world peace and the eventual elimination of nuclear arms despite our disagreements over the best way to achieve such goals.

I am not suggesting that all who agree with my peace and disarmament views should imitate my action of income tax withholding. I recognize that some who agree with me in their hearts find it practically impossible to run the risk of withholding taxes because of their obligations to those personally dependent upon them. Moreover, I see little value in imitating what I am doing simply because I am doing it. I prefer that each individual come to his or her own decision on what should be done to meet the nuclear arms challenge.

I am not pointing a finger of accusation at those who disagree with what I plan to do. I would hope, however, that such persons will respect those whose views differ from theirs. No one has answers that are absolutely certain in such complex matters. I am suggesting that we must maintain a continuing and open dialogue.

I am not attacking my country. I love my country. As I said in a previous pastoral letter on this subject (July 2, 1981):

It is true that as a general rule the laws of the state must be obeyed. However, we may peacefully disobey certain laws under serious conditions. There may even be times when disobedience may be an obligation of conscience. Most adults have lived through times and situations where this would apply.

Thus, Christians of the first three centuries disobeyed the laws of the Roman Empire and often went to their deaths because of their stands. They were within their rights. Similarly, in order to call attention to certain injustices, persons like Martin Luther King engaged in demonstrations that broke the laws of the state. The point is that civil law is not an absolute. It is not a god that must be obeyed under any and all conditions. In certain cases where issues of great moral import are at stake, disobedience to a law in a peaceful manner and accompanied by certain safeguards that help preserve respect for the institution of law is not only allowed but may be, as I have said, an obligation of conscience.

I am not encouraging those who wish to avoid paying taxes to use my action as a justification for their own personal gain. I plan to deposit what I withhold in a fund to be used for charitable peaceful purposes. There comes to mind the needs of those workers who will require assistance should they decide to leave their nuclear-war related jobs, the bona fide peace movements, the Academy of Peace and Conflict Resolutions, or programs for the aid of pregnant women who have chosen not to terminate their pregnancies by abortion.

I am saying by my action that in conscience I cannot support or acquiesce in a nuclear arms buildup which I consider a grave moral evil.

I am saying that I see no possible justification for the willingness to employ nuclear weapons capable of destroying humanity as we know it.

I am saying that everyone should think profoundly and pray deeply over the issue of nuclear armaments. My words and my action of tax withholding are meant to awaken those who have come to accept without thinking the continuation of the arms race, to stir even those who disagree with me to find a better path than the one we now follow, to encourage all to put in first place not the production of arms but the production of peace.

I urge all of you to pray and to fast, to study and to discuss, and then to decide what you shall do to combat the evil of the nuclear arms race. I cannot make your decision for you. I can and do challenge you to make a decision.

May God be with you: his joy, his peace, his love.

CHRIST IS RISEN FROM NUCLEAR HOLOCAUST

by James Douglass

On Easter Sunday 1981, I attended a sunrise service at Boron Federal Prison Camp in California's Mojave Desert. The new chapel was filled with prisoners and with visitors to the camp, many from the nearby Edwards Air Force Base community. The evangelical minister who preached the sermon was also from the Air Force community. With his back to a chapel window, where we could see the sun rising from the desert floor, the preacher warmed to the Good News of Christ's resurrection, finally proclaiming, "Brothers and sisters, I don't care if the whole world blows up! Because we believe in Jesus Christ, we are saved!"

I think our brother in the pulpit was preaching not good news but despair in Jesus' name. If we believe deeply enough with a living faith in the resurrection of Jesus Christ, we can be saved from the world's blowing up at all. The power of Christ's resurrection is the power to overturn death, not surrender to a nuclear war whose causes are already in our own lives. Jesus proclaimed that the kingdom of God is at hand, not on the far side of a holocaust accepted in his name. That kingdom with its confirmation in Jesus' resurrection means that God's redeeming presence is possible through the cross in our own history, today through the corporate choice of total nuclear disarmament. If we turn our lives away from a security founded on exploitation and missiles, and choose the cross instead, the kingdom of God can be realized now in inconceivable ways.

In the nuclear age we are at a point where the cross of Christ stands before us again. Two roads or ways leading from Jesus' cross involve different interpretations of what that cross means.

One way of the cross sees Jesus' death and his resurrection from the dead as unique events through which humankind has been saved from sin—yet sin retains so deep a hold over humanity that the global destruction of nuclear war is inevitable. Salvation in Christ parallels the race to nuclear holocaust like two railroad tracks to the

end of history. The two have no contact. God's infinite power of love makes no connection with our history of total self-destruction, except to pull particular individuals out of it. This first way of the cross establishes a hope for humanity beyond history, through the unique power of Jesus' death and resurrection. There is no hope for any new world within history—no hope for any breaking in of the kingdom of God before history has reached a totally destructive end.

A second way of the cross sees Jesus' death and resurrection as a continuing process of the Spirit that involves our own death and resurrection in the nuclear age. This view of the cross as a continuing process opens up our history today to possibilities of justice and peace that would otherwise be inconceivable. By offering up our lives in nonviolent action in obedience to Christ, we are given the power through the process of the cross to stand once again at an earlier crossroads of faith, that possibility of faith which Jesus pointed to when he said:

> Have faith in God. I tell you solemnly, if anyone says to this mountain, "Get up and throw yourself into the sea," with no hesitation in her heart but believing that what she says will happen, it will be done for her. I tell you therefore: everything you ask and pray for, believe that you have it already, and it will be yours. (Mark 11:22–24)

If faith in God can move mountains, it can stop nuclear war and create a just and nuclear-free world. It is not a question of whether such a transformation is possible. It is rather a question of who will have such faith and act on it. Those who see Jesus' cross as a process of the Spirit which has not yet been completed, as a continuing death which needs to be completed for the fullness of the resurrection in history, will build their lives on a faith which can move mountains, stop nuclear war, and create a new world.

In comparing these two ways of the cross, I do not mean to say that a Christian can be a peacemaker only by following the second way. Faithful obedience to a cross of Christ which is seen as taking one beyond history, rather than more deeply into it, should also mean resistance to that global murdering of Christ which is nuclear war. Our Easter sunrise preacher in fidelity to his own faith should have said, "Because we believe in Jesus Christ, we must care about the world's blowing up! Whatever we do to the least of these

through nuclear weapons, we do to Christ himself!"

The difference in the two views of the cross is not necessarily one of specific action—both can involve giving one's life for peace—but of how hopeful that action is seen to be in relation to history. The second view sees history, like Jesus' tomb, as being totally open to the power of God—through the cross. To enter more deeply the darkness of the cross and the tomb means that we can begin to touch through life and death the possible shape of the kingdom of God which is at hand.

The need to resist nuclear genocide takes one to the hardest teaching in the gospel, which is also its most central. Jesus taught that if anyone wanted to become a follower of his, that person had to renounce self and take up the cross. Each of our lives has its own personal way of being called to God, but according to Jesus, all our personal ways have one characteristic in common: the presence of the cross of love. Following Christ means the taking up of that cross. Thus we realize the kingdom of God which is at hand.

The literal meaning of the cross is that it was the means by which the Roman Empire executed its political prisoners. The state imprisoned and tortured its revolutionaries, then placed crosses on their shoulders, to be carried to the site of their own crucifixion. Jesus says that following him means acting in such a way as to bring about naturally one's own execution, and to do so out of love and truth, in obedience to God's will.

For citizens of a nation which is perfecting weapons that can already destroy all life on earth, the meaning of Jesus' teaching of the cross is not obscure. We are invited to act truthfully enough, and lovingly enough, to share in his suffering and death. We are invited to resist nonviolently the murder and suicide of the human family, thereby bringing about and accepting our cross at the hands of the modern state. The depth of the evil, and the depth of love we need to accept to overcome it, are both inconceivable. Through the process of resisting killing and accepting the cross of love, we are also invited to share in the new life of Jesus' resurrection. That double invitation of Jesus, to the cross and the hope that exists through and beyond it, is the very heart of nonviolence.

Peter's effort to repudiate Jesus' teaching, and to substitute a way of Christ without the cross, is rebuked by Jesus: "Get behind me, Satan! Because the way you think is not God's way but man's" (Mark 8:33). There is no way of Christ, no way of discipleship, without the cross. A deepening love of God, of all our sisters and

brothers in God, and a deepening way of discipleship, can expect persecution and execution by the state as a spiritual consequence. To think otherwise is not God's way but man's. And the term "man" is in this case accurate. Jesus renounces that way of men in the world which takes the standpoint of the state, imposer of the cross, rather than the way of Christ, prisoner of the state and bearer of the cross. God's way is the bearing of suffering out of love, giving up power through the cross. Man's way is the imposition of suffering and death, seeking and defending power through the sword.

The summit of this teaching of the cross for Jesus' disciples is given in Mark 8:35: "For anyone who wants to save one's life will lose it; but anyone who loses one's life for my sake, and for the sake of the gospel, will save it."

In the nuclear age, the way we Americans try to save our lives is by aiming tens of thousands of nuclear missiles at the rest of the people in the world. We want to save the American way of life by deterring any challenge to it (from the Third World at least as much as from the Russians), and by striking first with our missiles if and when a challenge is not deterred and becomes a crisis. There is an element of truth in the propaganda claim that our nuclear weapons are made not to be used, though we will certainly use them "when necessary." As Daniel Ellsberg has pointed out, even first-strike nuclear weapons are made primarily to threaten global terror on people whom we wish to control—the de facto political meaning of the propaganda word "deterrence."

Nuclear weapons function in U.S. foreign policy to keep millions of people in our economic empire or "sphere of influence," over against the Soviet Union and other powers. A nuclear-weapons-enforced empire in a world of growing revolution has given us a fortress mentality. We have become Hitler in his last days, now armed in his final bunker with the means of destroying the world. Anyone who wants to save one's life will lose it. Wanting to save the American way of life and our place in it will destroy our lives and all life on earth.

But the meaning of Jesus is that turning that process around, and losing one's life for the sake of God in the human family, will save life. It will save life itself. Losing our lives in the cross of love is the way, given by Jesus, which can save the human family's life on this earth.

We know so little about the meaning of Jesus' resurrection,

and we look for that meaning in the wrong places. Jesus' resurrection pointed to the truth that God's transforming presence is possible through the cross, in this our own history, and in inconceivable ways. But that truth is too much for us. The historical possibilities which Jesus' resurrection opened up have all been put back into the tomb. Christians seem to want a history whose limits are defined and determined by sin rather than by the God of Infinite Love who raised Jesus from death to life—and must be capable of doing the same for us in the nuclear age, were our faith and experience of the cross to go deeply enough.

The greatest power that nuclear weapons have, their power to kill us spiritually, can be taken from them right now by a living faith in Jesus' resurrection and the kingdom of God. Nuclear weapons have the power of spiritual death so long as we despair at overcoming their physical and political power. Nuclear weapons are killing us spiritually because our lives are in effect praying not "thy kingdom come" but "thy holocaust come," as if the will of God were to annihilate life on earth—or as if faith in God were powerless to prevent such annihilation.

The predominant attitude of Christians toward our own history is that Jesus' death and resurrection didn't make any difference. History is thought to be determined by sin, by evil, not by the overcoming of evil with God's love. We Christians have been brainwashed by the various cultures of "man's way" into thinking of love and truth as powerless against the forces of the world, somehow seeing a consistency between a view of love as powerless and a gospel which proclaims the overcoming of death itself through Jesus' resurrection. I think we have to make a choice. Either God *didn't* raise Jesus from the dead, which is consistent with the attitude that we are powerless against the evil and death summarized now in nuclear weapons, or God *did* raise Jesus, in which case God through our faith today can do whatever is necessary in our lives to overcome nuclear war.

The loving, suffering acceptance of our own death through prayer and nonviolent action is a divinely given process which, according to Jesus' teaching, makes a new world possible in utterly unpredictable ways. The kingdom of God is at hand. The way into the kingdom is through the deepening darkness of the cross, where our absolute powerlessness, dependence, and emptiness can give our lives over to the transforming power of God's love. The kingdom of God which is at hand now, a nuclear-free world, will call for many

Christians offering up our lives for peace—dying for peace—in faithful obedience to Jesus' way of the cross.

Taking the cross and the resurrection as openings to a new history would mean seeing nonviolent action such as civil disobedience less as a political tactic with high risks than as a way of life with high hopes. The kingdom of God is at hand. The new reality of a nuclear-free world is possible. That new world can be touched through faithful action. The new reality is no farther away than the possibilities inherent in our own lives, at the point where nonviolent civil disobedience can deliver our lives into the truth of total insecurity. Civil disobedience is a way of prayer into the kingdom.

Thomas Merton once described the way of life of the desert fathers and mothers of the fourth century in terms which can deepen our understanding of nonviolent civil disobedience as a calling into prayer. Merton said that the wisdom of the desert contemplatives consisted in making a "clean break with a conventional, accepted social context in order to swim for one's life into an apparently irrational void." The contemplatives who laid the foundations for Western monasticism saw the need to become outcasts from society in order to lose all preoccupation with a false or limited self and become one with God. The beginning of monasteries as we know them today was this radical commitment to seek God alone in the wilderness, in an abandonment of personal security and self which the world saw as crazy.

We need such craziness (or purity of heart) in the nuclear age. But to follow that contemplative vocation of abandoning one's self to God alone, it is necessary to break open the monastic spirituality of our time. Because prayer is the simple awareness of one's absolute poverty and dependence upon God, we need to pray in a situation and place where that radical poverty of self will come home to us. The place for that in the fourth century was the desert. Today in America, a corresponding place of abandonment and poverty of self is jail. Just as the desert once gave birth to the radical commitment of contemplative prayer, today the metropolitan wilderness of jail can revive that commitment in a transforming way.

In a society where the organized crime of war-making is protected by police and courts, one can become eligible for a prayerful stay in jail simply by making peace—by living out one's faith in the kingdom of God. Many people in the area where I live have made peace with themselves and the world by the simple act of climbing a fence and walking into another desert, the construction site of the

Trident submarine base. They thereby stated in action their refusal to participate any longer in (or condone by silence) the mortal sin of our society, preparing for thermonuclear war. And they abandoned self in a way which reopened the possibilities of prayer in a radically new way, in the experienced freedom of a God of peace and love. So long as we rely on missiles for our security, we are unable to experience the power of God.

The wisdom of the desert, a total abandonment to God, was considered insane by the society of the fourth century. Today that wisdom, or insanity, can be rediscovered by transforming our jails into monasteries—by realizing that our own abandonment to God lies along a contemplative path of peacemaking, struggling for justice, and learning to live with the poor (and our own poverty) in jail.

The kingdom of God is at hand in the nuclear age when we are willing to put our lives in God's hands. One simple way to do that, through nonviolent civil disobedience, is to climb the highest security fences protecting nuclear weapons, so as to pray at the physical sites of the greatest evil in history. Those atrocious places exist through our silence, complicity, and moral cowardice. We need to seek them out, climb their fences, and from those centers of evil pray for God's forgiveness for our having allowed such horrors to come into being. There is no Auschwitz or Buchenwald which could begin to match the future atrocities of a Trident submarine base.

Faith in our nuclear age is an invitation to enter the cross more deeply, as our way into the kingdom of God which is a transformed self and world. There are suggestions in the Gospels that when Jesus received his invitation to the cross, he may have thought he was living at the end of the world. Perhaps he was. Perhaps it was his death and resurrection which reopened history. The spiritual death which nuclear weapons have already worked in our own history can also be transformed into new life and hope. Jesus' death and resurrection today open up the process and possibility of a new humanity through which divine love can transform history into a nuclear-free world. We can live in faith so that Christ in us is risen from nuclear holocaust. Jesus' resurrection and the inconceivable growth of his band of disciples is testimony to the Christian in the nuclear age that for God anything is possible within history, but only through the total gift of our lives.

WHOM DO WE OBEY?
Questions for Thought and Discussion

1. Stoner argues that it's time for the churches to stop paying for war while praying for peace. Do you see the state's demand of taxes for war in conflict with Jesus' call to love your enemies?

2. At what point is a Christian obliged to disobey the laws of the state? What would be the implications of war tax resistance for you and your church?

3. What is the connection between losing one's life for the sake of the gospel, and civil disobedience? Between Jesus' cross and resurrection, and actions of nonviolent resistance?

EPILOGUE:

A Dream
by Jim Wallis

(Sometime in the Future)

The government is worried. It used to be that the churches were satisfied with issuing statements and declarations about world peace. Everyone knew they didn't mean very much; church members were as scared of the Russians as everybody else. Christians, too, wanted to hang on to the style of life they had become accustomed to in this country. They were as glad for the nuclear arsenal as the rest of us, no matter what their church offices in New York and Washington said.

Anyway, their denominational leaders had church money invested in the big weapons companies. They paid their war taxes and fought for power and influence just as hard as all the other lobby groups in Washington, D.C. The only real difference between the church lobbies and the National Rifle Association was that the churches couldn't deliver their constituency.

That was before it all happened. They say it's a revival—just like what happened more than a hundred years ago when a lot of Christians turned against slavery. Whatever it is, it's got the government worried.

Evangelists are springing up all over. They're preaching the gospel and saying that our country's nuclear policy is a sin. A sin, mind you, not merely a social or political problem.

It's idolatry, they say, to put your own nation ahead of the lives of millions of other people. They're going all over the country saying that to turn to Jesus means to turn away from nuclear weapons.

The Christians are no longer happy just giving the government good advice about international cooperation. They say they must first put their own house in order. Pastors are telling people that the Lord wants them to quit supporting the arms race. And the people are quitting.

They're calling it repentance. Engineers, businessmen, and workers have formed groups to pray and study the Bible on the issue of peace. They're telling their employers that they will no

longer make nuclear weapons and that they will quit if their companies continue to do so.

This is presenting quite a problem for management. Many of these Christians are in key positions. Even after they quit or are fired, they keep coming back to talk to the other employees. Evangelism, they call it.

Christian scientists, researchers, and professors are saying that their God-given responsibility is to save lives and to protect the earth, not to destroy creation. They refuse to work on military projects.

Even in the military, Christian soldiers and officers are saying that they won't use nuclear weapons. Most are leaving the military altogether. Many chaplains have been relieved of their duties after giving sermons on the need for peace.

For years, the Pentagon has been honeycombed with prayer groups. But their members never talked or prayed about their work before this. They thought politics should be kept out of prayer. Now they claim that their faith is causing them to re-examine their jobs. Many of the Christians on the inside are beginning to join the protesting Christians on the outside. They are vowing never to return to their former work.

There were always a few here and there who wouldn't pay their war taxes. But now there are thousands of Christians who have decided that taxes for war are not part of what they should render to Caesar. Churches are holding workshops on tax resistance right after the Sunday school hour.

Most startling of all is the way in which Christians are converging on nuclear sites all over the country. They call it "moving the geography of worship and prayer." What better place to confess their faith in the true God, they ask, than at the altars and idols of the false gods?

No nuclear facility, military base, or weapons plant is spared the regular presence of Christians, especially at important dates in the religious calendar, and on August 6 and 9, of course. Whole congregations have come out. They call it their peace ministry.

Many of them have been arrested and charged with illegal entry. The Christians say it helps to make visible what the government wants to keep invisible and to make public what has been hidden from view.

But that's causing problems in the jails. These Christians go

253

on having their Bible studies and prayer meetings inside. Some of them say that's the best place to have them. Other inmates are joining them, and new groups have formed called "Prisoners for Peace." Even some of the guards are involved.

And there's trouble with Christian police who don't want to arrest their fellow Christians. Recently a judge broke down in tears, right in the courtroom. He said he would no longer convict anyone for protesting nuclear weapons. One prosecutor, out West somewhere, has dropped charges against Christians who were praying at a nuclear weapons plant and instead has filed charges against the plant for violating international law by making weapons of total destruction in his county.

Some of the churches have even made contact with Russian churches—bypassing all proper diplomatic channels. They say that Russian Christians are part of the body of Christ too. They claim that their bonds with Christians in Russia are stronger than their loyalty to their own country. Maybe, they say, if U.S. and Russian Christians began to act like brothers and sisters, their governments might wake up.

Finally, they have told the government that it must stop the arms race. Just stop, they say. They vow to withhold all political support from any public official who won't promise to do that.

This has all happened because the Christians have the idea that their faith is tied up in this nuclear thing. It was a lot easier when they regarded nuclear war as a political issue, gave it to a committee, and had educational seminars on it. Now they worship about it, pray over it, and act like their faith is at stake in it all. They say that to follow Jesus is to be a peacemaker. The idea is spreading. And the government is worried.

A COVENANT AND A DREAM:
Question for Thought and Discussion

1. What would it take for Wallis' dream to become a reality for you, your family, your church, and this nation?

Now that you have finished *Waging Peace,* flip back to the New Abolitionist Covenant. The Covenant has already been used by thousands of people. As a follow-up to *Waging Peace,* it is an excellent basis for further reflection and action. Make this covenant yourself and join the New Abolitionist Movement.

GLOSSARY

ABM Treaty: the 1971 treaty (with its 1974 protocol) which limited the U.S. and USSR to one ABM *deployment* area each; due to the inviability of anti-ballistic missiles, the U.S. dismantled its one site.

A-bomb: atomic bomb; uses the energy released with the splitting of the atom, or *fission.*

air-burst: the explosion of a nuclear weapon thousands of feet above the ground to maximize the area of *blast destruction;* both the Hiroshima and Nagasaki blasts were air-bursts.

anti-ballistic missile (ABM): a defensive missile intended to intercept incoming *warheads.*

anti-submarine warfare (ASW): the use of nuclear and conventional weapons to seek and destroy the opponent's submarines; an essential component of a first-strike strategy since effective ASW would remove the opponent's ability to retaliate (see *disarming first strike*).

ballistic missile: a missile that, after propulsion force is ended, continues to its target without relying on wings or other aerodynamic surfaces to produce lift (as opposed to *cruise missile*).

blast destruction: the damage caused by the intense pressure wave generated by an explosion.

circular error probability (CEP): a measure of the accuracy of a weapon system; the radius of a circle within which half of the warheads are expected to fall.

civil defense: programs intended to protect civilians in the event of an enemy attack. In the past, emphasis was on fallout shelters; recent administration plans have stressed evacuation.

conventional weapons: non-nuclear weapons. With the development of increasingly lethal weapons such as napalm, chemical and biological weapons, anti-personnel cluster bombs, and other extremely explosive devices, many feel the gap between the horror of nuclear weapons and conventional weapons is diminishing.

conversion: the process of switching industry from military to civilian production and employment.

cost-plus contracts: most military contracts are now on a cost-plus basis; contractors are paid whatever it costs to produce plus a guaranteed amount for profit.

counterforce (countervailing): official U.S. government nuclear strategy whereby attack missiles are aimed at opponent's military emplacements; essentially a first-strike policy since, if fired second, the missiles would strike opponent's empty missile silos (see *pre-emptive strike; Presidential directive 59*).

cruise missile: a small, pilotless, jet-powered aircraft that flies underneath radar coverage at extremely low altitudes; based on the same concept as German buzz-bombs of World War II, the latest versions are extremely accurate and may be launched from airplanes, trucks, surface ships, and submerged submarines.

Cuban Missile Crisis: two weeks of extreme tension in October 1962, when

President John Kennedy threatened to use nuclear weapons in response to a Soviet attempt to place nuclear weapons in Cuba. The crisis was averted when Soviet Premier Nikita Khruschev backed down from his decision to place the missiles; USSR Premier Leonid Brezhnev has referred to the forthcoming placement of U.S. Pershing 2 missiles in Europe as the "Cuban Missile Crisis in reverse" (see *NATO "Modernization" Decision*).

deployment: officially refers to the transfer of nuclear weapons from the Department of Energy to the Department of Defense; in common usage it means the placing of weapons in a ready-to-use posture.

disarming first strike: a surprise attack on opponent's missile silos, bomber bases, and ballistic-missile submarines that would theoretically prevent retaliation; in reality, this would be impossible as submarines at sea are virtually invulnerable and destruction of the opponent's total land- and air-based arsenal could not be guaranteed (see *anti-submarine warfare; counterforce*).

firestorm: in the wake of an atomic blast, massive fires would generate inrushing winds that would further intensify the flames and create a rolling sea of fire.

fission: the splitting of the nucleus of an atom, which releases the large amounts of energy that bind the atom together.

fissionable material: the fuel for nuclear weapons (see *uranium, plutonium*).

fission bomb: atomic bomb (see *fission*).

fusion: the process whereby the nuclei of light elements combine to form the nucleus of a heavier element, releasing tremendous amounts of energy.

fusion bomb: hydrogen bomb (see *fusion*).

ground-burst: a nuclear weapon exploded at ground level; the debris of the blast would be thrown into the air and would settle back down as lethal radioactive fallout.

ground zero: the point on the surface of the earth directly below the center of a nuclear explosion.

hair-trigger: likely to be set off by the slightest disturbance; on a hunting rifle, a hair-trigger allows for instant firing upon the slightest pressure from the trigger-finger.

hardened missile silo: a missile silo "protected" with steel-reinforced concrete or layers of earth; no hardening would protect against a direct strike with a nuclear weapon.

H-bomb: hydrogen bomb; triggered by a fission reaction, the hydrogen bomb is the release of energy from the *fusion* of atoms.

Intercontinental Ballistic Missile (ICBM): a *ballistic missile* with a range of more than 3,000 miles.

kiloton: having the equivalent explosive power of 1,000 tons of TNT. (Note: the largest *conventional weapon* regularly used in World War II, the "blockbuster," had the explosive power of about one ton of TNT.)

launch on warning: a strategic weapons policy stating that a nation will launch its nuclear weapons at the first warning of an enemy attack so as not to have its weapons destroyed in their silos (see *hair trigger*).

lethality: a product of the accuracy and explosive yield of a nuclear weap-

on; indicates the probability of destroying a hardened target.

limited nuclear war: the concept that nuclear weapons could be used in a battlefield situation without the escalation to larger yield or to strategic weapons; sometimes used to refer to using a portion of available nuclear weapons to strike against military targets in opponent's homeland.

Maneuvering Reentry Vehicle (MARV): a *reentry vehicle* capable of performing preplanned maneuvers as it approaches its target.

Mark 12-A Reentry Vehicle: called "the most heinous weapon ever invented" by Congressman Ron Dellums because of its accuracy and explosive power, the Mark 12-A has been deployed on Minuteman III missiles and will likely be the *reentry vehicle* for the MX missile.

megaton: having the equivalent explosive power of one million tons of TNT.

military-industrial complex: a phrase coined by President Dwight Eisenhower to refer to the close relationship between the U.S. military and defense contractors; Eisenhower warned of the "undue influence" of this self-perpetuating association.

missile silo: the "launching pad" for an intercontinental missile; usually buried in the earth and *"hardened"* with steel-reinforced concrete.

Multiple Independently Targetable Reentry Vehicle (MIRV): two or more warheads carried by a single missile, each one capable of attacking a different target.

Mutual Assured Destruction (MAD) (deterrence, balance of terror, massive retaliation): a phrase coined by Defense Secretary Robert McNamara in 1965 to refer to the nuclear strategy based on threatening "massive and unacceptable retaliation" against an opponent if the opponent strikes first; McNamara stated that 400 megatons would be adequate deterrent (see *overkill*); in 1980 MAD was officially replaced with a *counterforce* policy (see *Presidential Directive 59*).

NATO (North Atlantic Treaty Organization): military and political alliance of 15 U.S. and European allies; formed 1949 (see *Warsaw Pact*).

NATO "Modernization" Decision: the 1979 decision by NATO defense ministers to place U.S. Pershing 2 missiles and *cruise missiles* in Europe (see *Cuban Missile Crisis*).

Navstar Global Positioning System: a network of 24 satellites that will allow pinpoint accuracy for U.S. weapons by providing precise navigation and velocity information; to be launched by space shuttle during the 1980s. (Note: the primary purpose of the Space Shuttle is military; the FY 1983 Military Posture Statement of the Joint Chiefs states that "DOD [Department of Defense] planning includes the transition of all national security spacecraft launches to the shuttle by FY 1987.")

Non-Proliferation Treaty (NPT): signed in 1968 and since ratified by more than 100 nations; the nuclear nations (including the U.S. and USSR) pledged to "pursue negotiations in good faith" for the "cessation of nuclear arms race at an early date," and the non-nuclear nations promised not to produce or purchase nuclear weapons.

nuclear fuel cycle: consists of uranium mining and milling, fuel processing, fabrication, reprocessing, waste management and storage, and transporta-

tion; each stage is an essential and dangerous component in the production of a nuclear weapon.

nuclear strategy: operational policy governing the production, deployment, and use of nuclear weapons.

overkill: the ability to destroy a target more than once (e.g., the nuclear weapons of the U.S. and USSR could destroy every city in the world seven times over).

parity (essential equivalence): approximate equality between two sides in overall strategic capabilities despite differences in the types of weapons possessed by each side.

plutonium: a human-made radioactive element, the primary fuel for most fission (atomic) bombs and the "trigger" or detonator in fusion (hydrogen) bombs; produced by fission in a nuclear reactor.

pre-emptive strike: an attack on opponent's missile silos, command centers, and other military sites in order to pre-empt attack by the opponent (see *counterforce; disarming first strike*).

Presidential Directive 59 (P.D. 59): the August 6, 1980 declaration by President Jimmy Carter that U.S. targeting strategy had changed from aiming at Soviet cities to aiming at missile silos and other military targets in the Soviet Union; seen as a provocative policy since aiming at missile silos necessitates striking them before opponent's missiles are fired, and thus constitutes a "first-strike" policy (see *counterforce*).

proliferation, horizontal: the acquisition of nuclear capability by non-nuclear nations.

proliferation, vertical: increase in the nuclear arsenals of the superpowers (i.e., the U.S. and USSR).

radiation sickness: the disease caused by exposure to excessive amounts of radioactive material; symptoms include hair loss, bleeding from gums and through skin, diarrhea and vomiting, and death within weeks from decay of internal organs.

reentry vehicle: the part of a missile that reenters the atmosphere on the last part of its flight.

reliability (of nuclear weapons): likelihood that weapons will perform as planned; e.g., the reliability of U.S. Minuteman III is 80 percent; the reliability of Soviet SS-18 is 75 percent.

Strategic Arms Limitation Talks (SALT): negotiating sessions between the U.S. and USSR from 1969 to 1979; SALT I resulted in the *ABM Treaty;* SALT II, still unratified by the U.S. Senate, provides that each side increase its arsenal of strategic warheads by more than 4,000 and places no limit on tactical nuclear weapons or on accuracy improvements.

Strategic Arms Reduction Talks (START): the acronym the Reagan administration has chosen for the next stage in strategic arms talks; contrary to the name, the administration has promised continued buildup of U.S. nuclear forces so as to negotiate from a "position of strength."

strategic nuclear weapons: designed to attack targets in the enemy's homeland; the strategic triad of both the U.S. and USSR consists of land-based ICBMs, airborne intercontinental bombers and cruise missiles, and submarine-launched ballistic missiles.

submarine-launched ballistic missiles (SLBM): a ballistic missile launched from a submarine.

tactical nuclear weapons: as opposed to *strategic* weapons, refers to short-range battlefield weapons; the U.S. has more than 6,000 tactical nuclear weapons in Europe today.

targeted: aimed at.

theatre nuclear weapons: refers to mid-range nuclear weapons, with a range of from 200 to 3,000 miles; with the deployment of U.S. mid-range nuclear weapons within striking distance of the heartland of the Soviet Union, the distinction between theatre and strategic weapons becomes academic.

uranium: the heaviest natural element; the basic raw material of nuclear power; used as fuel in the Hiroshima atomic bomb.

uranium enrichment: the process of refining natural uranium to increase the amount of U-235, the fissionable isotope; weapons-grade uranium has about 90 percent U-235 (as opposed to 3 percent in power reactor fuel).

warhead: the part of the weapon that contains the explosive device.

Warsaw Pact: military and civilian alliance formed by the Soviet Union and six Eastern European nations in 1955 in response to the establishment of *NATO*.

APPENDIX A:
Resources for Action

GROUPS FOR FURTHER INVOLVEMENT

The following list of national peace groups is not exhaustive; rather, it offers opportunities for further exposure to these issues and involvement in them. Listing regional and local groups would be an impossible task—there are countless anti-nuclear groups in the country, varying greatly in emphasis and action. Many of these national organizations have information concerning local and regional groups with which they are associated.

National Organizations

American Friends Service Committee. An organization with regional offices, which emphasizes education and nonviolent action against war and militarism. 1501 Cherry St., Philadelphia, PA 19102.
Atlantic Life Community. A network of communities which, along with other groups around the country, work against nuclear weapons through nonviolent direct action. 1933 Park Ave., Baltimore, MD 21217.
Clergy and Laity Concerned. An interfaith organization that works for peace and justice. 198 Broadway, New York, NY 10038.
Fellowship of Reconciliation. A religious pacifist organization committed to nonviolent methods of social change. Box 271, Nyack, NY 10960.
Mennonite Central Committee. This denomination's center for education and coordination of its peace witness. 21 South 12th St., Akron, PA 17501.
Mobilization for Survival. A coalition of groups that emphasize grassroots organization and action. 48 St. Marks Place, New York, NY 10003.
New Call to Peacemaking. A renewal movement within the historic peace churches (Mennonite, Brethren, and Quaker), committed to deepening their peace witness. Box 235, Plainfield, IN 46168.
Nuclear Weapons Facilities Task Force. A network of groups around the country that organize locally to convert nuclear weapons facilities to socially useful production. FOR/AFSC, 1428 Lafayette St., Denver, CO 80218.
Nuclear Weapons Freeze Campaign. The national headquarters for this locally based campaign for a bilateral nuclear weapons freeze provides information and resources to local and regional groups as well as members of Congress, the press, and national organizations. National Clearinghouse, 4144 Lindell Blvd., Suite 404, St. Louis, MO 63108.
Pacific Life Community. A network of West Coast communities which, with other groups around the country, works against nuclear weapons through nonviolent direct action. 2118 8th St., Berkeley, CA 94710.
Pax Christi. The international Catholic peace organization. 3000 N. Mango, Chicago, IL 60634.
Physicians for Social Responsibility. An organization of physicians, medical students, and other health professionals whose purpose is to provide

information to assess the hazards of nuclear power and weaponry. P.O. Box 144, Waterton, MA 02172.

Prolifers for Survival. A pro-life organization working for nuclear disarmament. 345 East 9th St., Erie, PA 16503.

Religious Task Force/MFS. A group working with an interfaith constituency for a religious witness against the arms race. 85 South Oxford St., Brooklyn, NY 11217.

Riverside Church Disarmament Program. Provides speakers and resources for local disarmament education. 490 Riverside Dr., New York, NY 10027.

SANE. Mobilizes grassroots support for peace and disarmament while emphasizing planned economic conversion. 514 C St., NE, Washington, D.C. 20002.

Sojourners. An evangelical and ecumenical Christian community which, through its Peace Ministry, offers resources and help to those who are raising peace issues as central to the church's life (see the Publications section of this appendix). 1309 L St., NW, Washington, D.C. 20005.

War Resisters League. A pacifist organization whose members oppose armaments, conscription, and war. 339 Lafayette St., New York, NY 10012.

Women's International League for Peace and Freedom. An international organization that emphasizes nonviolent solutions to domestic and international problems. 1213 Race St., Philadelphia, PA 19107.

Women Strike for Peace. An organization composed of women dedicated to achieving international disarmament under effective controls. 145 South 13th St., Philadelphia, PA 19107.

World Peacemakers. A mission group of the Church of the Savior that seeks to establish local groups both in their own churches and across denominational lines. 2852 Ontario Rd., NW, Washington, D.C. 20009.

Research and Lobby Groups

Center of Concern. An independent, interdisciplinary group engaged in social analysis, religious reflection, and public education around questions of social justice. 3700 13th St., NE, Washington, D.C. 20017.

Center for Theology and Public Policy. A study and research group that relates current political issues to Christian theology. 4400 Massachusetts Ave., NW, Washington, D.C. 20016.

Center for Defense Information. A research and educational outreach organization that supports a strong defense but opposes excessive expenditures of forces. Capitol Gallery West, Suite 303, 600 Maryland Ave., SW, Washington, D.C. 20024.

Center on Law and Pacifism. Provides advice and materials for war tax resisters. P.O. Box 1584, Colorado Springs, CO 80901.

Central Committee for Conscientious Objectors. Provides information and support for conscientious objectors and non-registrants, including legal advice and material. P.O. Box 15796, Philadelphia, PA 19103.

Coalition for a New Foreign and Military Policy. A coalition whose Washington-based office researches, lobbies, and produces materials on disarma-

ment and human rights issues. 120 Maryland Ave., NE, Washington, D.C. 20002.

Council for a Livable World. A public interest group that lobbies on arms control and military budget issues. 100 Maryland Ave., NE, Washington, D.C. 20002.

Council on Economic Priorities. A research organization that provides information about dependency on defense spending and about conversion. 84 Fifth Ave., New York, NY 10011.

Federation of American Scientists. An organization of scientists that does research and education on issues including nuclear arms control. 307 Massachusetts Ave., NE, Washington, D.C. 20002.

Friends Committee on National Legislation. A lobby/educational outreach group that seeks to influence policy-makers on a broad range of foreign and domestic issues. 245 Second St., NE, Washington, D.C. 20002.

Institute for Defense and Disarmament Studies. A research and public education center studying the nature and purposes of military forces. 251 Harvard St., Brookline, MA 02146.

Institute for Policy Studies. A research and public education organization concerned with international issues. 1901 Q St., NW, Washington, D.C. 20009.

Institute for World Order. A group that does research and education toward establishing practical steps to abolish war as an acceptable institution. 777 United Nations Plaza, New York, NY 10017.

NARMIC (National Action/Research on the Military Industrial Complex). A research and public education group on the defense industry. 1501 Cherry St., Philadelphia, PA 19102.

National Interreligious Service Board for Conscientious Objectors. Counsels and researches for the benefit of COs as well as acts as a liaison to the Selective Service. 550 Washington Building, 15th and New York Ave., NW, Washington, D.C. 20005.

Network. Catholic lobby group on social justice and peace issues. 806 Rhode Island Ave., NE, Washington, D.C. 20018.

Nuclear Information and Resource Service. A network center and a national clearinghouse for those concerned with nuclear issues; NIRS maintains lists of antinuclear groups. 1536 16th St., NW, Washington, D.C. 20036.

Union of Concerned Scientists. Runs public education programs on health and safety issues related to nuclear energy and weapons. 1384 Massachusetts Ave., Cambridge, MA 02238.

Local Groups

You may be able to be referred to other groups in your geographical area by writing to the following offices.

- Denominational committees and task forces on peace issues: write to your church's national office.
- Denominational peace fellowships: write to the Fellowship of Reconciliation, Box 271, Nyack, NY 10960.

• Catholic Worker houses in your area: write *The Catholic Worker*, 36 E. First St., New York, NY 10003.

• Local offices of the American Friends Service Committee, Clergy and Laity Concerned, Fellowship of Reconciliation, Mobilization for Survival, Pax Christi, War Resisters League, and World Peacemakers: write to the national offices listed under National Organizations and Research and Lobby Groups.

• Local and statewide campaigns for a bilateral nuclear weapons freeze: write the Nuclear Weapons Freeze Campaign, National Clearinghouse, 4144 Lindell Blvd., Suite 404, St. Louis, MO 63108.

• Local campaigns against specific nuclear weapons facilities: write to the Nuclear Weapons Facilities Task Force, FOR/ASC, 1428 Lafayette St., Denver, CO 80218.

• Churches, communities, local groups and fellowships working in peace issues: write to Sojourners Peace Ministry, 1309 L St., NW, Washington, D.C. 20005.

Professional Groups

In the past year, over half a dozen new constituency groups that focus exclusively on preventing nuclear war have sprung up in the Boston area. Some are local in scope, others hope to establish chapters around the country.

Business Alert to Nuclear War, Box 7, Belmont, MA 02178.
Physicians for Social Responsibility, 639 Massachusetts Ave., Cambridge, MA 02139.
Lawyers' Alliance for Nuclear Arms Control, P.O. Box 9171, Boston, MA 02114.
Nurses Alliance for the Prevention of Nuclear War, c/o Elizabeth Johnson, 48 Addington Rd., Brookline, MA 02146.
Educators for Social Responsibility, c/o Bobbi Snow, ESR, Box 1041, Brookline Village, MA 02147.
Student Network for Nuclear Disarmament, c/o the Freeze Clearinghouse or Roseria Solerno, Boston College, McElroy 215, Chestnut Hill, MA 02167.
High-Technology Professionals for Peace, c/o Warren Davis, Hi-Tech Professionals for Peace, 2161 Massachusetts Ave., Cambridge, MA 02140.
Artists for Survival, c/o Mitchell Kamen, Artists West, 144 Moody Street, Waltham, MA 02154.

APPENDIX B:

The Canadian Churches Respond to Militarism

by Ernest Regehr

No recent event has dramatized Canadian complicity in the international arms race as clearly as the news that Canada is in the process of arranging for U.S. cruise missiles to be tested in Canada. Another dimension of Canadian complicity with the cruise was already well known, and Canadian churches had been active in varying degrees in opposing the production of components for the missile's electronic guidance system in a plant near Toronto. The news of plans for testing the missile, however, came just as a Committee of the House of Commons was completing public hearings on appropriate Canadian policies for the Second UN Special Session on Disarmament. A particular item for review by this committee was the 1978 proposal of Prime Minister Trudeau that the arms race be suffocated by, among other things, banning the flight-testing of new nuclear weapons strategic delivery vehicles.

Representatives of several national church organizations testified before the committee, all of them recommending increased diplomatic efforts in support of this "strategy of suffocation." They and other Canadians felt a special sense of betrayal when it became known, as the result of a U.S. state department leak to an American newspaper, that all along the government was pursuing a policy that blatantly violated its own strategy.

That event brought many Canadian church people out of the closet. Churches in Alberta, a part of the country not known as a hotbed of radicalism, responded quickly. Churches near Cold Lake, Alberta, the site of the proposed testing, moved quickly to organize demonstrations and other means of voicing their displeasure.

The cruise missile highlights the Canadian security dilemma. Since World War II it has been the conventional wisdom that Canada is, on its own, incapable of arranging for its own defense and,

given the political and economic realities of the continent, must rely upon the United States.

While the conventional wisdom holds Canadian security to be inextricably linked to the United States (through NORAD—the North American Aerospace Defense Agreement) and NATO (the North Atlantic Treaty Organization), Canada's own defense preparedness consists almost entirely of providing token contributions to the "common defense" that is represented by these two alliances.

That is where the cruise missile comes in. The most common government rationale for the plan to test the cruise in Canadian airspace is that this is part of our NATO commitment. In fact, of course, there is no formal Canadian commitment to NATO to test weapons of its alliance partners here. In practice, however, Canadian political and military leaders feel a keen sense of obligation. Defense spending in Canada as a percentage of gross national product (though not in absolute terms) has not been high, so Canadian officials are keen to make Canadian territory available as a kind of compensation—British and German forces have been training in Canada for some time.

Many within the churches, however, see the matter rather differently. In the first place, they see Canadian reliance upon its alliances to be more than shared defense agreements. Through its alliances Canada has essentially forfeited the role of formulating an indigenous national security policy. It has given this task over to the alliance in exchange for a certain level of participation in the production of hardware and weapons systems for the alliance (Canada and the United States also have Defense Production Sharing Arrangements [DPSA] by which the North American defense industry is considered to be a single integrated industry in which Canada functions as a supplier of components according to the specifications handed down by the U.S. defense department). This has meant a *de facto* loss of independence, if not of sovereignty, whereby Canada is implicated not only in alliance cold war politics but specifically in the relentless build-up of nuclear weapons.

There is a strong tradition within Canadian diplomacy of Canada as mediator, peacekeeper, and compromiser, a tradition that reached its zenith in former Prime Minister Lester B. Pearson's efforts to develop the United Nations' peacekeeping function. Canada's role as a peacekeeper may never have been quite so significant as Mr. Pearson's Nobel Prize and Canadian folklore sug-

gest, but it remains a prominent element within Canadian mythology—a myth that becomes increasingly difficult to sustain in the face of alliance politics and defense policies.

Accordingly, a prominent thrust of the Canadian peace movement and of Canadian churches as a force within the movement has been the push for a more independent foreign policy in which Canada is not regarded simply as an addendum to U.S. policies and initiatives but as a creative diplomatic presence from which alternatives to superpower posturing may be forthcoming.

Opposition to the testing of cruise missiles in Canada has become a symbol of this search for a third way (the feeling of betrayal by the Trudeau government is heightened by the fact that it was this same government that a decade ago switched Canada to a nonnuclear role within NATO and, with much fanfare, announced it was pursuing a "third option" in foreign policy—which at the time meant an attempt to distance Canada from U.S. influence).

This year, Good Friday prayers and a vigil outside the gates of the manufacturing plant that builds cruise components attracted 2,000 people—a major crowd by Canadian demonstration standards. Earlier, before the cruise testing issue became public, the Canadian Conference of Catholic Bishops told the House of Commons Standing Committee on External Affairs and National Defence that Canada's record in support of its "strategy of suffocation" "leaves something to be desired. Nuclear weapons are located on Canadian soil (e.g., Commox, British Columbia); U.S. nuclear weapon submarines (e.g., Trident) are permitted to pass freely through Canadian waters. Canadian industries are engaged in manufacturing component parts for nuclear weapon systems (e.g., the cruise missile). And serious questions are being raised about the 'safeguards' involved in the export of Canada's CANDU technology to certain countries (e.g., India, Argentina, South Korea)."

The United Church of Canada is perhaps the most vigorous of Canadian churches in bringing issues of militarism to the attention of its members. The United Church has given particular leadership in the area of human rights, and this work has led naturally to a greater focus on issues of militarism.

Ecumenically, the Canadian churches support an interchurch group under the sponsorship of the Canadian Council of Churches, known as Project Ploughshares. The Project was initiated in the mid-1970s as a project on "militarism and underdevelopment." The

Project is a member of a consultative group that meets twice-yearly with the arms control and disarmament division of the Canadian Department of External Affairs, is associated with the United Nations' Department of Public Information, and is represented on the Bureau of the Non-Governmental Committee on Disarmament at the United Nations in New York.

A special focus of the Project during the past year (and continuing for the next two or three years) has been a proposal to make Canada a Nuclear Weapon Free Zone (NWFZ). The proposal fits squarely into that part of the Canadian foreign policy tradition that seeks the "third option." Canadian foreign policy in the years after World War II has had two major, even though contradictory, preoccupations. One is what historians have called the attempt to negotiate a position of privilege within the American imperium (that is, the search for a special status within the American sphere of influence). The other is the attempt to draw back from the U.S. sphere of influence (that is, the search for the third way).

The NORAD alliance and the DPSA are clearly a part of that first focus, the search for special status from a position squarely within the "empire." Canadian membership in NATO was originally conceived as a way of developing closer ties with Europe and therefore reducing American influence over Canadian foreign and defense policies. It didn't work out quite that way, NATO having become a prominent tool of American foreign policy and Canada rarely publicly disagreeing with U.S. NATO policies.

The proposal to make Canada a NWFZ is a proposal to develop alternative diplomatic opportunities for Canada. The proposal calls for the elimination of nuclear weapons from Canadian territory (Canadian fighter aircraft assigned to NORAD now carry air-to-air nuclear missiles; however, the Government is already committed to getting rid of these by the mid-1980s); no transit of nuclear weapons through Canadian territory; no Canadian support systems for nuclear weapons (this would eliminate Canadian participation in the operation of communications and other facilities for U.S. nuclear weapons systems); and no Canadian production of components for nuclear weapons (in addition to the cruise, Canadian firms supply components for the Trident system, the Lance missile, and various nuclear-weapons-carrying aircraft).

Canada's current involvements are viewed by the proponents of the NWFZ as compromising Canadian diplomacy. In the case of

the deployment of cruise missiles in Europe, for example, there is little possibility of Canada taking an objective look at the security issues involved as long as Canadian industry is being encouraged to participate in the production of components for the cruise. In fact, while the Department of External Affairs was considering its position on the cruise in Europe, the Canadian Department of Industry, Trade and Commerce was assisting a Canadian firm, Litton Systems (Canada), in acquiring a contract for cruise navigational components. Under its industrial grants programs, the Department of Industry, Trade and Commerce provided the company with a grant of $26.4 million and an interest-free loan of $22.5 million specifically for the cruise work. Contracts actually to be awarded to the Canadian company depend upon extensive deployment of the missile. To date, contracts worth $110 million have been signed. Clearly, if the Government wishes to make its $48.9 million a responsible investment it will be promoting deployment of the cruise in order to win maximum orders for Canadian industry.

Similarly, Canada is being encouraged to participate in an internationally controlled space-based surveillance system to monitor nuclear arsenals, verify reduction agreements, and help to create an international climate of strategic stability and increased confidence. It is doubtful whether Canada could play a constructive role in such an international venture as long as it continues to assist one of the sides in the nuclear confrontation in the build-up of its arsenal.

Another area of concern for the churches is Canada's increasing volume of exports of military commodities to the United States, other NATO partners, and to the third world. This is linked to the integration of Canada's defense industry with that of the United States, which is itself simply another expression of the overall Canadian predicament. The Canadian economy is dominated by the United States, and the two nations share a number of political interests. While this unquestionably works to Canada's benefit in many ways, it nevertheless poses a constant and, now, increasing threat to Canadian independence. Canadian military sales illustrate the point.

For many Canadians, the current arms boom, generated by the policies of the present U.S. administration, spells prosperity. In Toronto the chairman of an auto parts and defense equipment manufacturer told a group of financial analysts that he expects defense

sales to restore the firm's declining growth rate and that defense orders will increase from twenty-five percent of revenue to as high as fifty percent. "We feel," he said last year, "that right now we're seeing the beginning of an enormous capital spending on military hardware, especially with the election of Ronald Reagan."

A front-page story in the Canadian *Financial Post* proclaimed that "defence firms eye US moves," and then went on to describe the efforts of Canadian government officials to have President Reagan "reaffirm" the Canada/U.S. Defense Production Sharing Arrangement (DPSA). A financial analyst assured investors that increased defense spending would enhance the profitability of a Canadian electronics firm. He added that military spending looks "encouraging" at least until the middle of the decade.

Canadian firms are anxious to cash in on the American arms boom, but the Canadian churches, quite apart from serious moral compunction, offer compelling political and economic reasons why the arms boom is not an unmitigated benefit to Canada. In particular, the integration of the Canadian industry with that of the United States through the DPSA includes a deal whereby the military trade across the border must be kept in rough balance—in other words, Canada must buy as much military equipment from the United States as it sells. Hence, as Canadian sales to the United States increase in "boom" years (that happened during the Vietnam war and is now happening again), increased Canadian purchases from the United States must inevitably follow. This places artificial pressure on Canada's military equipment budget and, particularly, presupposes that Canada will buy U.S. equipment when it does go shopping for new equipment. This, in turn, has direct implications for Canadian policy. It is increasingly recognized that military equipment has strategic assumptions built into it. In other words, the more Canada relies upon U.S. military equipment, the more it tends to see the world, and strategic threats, through the lens of its U.S. equipment.

The Canadian response to militarism is not easily separated from the recurring issue of Canadian independence on a continent dominated by a superpower. Canadians have never been certain whether it is more appropriate to speak of the Finlandization of Canada or the Canadization of Finland, and it is in the matter of national security that Canada/U.S. integration is perhaps the most advanced.

A broad spectrum of Canadian churches, from the historic peace churches to the Roman Catholic and mainline Protestant churches, have come together in an ecumenical setting to bring the issues of militarism (and all that they imply) to the attention of the Canadian people. Obviously, such a gathering includes a wide range of concerns and perspectives, not all of which are critical of current Canadian policy, but developments within the past few months have established these issues firmly near the top of the contemporary church agenda.

Canadian Resources for Action

Canadian Catholic Organization for Development and Peace. An organization within the Catholic Church working for education on militarism and development within third world countries. 67 Bond St., Toronto, Ontario.

Canadian Friends Service Committee. An organization within the Quaker Church committed to peace education. 60 Lowther Ave., Toronto, Ontario.

Christian Movement for Peace. An international organization working to raise people's awareness of social injustices. 427 Bloors St. West, Toronto, Ontario, M5S 1X7.

Cruise Missile Conversion Project. An organization working to raise the awareness of and halt Canadian complicity in the development of cruise missiles. P.O. Box 5676, Station A, Toronto, Ontario.

Edmontonians for a Non-Nuclear Future. A local group working to promote peace and disarmament. 8902 120th St., Edmonton, Alberta, T6G 1X5.

Hiroshima-Nagasaki Relived. A group dedicated to keeping alive the memory of the Bomb and to educate people on the dangers of nuclear arms development. 69 Olson Dr., Don Mills, Ontario, M3A 3J4.

Operation Dismantle. An organization whose purpose is to promote a world referendum on disarmament. Box 3887, Station C, Ottawa, Ontario, K1H 4M5.

Peace Network. A regional group working to raise people's awareness of the danger of nuclear power and weaponry. 313 Williston Ave., Newcastle, New Brunswick, E1V 1E4.

Peace Research Institute. An organization that researches the causes of war and publishes reviews of current peace issues as well as abstracts of articles on the peace movement. 25 Dundana Ave., Dundas, Ontario. L9H 4ES.

Peace and Social Concerns Committee. A branch of the Mennonite Central Committee that promotes peace education. 201-1483 Tembina Highway, Winnipeg, Manitoba, R3T 2C8.

Peace Tax Fund Committee. An organization working to promote a peace tax as an alternative to a tax for defense. 1831 Fern St., Victoria, British Columbia, V8R 4X4.

People's Assembly on Canadian Foreign Policy. A coalition of various Canadian peace groups. 109 Wilton St., Toronto, Ontario.

Physicians for Social Responsibility. An organization of health professionals and medical students whose purpose is to provide information to assess the hazards of nuclear power and weaponry. 360 Bloors St. West, Toronto, Ontario, M5S 1X1.

Project Ploughshares. An organization sponsored by the Canadian Council of Churches and supported by various other peace groups whose purpose is education and research militarism. *The Ploughshares Monitor* is a periodical published by this group that provides an analysis of current peace issues, and *The Ploughshares News Report* provides news on the Canadian peace movement.

Institute of Peace and Conflict Studies. Conrad Grebel College, University of Waterloo, Waterloo, Ontario, N2L 3G6.

Regina Group for a Non-Nuclear Society. A local group working to promote peace and disarmament. 2230 Smith St., Regina, Saskatchewan, S4P 2P4.

Science for Peace. An organization of science professionals working to educate and promote issues of peace and disarmament. University of Toronto, Department of Physics, Toronto, Ontario, M5S 1A7.

World Conference on Religions for Peace. An interfaith peace organization. 11 Madison Ave., Toronto, Ontario, M5R 2S2.

World Federalists of Canada. A group lobbying for disarmament and a stronger United Nations. 46 Elgin St., Ottawa, Ontario, K1P 5PG.

Vancouver Coalition for World Disarmament. A local group working to promote peace and disarmament. 1811 West 16th Ave., Vancouver, British Columbia, V6J 2M3.

Voice of Women. A national women's organization, formed in the sixties, working for peace and disarmament. 175 Carlton St., Toronto, Ontario, M5A 2K3.

APPENDIX C:
Map and Legend—Nuclear America

Nuclear America

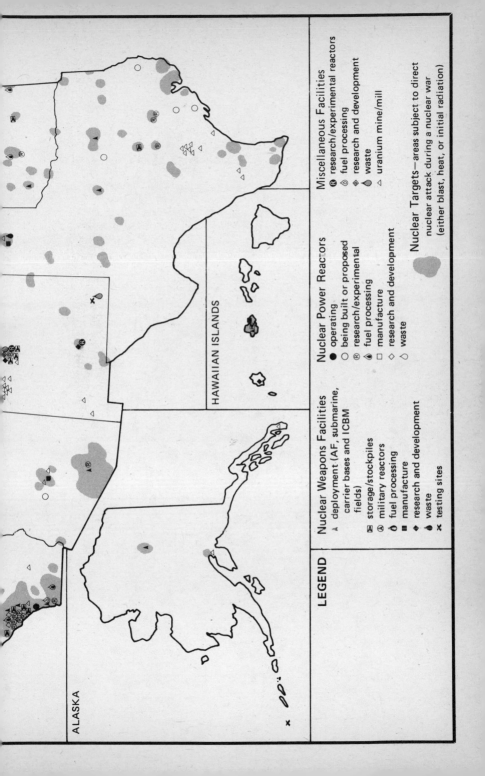

ALASKA

HAWAIIAN ISLANDS

LEGEND

Nuclear Weapons Facilities
⊿ deployment (AF, submarine, carrier bases and ICBM fields)
⊠ storage/stockpiles
Ⓐ military reactors
♦ fuel processing
■ manufacture
♦ research and development
◗ waste
✕ testing sites

Nuclear Power Reactors
● operating
○ being built or proposed
Ⓡ research/experimental
◗ fuel processing
□ manufacture
◇ research and development
◁ waste

Miscellaneous Facilities
Ⓡ research/experimental reactors
◗ fuel processing
✦ research and development
◗ waste
△ uranium mine/mill

Nuclear Targets—areas subject to direct nuclear attack during a nuclear war (either blast, heat, or initial radiation)

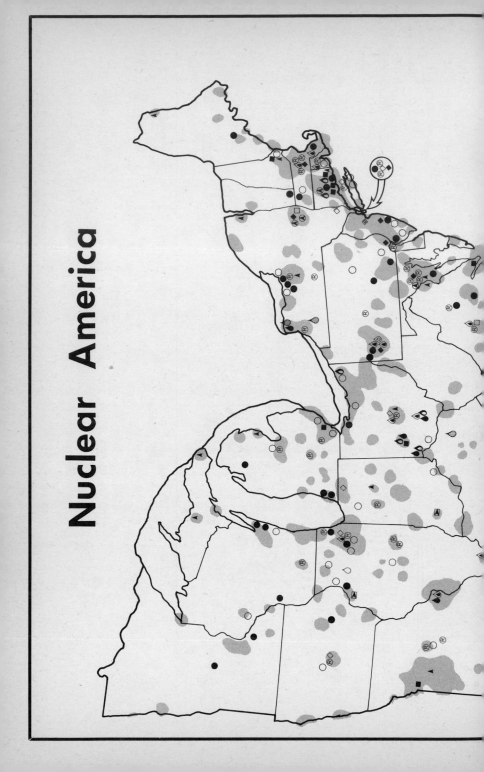

Nuclear America

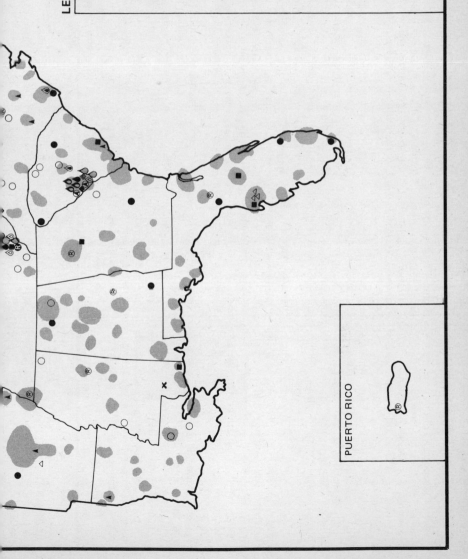

LEGEND

Nuclear Weapons Facilities
- ▲ deployment (AF, submarine, carrier bases and ICBM fields)
- ◮ storage/stockpiles
- ⊛ military reactors
- ◆ fuel processing
- ■ manufacture
- ◆ research and development
- ◆ waste
- ✕ testing sites

Nuclear Power Reactors
- ● operating
- ○ being built or proposed
- ® research/experimental
- ◈ fuel processing
- □ manufacture
- ◇ research and development
- ◇ waste

Miscellaneous Facilities
- ® research/experimental reactors
- ◈ fuel processing
- ◈ research and development
- ◈ waste
- △ uranium mine/mill

Nuclear Targets—areas subject
to direct nuclear attack during
a nuclear war (either blast,
heat or initial radiation)

PUERTO RICO

Map Explanation and Resource List

Nuclear Weapons Facilities. The sources used for identification of nuclear weapons facilities were *The ERDA Facilities: A National Resource for Resolving Energy Problems* (National Technical Information Center of Department of Commerce, Springfield, Virginia, August 1977), "Guide to USAF Bases" (*Air Force Magazine*, May 1977), "The Great American Bomb Machine" (a flier on nuclear warhead production and research facilities, NARMIC, 1501 Cherry Street, Philadelphia, PA 19102, November 1977), *The Defense Monitor* (February 1975 issue contains a map of nuclear weapons and nuclear facilities in the U.S., Washington, D.C.).

Because of the secrecy surrounding nuclear weapons facilities, it is difficult to determine where nuclear weapons are stored and deployed. We assumed that all Strategic Air Command (SAC) bases are equipped with nuclear weapons. Also included are bases which are in direct support of the SAC bases. Where the words "weapons" or "bomb" appear in the list, the word "nuclear" is implied.

Nuclear Power Plants. The source used for identification of nuclear reactors was *Nuclear Reactors Built, Being Built or Planned in the United States as of December 31, 1978* (Technical Information Center of the Department of Energy, Oak Ridge, NY). This list does not contain reactors which have been shut down or the 168 operating or planned reactors in nuclear submarines or carriers. Only one symbol has been used per location. However, the number of reactors at that location is indicated by the number of startup dates listed.

Miscellaneous Facilities. This category services both nuclear weapons and nuclear reactors. Medical and radiopharmaceutical facilities and companies which service reactors or transport and receive radioactive materials are not listed. We do this not because we feel that those items or functions are not dangerous, but because to add them would dilute our focus and organizing efforts on the much more serious categories of weapons and plants. Furthermore, our information on those items is not reliable.

When the word "fuel" is used, the word "nuclear" is implied. Only one symbol has been used per mining and milling location, though there may be several companies operating there. The number of companies is indicated in the listing. The sources used were DoE lists and *The ERDA Facilities*.

Targets. The shaded areas of the map represent potential targets in a nuclear war, as determined by *High Risk Areas for Civil Preparedness Nuclear Defense Planning Purposes* (Defense Civil Preparedness Agency, Washington, DC, November 1977). Potential targets were determined on the bases of key military bases, military support facilities, basic industries, and large populations.

This map is adapted from the second edition (June 1979) map "Nuclear America," prepared by Ed Hedemann, Grace Hedemann, Gale Jackson, Jennifer Kraar, and Jo Moody of War Resisters League, with special thanks to Hope Harle of Clergy and Laity Concerned and Elaine Douglass. Adaptations and typesetting by Econographics, San Francisco, CA.

Reactor Codes:	BW	boiling water	H	homogeneous
	PW	pressurized water	HW	heavy water
	HS	homogeneous solid		

Location	Name/Owner or Contractor	Description (reactor:type, startup)		
▲ Fairfield	Travis AFB	MAC base		
⊛ Hawthorne	Northrop	U-Zr	1963	
⊛ Irvine	U. of California	U-Zr	1969	
⊛ La Jolla	General Atomic	U-Zr	1958,60

Location	Name/Owner or Contractor	Description (reactor:type, startup)
ALABAMA		
● Decatur	Brown's Ferry (TVA)	BW 1974,75,77,77
● Dothan	Joseph Farley (APCo)	PW 1977,80
○ Scottsboro	Bellefonte (TVA)	PW 1981,82

® Tuskegee	Tuskegee Institute	HS	195?

ALASKA

✕ Amchitka	DoE/DoD	underground test site	
△ Anchorage	Seraphin Eng.	uranium mine/mill	
▲ Fairbanks	Eielson AFB	Alaskan Air Command	
△ Ketchikan	Cotter/Kendrick Bay	uranium mine/mill	

ARIZONA

△ Miami	Pinal	uranium mine/mill	
△ Monument Valley		uranium mine/mill	
△ Orphan Lode		uranium mine/mill	
△ Phoenix	JRJ Joint Ventures	uranium mine/mill	
■ Scottsdale	Motorola	nuclear artillery fuze	
△ Tuba City		inactive mill site	
▲ Tucson	Davis-Monthan AFB	TAC base; ICBM field	
® Tucson	U. of Arizona	U-Zr	1958
○ Wintersburg	Palo Verde (APSCo)	PW	1982,84,86,88,90

ARKANSAS

▲ Blytheville	Blytheville AFB	SAC base	
▲ Hot Springs	Union Carbide	uranium mine/mill	
▲ Little Rock	Little Rock AFB	MAC base; ICBM field	
● Russellville	Arkansas Nuc. I (AP&LC)	PW	1974,78

CALIFORNIA

▲ Alameda	Naval Air Station	nuclear carrier dock	
▣ Alameda	US Navy	weapons storage	
△ Anaheim	Holmes & Narver	uranium mine/mill	
▣ Angeles Nat'l Forest	Army 19th Artillery	weapons storage	
®◇ Berkeley	U. of California	U-Zr	1966
◇ Canoga Park	Atomics Int.	fuel processing/R&D	
® Canoga Park	Rockwell/DoE	H	1958
▣ Clay Station	Rancho Seco (SMUD)	PW	1975
▣ Concord	Naval Weapons Depot	weapons storage	
○ Diablo Canyon	Diablo Canyon (PG&E)	PW	1979,79
△ Eagle Meadows		uranium mine/mill	
● Eureka	Humboldt Bay (PG&E)	BW	1963
	U. of Calif./DoE	tank	195?
® Livermore	Lawrence Livermore Lab	nuclear weapons R&D	
◆ Livermore	Lawrence Livermore Lab	low level waste burial	
▲ Lompoc	Vandenberg AFB	SAC base; ICBM field	
▲ Long Beach	US Navy	nuclear sub base	
▣ Los Angeles	US Army	weapons storage	
® Los Angeles	UCLA	graphite/water	1960
■ Mare Island	US Navy	nuclear shipyard	
▲ Marysville	Beale AFB	SAC base; ICBM	
◆ Menlo Park	SRI	weapons research	
◇ Menlo Park	SRI	reactor accident studies	
▲ Merced	Castle AFB	SAC base	
△ Miracle Hot Spr.	Great Lakes Chem.	uranium mine/mill	
◆ Mountain View	Acurex	weapons effects	
▣ Oakland	US Army	poss. weapons storage	
▣ Orange	US Navy	weapons storage	
® Pleasanton	GE Nuclear Test	light water	1957
▲ Riverside	March AFB	SAC base	
▲ Sacramento	Mather AFB	Air Training Command	
● San Clemente	San Onofre (SCE)	PW	1968,81,83
▲ San Diego	US Navy	nuclear sub base	
◈ San Diego	General Atomic	nuclear fuels processing	
□ San Jose	General Electric	reactor components/fuels processing	
® San Luis Obispo	Calif. State Poly.	HS	1973
▲ San Ramon	Aerotest Op.	pool, triga	1965
▣ Santa Barbara	U. of California	H	unknown
▣ Santa Susana	Rockwell	H	1952
◇ Santa Susana	Liq. Metal Eng. Lab (Rockwell/DoE)	breeder reactor (R&D)	
▣ Seal Beach	US Navy	weapons storage	
▣ Solano	US Air Force	weapons storage	
△ Strawberry		uranium mine/mill	
◆ Sunnyvale	Lockheed/Westinghouse/United Tech./ESL	weapons research; Trident Missile (R&D)	
◈ Vallecitos	General Electric	plutonium processing	

Location	Name/Owner or Contractor	Description (reactor:type, startup)
▲ Ventura	US Navy	weapons storage
○ Unsited	Units 1 & 2 (PG&E)	indefinite
COLORADO		
◁ Beadrock	Jones & Hopper	uranium mine/mill
◁ Broomfield	Forward Drilling	uranium mine/mill
◁ Cahone	Laura Mining	uranium mine
◁ Canon City	Cotter/Benson	uranium mine/mill
◁ Cedaredge	Jack Thompson	uranium mine/mill
◁ Clifton	Plateau	uranium mine/mill
▲ Colorado Springs	Ft. Carson (US Army)	weapons storage
◆ Colorado Springs	Kaman Sciences	weapons reliability stdy.
◁ Cory	John Beres	uranium mine
® Denver	US Geological Survey	U-Zr 1969
◁ Denver	2 companies	uranium mine/mill
▲ Denver	Lowry AFB	ICBM
◁ Durango		uranium mine/mill
◁ Englewood	Rampart Explor.	uranium mine/mill
◁ Gateway	5 companies	uranium mine/mill
◁ Golden	2 companies	uranium mine/mill
◁ Grand Junction	7 companies	uranium mine/mill
◁ Gunnison	Homestake Mining	uranium mine/mill
◁ Lakewood	Wyoming Mineral	uranium mine/mill
◁ Marshall Pass		uranium mine/mill
◁ Maybell	Union Carbide	uranium mine/mill
◁ Meeker	Harps & Harry	uranium mine/mill
◁ Montrose	KMSU Mining	uranium mine/mill
◁ Montville	3 companies	uranium mine/mill
® Naturita	8 companies	uranium mine/mill
◁ Norwood	3 companies	uranium mine/mill
◁ Nucla	10 companies	uranium mine/mill
◁ Palisade	Hisel-Miller	uranium mine/mill
◁ Paradox	C & H Mining	uranium mine/mill
● Platteville	Fort St. Vrain (PSC)	high temp. 1978

Location	Name/Owner or Contractor	Description (reactor:type, startup)
▲ Tampa	Farmland Ind.	uranium mine/mill
GEORGIA		
® Atlanta	Georgia Tech.	HS, HW 1957,64
● Baxley	Edwin Hatch (GPCo)	BW 1975,78
○ Waynesboro	Alvin Vogtle (GPCo)	PW 1984,87
■ Winder	Westhold of Georgia	bomb dispenser adapter
HAWAII		
◆ Barking Sands	Sandia Lab/DoE	nuclear weapons R&D
■▲ Pearl Harbor	US Navy	nuclear sub base/shipyd
▲ West Loch	US Navy	weapons storage
IDAHO		
® Idaho Falls	DoE/Idaho National Engineering Lab (INEL)	12 experimental reactors incl. a sodium, fast breeder 1953–78
◈ Idaho Falls	INEL/DoE	reprocessing plant
◈□ Idaho Falls	INEL/DoE	reactor research; five critical assy. facilities
◈ Idaho Falls	INEL/DoE	waste mgmt./burial
◈ Idaho Falls	US Navy	nuclear pwr.training ctr.
▲ Mountain Home	Mountain Home AFB	ICBM field
® Pocatello	Idaho State U.	HS 1967
ILLINOIS		
® Argonne	Argonne Lab/DoE	HW, Therm., tank 1954,57,64
◇ Argonne	Argonne Lab/DoE	reactor R&D
○ Braidwood	Braidwood (Com Ed)	PW 1981,82
○ Byron	Byron (Com Ed)	PW 1981,82
® Champaign	U. of Illinois	U-Zr 1960
○ Clinton	Clinton (IPC)	BW 1982,88
◈ Cordova	QuadCities (Com Ed)	BW 1973,73
● Metropolis	Allied Chemical	fuel processing
● Morris	Dresden (Com Ed)	BW 1960,70,71
◈ Morris	General Electric	fuel processing

△ Redvale	3 companies	uranium mine/mill	
△ Rifle	United Nuclear	uranium mine/mill	
■ Rocky Flats	DoE (Rockwell)	plutonium triggers for weapons	
♦ Rocky Flats	DoE (Rockwell)	waste mgmt./burial	
△ Slick Rock		2 inactive mill sites	
△ Tallahasse Creek	2 companies	uranium mine/mill	
△ Uravan	2 companies	uranium mine/mill	
CONNECTICUT			
▲ Groton	US Navy	nuclear sub base	
■ Groton	DoE/Electric Boat (General Dyn.)	nuclear sub constr.	
● Haddam Neck	Haddam Neck (CYAP)	PW	1968
■ Middletown	Raymond Eng.	locking devices for	
■ Montville	United Nuclear	sub components	
◊ Montville	United Nuclear	fuel processing	
● Waterford	Millstone (NENE)	BW, PW, BW	1971,75,86
◊ Windsor	Knolls Lab/ Combustion Eng.	fuel processing/fab.	
Ⓐ Windsor	DoE/Small Sub.	PW	1959
DELAWARE			
® Newark	U. of Delaware	HS	1958
DISTRICT OF COLUMBIA			
® Washington	Catholic U.	HS	1957
▲ Washington	The White House	sets national nuclear policy	
FLORIDA			
● Florida City	Turkey Point (FPL)	PW	1972,73
● Ft. Pierce	St. Lucie (FPL)	PW	1976,83
® Gainesville	U. of Florida	graphite/water	1959
△ Mulberry	Uranium Recovery	uranium mine/mill	
■ Orlando	Martin Marietta	bomb delivery tech.	
△ Pierce	Farmland Ind.	uranium mine/mill	
■ Pinellas	General Electric	electric comp. for H-bombs	
● Red Level	Crystal River (FPC)	PW	1977

⧈ Rock Island	Rock Island Arsenal (US Army)	weapons storage	
○ Savanna	Carroll Cty. (Com Ed)		1987,88
○ Seneca	LaSalle (Com Ed)	BW	1979,80
◊ Sheffield	Nuc. Fuels Eng.	low level burial	
® Urbana	U. of Illinois	U-Zr	1971
® Zion	Westinghouse	unknown	1972
● Zion	Zion (Com Ed)	PW	1973,74
INDIANA			
⧈ Crane	US Navy	weapons storage	
○ Madison	Marble Hill (PSI)	PW	1982,84
▲ Peru	Grissom AFB	SAC base	
◇ South Bend	DoE/Notre Dame Lab	rad. effects research	
○ Westchester	Bailly (NIPSC)	BW	1984
® West Lafayette	Purdue U.	pool	1962
IOWA			
® Ames	Iowa State U.	graphite/water	1959
◇ Ames	Ames Lab/DoE	reactor research	
● Palo	Duane Arnold (IELPC)	BW	1975
○ Vandelia	Vandelia (IPLC)	PW	indefinite
KANSAS			
○ Burlington	Wolf Creek (KG&E)	PW	1983
® Lawrence	U. of Kansas	pool	1961
® Manhattan	Kansas State U.	U-Zr	1962
▲ Wichita	McConnell AFB	SAC base; ICBM field	
KENTUCKY			
◈ Morehead	Maxcey Flats	waste burial	
◊ Paducah	DoE/Gaseous Diffusion Plant (Union Carbide)	uranium enrichment for weapons and reactors	
◈ Paducah	DoE (Union Carbide)	low level burial	
LOUISIANA			
▲ Bossier City	Barksdale AFB	SAC base	
○ St. Francisville	River Bend (GSU)	BW	1984, indef.
○ Taft	Waterford (LP&L)	PW	1981

Location	Name/Owner or Contractor	Description (reactor:type, startup)
MAINE		
▲ Limestone	Loring AFB	SAC base
● Wiscasset	Maine Yankee (MYAP)	PW 1972
MARYLAND		
® Aberdeen	Aberdeen Pulsed Reactor Facility	bare, fast 1968
◆ Adelphi	Harry Diamond Labs	prompt burst
Ⓐ Bethesda	Armed Forces Radiobiology Research Inst.	bomb fuse design
® College Park	U. of Maryland	tank 1960
® Gaithersburg	Bureau of Standards	HW 1967
● Lusby	Calvert Cliffs (BG&E)	PW 1975,77
MASSACHUSETTS		
Ⓐ Attleboro	Texas Instruments	fuel processing
® Cambridge	MIT	HW 1958
◆ Cambridge	Draper Labs	weapons syst. design
® Lowell	U. of Lowell	pool 1961
○ Montague	Montague (NEU)	BW indef., indef.
● Plymouth	Pilgrim (BE)	PW, BW 1972,85
● Rowe	Yankee (YAEC)	PW 1961
Ⓐ West Concord	Nuc. Metals (Whittaker)	fuel processing
® Worcester	Worcester Polytechnic	pool 1959
MICHIGAN		
® Ann Arbor	U. of Michigan	pool 1957
● Big Rock Point	Big Rock Point (CPC)	BW 1963
● Bridgman	Donald Cook (I&MEC)	PW 1975,78
® East Lansing	Michigan State	U-Zr 1969
▲ Marquette	K.I. Sawyer AFB	SAC base
® Midland	Dow Chemical	U-Zr 1967
○ Midland	Midland (CPCo)	PW 1982,81
○ Newport	Enrico Fermi (DEC)	BW 1980
▲ Oscoda	Wurtsmith AFB	SAC base
▲ Sault Ste. Marie	Kincheloe AFB	SAC base

(NV)

Location	Name/Owner or Contractor	Description (reactor:type, startup)
▲ Las Vegas	Defense Atomic Support	weapons storage
✕ So. Nevada	Nevada Test Site	undergrnd. weapns tests
● So. Nevada	NTS	low level waste storage
NEW HAMPSHIRE		
▲ Portsmouth	Pease AFB	SAC base
■ Portsmouth	US Navy	nuclear shipyard
○ Seabrook	Seabrook (PSCo)	PW 1983,85
NEW JERSEY		
◆ Dover	US Army (Picatinny)	warhead design
○ Forked River	Forked River (JCP&L)	PW 1984
○ Little Egg Inlet	Atlantic (PSE&G)	PW 1988,90
◈ New Brunswick	New Brunswick Lab	plutonium security
● Salem	Salem (PSE&G)	PW 1977,79
○ Salem	Hope Creek (PSE&G)	BW 1984,86
● Toms River	Oyster Creek (JCP&L)	BW 1969
NEW MEXICO		
® Albuquerque	U. of New Mexico	HS 1957
△ Albuquerque	2 companies	uranium mine companies
▲ Albuquerque	Defense Nuclear Agency	weapons stockpile supv.
◆ Albuquerque	DoE/Sandia Labs	weapons development
◈ Albuquerque	DoE/Sandia Labs	waste mgmt./burial
Ⓐ Albuquerque	DoE/Sandia Labs	reactor research
Ⓑ Albuquerque	DoE/Sandia Labs	prompt burst 1967,75
▲ Albuquerque	Kirtland AFB	weapons storage
Ⓑ Albuquerque	DoE/Kirtland AFB	UO_2 BeO 1978
△ Ambrosia Lake	United Nuclear	uranium mine/mill
△ Bluewater	Anaconda	uranium mine/mill
✕ Carlsbad	DoE	underground test site
◈ Carlsbad	DoE (Westinghouse)	poss. waste burial site
△ Cebolleta	Sohio	uranium mill
△ Church Rock	2 companies	uranium mine/mill
✕ Farmington	DoE	underground test site
△ Gallup		uranium mine/mill

MINNESOTA

	Location	Operator	Notes	Date
○	St. Clair County	Greenwood (UEC)	PW	1987,89
■	Sterling Heights	US Army	Army missile plant	
●	South Haven	Palisades (CPC)	PW	1971
●	Monticello	Monticello (NSP)	PW	1971
●	Red Wing	Prarie Island (NSP)	PW	1973,74

MISSISSIPPI

	Location	Operator	Notes	Date
○	Corinth	Yellow Creek (TVA)	PW	1985,86
■	Pascagoula	Ingalls (US Navy)	nuclear shipyard	
●	Port Gibson	Grand Gulf (MP&L)	BW	1981,84
®	State College	Mississippi State U.	H	unknown
✕	Tatum Salt Dome	DoE	underground testing	

MISSOURI

	Location	Operator	Notes	Date
®	Columbia	U. of Missouri	tank	1966
○	Fulton	Callaway (UEC)	PW	1983,87
◈	Hematite	Babcock & Wilcox	fuel processing	
■	Kansas City	Bendix Corp./DoE	electronic parts for nuclear weapons	
▲	Knob Noster	Whiteman AFB	SAC base; ICBM field	
®	Rolla	U. of Missouri	pool	1961
◆	Weldon Springs	DoE	weapons waste dump	

MONTANA

	Location	Operator	Notes	Date
✕	Carter County		poss. underground test.	
▲	Great Falls	Malmstrom AFB	SAC base; ICBM field	

NEBRASKA

	Location	Operator	Notes	Date
●	Brownville	Cooper (NPPD)	BW	1974
●	Fort Calhoun	Ft. Calhoun (OPPD)	PW	1973
®	Omaha	Omaha VA Hospital	U-Zr	1959
▲	Omaha	Offutt AFB	SAC Headquarters	

NEVADA

	Location	Operator	Notes	Date
◈	Beatty	Nuclear Engineering	low level burial	
◼	Hawthorne	US Navy	weapons storage	
◉	Hot Creek	DoE/Nevada Test Site (NTS)	prompt burst	1964
▲	Indian Springs	Indian Sprgs. AF Aux.	TAC base	

NEW MEXICO (cont.)

	Location	Operator	Notes	Date
△	(——)		uranium mine/mill	
△	Laguna		uranium mine/mill	
△	L-Bar Ranch	Schio Petro.	uranium mine/mill	
△	Lordsburg	Federal Resources Corp.	uranium mine/mill	
●	Los Alamos	DoE/Los Alamos Sci. Lab	weapons design	
△	Los Alamos	DoE/LASL	waste management	
◇	Los Alamos	DoE/LASL	reactor research	
®	Los Alamos	DoE/LASL	tank	1956
△	Milan	M3M Comp.	uranium mine/mill	
▣	Manzano Mts.	US Air Force	weapons storage	
△	SaNoStee	Williams Ray	uranium mine/mill	
△	San Mateo	Harrison Western	uranium mine/mill	
△	Shiprock		uranium mine/mill	
△	Silver City	Hamilton James	uranium mine/mill	
△	Thoreau	Gulf/Western	uranium mine/mill	
®	White Sands	Army Missile Range	fast, burst	1964
◆	White Sands	US Navy	ordnance missile test	

NEW YORK

	Location	Operator	Notes	Date
○	Brookhaven	Shoreham (LILCo)	BW	1981
●	Buchanan	Indian Point (Con Ed/PASNY)	PW	1973,76
®	Buffalo	State U. of New York	pool	1961
®	Ithaca	Cornell	U-Zr, tank	1962,62
○	Jamesport	Jamesport (LILCo)	PW	1988,90
◆	Lewiston	DoE	weapons waste dump	
®	New York	Columbia	U-Zr	indef.
®	New York	Manhattan College	tank	1964
◇	New York	S.M. Stoller	nuclear consultants	
◆	New York	Riverside Research Inst.	weapons think tank	
◗	New Haven	Urits 1 & 2 (NYSE&G)	PW	1994,96
◗	Niagara Falls	DoE (National Lead)	low level burial	
○	Ontario	R.E. Ginna (RG&E)	PW	1970
○	Oswego	Sterling (RG&E)	PW	1988
◇	Pawling	United Nuclear	reactor development	
▲	Plattsburg	Plattsburg AFB	SAC base	
▲	Rome	Griffiss AFB	SAC base	

Location	Name/Owner or Contractor	Description (reactor:type, startup)
Schenectady	Thermal Test Reactor/DoE	graphite 1951
Schenectady	Knolls Atomic Power Lab (DoD/DoE)	design, development, testing of nucl. propulsion
Scriba	Nine Mile Point (NMPC)	BW 1969,83
Scriba	James Fitzpatrick (PASNY)	BW 1975
Sterling Forest	Union Carbide	pool 1961
Troy	Rensselaer Inst.	critical assy. facilities
Upton	Brookhaven High Flux/ DoE	HW, tank 1965,59
Upton	Brookhaven/DoE	reactor research
West Milton	Knolls Lab (US Navy/DoE)	PW 1958,62,76
West Valley	Nuclear Fuel Services	waste storage

NORTH CAROLINA

Location	Name/Owner or Contractor	Description (reactor:type, startup)
Bonsal	Shearon Harris (CP&L)	PW 1984,86,90,88
Cowans Ford Dam	Wm. McGuire (Duke)	PW 1979,81
Davie County	Perkins (Duke)	PW 1988,91,93
Fayetteville	US Army	Army Strike Command
Goldsboro	Seymour Johnson AFB	TAC base
Raleigh	N.C. State U.	pool 1972
Southport	Brunswick (CP&L)	BW 1977,75
Wilmington	General Electric	fuel processing
Youngsville	General Atomic	fuel processing
Unsited	Units 1 & 2 (CP&L)	PW indef.

NORTH DAKOTA

Location	Name/Owner or Contractor	Description (reactor:type, startup)
Dakota Plains		uranium mine/mill
Grand Forks	Grand Forks AFB	SAC base; ICBM field
Minot	Minot AFB	SAC base; ICBM field

OHIO

Location	Name/Owner or Contractor	Description (reactor:type, startup)
Ashtabula	DoE/Extrusion Plant (Reactive Metals)	fuel processing for weapons
Berlin Heights	Erie (Ohio Ed)	PW 1986,88
Columbus	Battelle Memorial Inst.	fuel R&D
Columbus	Ohio State U	pool 1961

Location	Name/Owner or Contractor	Description (reactor:type, startup)
Middletown	Three Mile Island (Met Ed/JCP&L)	PW 1974,78 (temp. shutdown)
Parks	Babcock & Wilcox	plutonium processing
Peach Bottom	Peach Bottom (PECo)	BW 1974,74
Philadelphia	General Electric	Mark 12 warhead devpt.
Pottstown	Limerick (PECo)	BW 1983,85
Shippingport	Shippingport/DoE	PW 1957
Shippingport	Beaver Valley (DL-OE)	BW 1976,84
University Park	Penn State	pool, triga 1965
Waltz Mill	Westinghouse	plutonium processing
West Mifflin	Bettis Atomic Power Lab (DoE/DoD)	R&D for Naval reactors

RHODE ISLAND

Location	Name/Owner or Contractor	Description (reactor:type, startup)
Charlestown	New England (NEP)	PW 1986,88
Ft. Kearney	Nuclear Science Center	pool 1964
Wood River Junct.	United Fuels Service	fuel processing

SOUTH CAROLINA

Location	Name/Owner or Contractor	Description (reactor:type, startup)
Aiken	Savannah River Plant DoE/DoD	weapons research
Aiken	SRP; C, K, & P reactors (DoE/Du Pont)	production of nuclear materials for weapons since 1955,54,54
Aiken	SRP: 4 process development reactors (DoE)	weapons production since 1967,53,53,53
Aiken	Savannah River Plant	waste mgmt./storage
Aiken	Savannah River Lab	reactor R&D
Aiken	Savannah River Plant	reprocessing
Barnwell	Allied-General Nuclear	reprocessing
Barnwell	Allied-General Nuclear	spent fuel storage
Barnwell	Chem-Nuclear Services	low level waste burial
Charleston	US Navy	nuc. sub base/shipyard
Cherokee Cnty.	Cherokee (Duke)	PW 1985,87,89
Columbia	Westinghouse	fuel processing
Hartsville	H.3.Robinson (CP&L)	PW 1971

	City	Facility	Type / Notes	Date
▲	Columbus	Rickenbacker AFB	SAC base	
◊	Fernald	DoE/Feed Materials (National Lead)	fuel processing for weapons	
◆	Fernald	DoE/Feed Materials	waste disposal	
■	Miamisburg	DoE/Mound Lab (Monsanto)	manufactures nuclear weapons detonators	
◆	Miamisburg	DoE/Mound Lab	waste management	
◊	Miamisburg	DoE/Mound Lab	fuel proc. for weapons	BW 1980
○	Moscow	Wm. Zimmer (CG&E)	PW	1977,85,87
●	Oak Harbor	Davis-Besse (TE-CEI)	BW	1981,83
○	Perry	Perry (CEI)	uranium enrichment for weapons	
◊	Piketon	DoE/Portsmouth Gaseous Diffusion (Goodyear)		
◆	Piketon	DoE/Portsmouth	waste disposal	
◈	Piketon	DoE/Portsmouth Gas Centrifuge Plant	uranium enrichment for reactors (under constr.)	
◈	West Jefferson	Batelle Mem. Inst.	plutonium processing	

OKLAHOMA

	City	Facility	Type / Notes	Date
▲	Altus	Altus AFB	MAC base	
◈	Crescent City	Kerr-McGee	fuel processing (temp. closed)	
○	Inola	Black Fox (PSC)	BW	1984,86
▣	McAlester	US Navy	weapons storage	
®	Norman	U. of Oklahoma	HS, pool	1958
◈	Sequoyah	Kerr-McGee	fuel processing	

OREGON

	City	Facility	Type / Notes	Date
○	Arlington	Pebble Springs (PGE)	BW	1987,89
®	Corvallis	Oregon State U.	HS, U-Zr	1958,67
△	Lakeview		inactive mill site	
®	Portland	Reed College	U-Zr	1968
●	Prescott	Trojan (PGE)	PW	1976

PENNSYLVANIA

	City	Facility	Type / Notes	Date
◈	Apollo	Babcock & Wilcox	fuel processing	
○	Berwick	Susquehanna (PP&L)	BW	1981,82
◈	Cheswick	Westinghouse	plutonium processing	

	City	Facility	Type / Notes	Date
○	Lake Wylie	Catawba (Duke)	PW	1981,83
●	Seneca	Oconee (Duke)	PW	1973,74,74

SOUTH DAKOTA

	City	Facility	Type / Notes	Date
△	Black Hills		uranium mine/mill	
✗	Butte County		poss. undg. test site	
△	Custer	Pacer Corp.	uranium mine/mill	
△	Edgemont	Silver King	uranium mine/mill	
△	Ft. Pierre	Johnson Bros.	uranium mine	
△	Lignites		uranium mine/mill	
▲	Rapid City	Ellsworth AFB	SAC base; ICBM field	

TENNESSEE

	City	Facility	Type / Notes	Date
▲	Clarksville	US Army	Army Strike Command	
▲	Clarksville	Defense Atomic Support	weapons storage	
○	Daisy	Sequoyah (TVA)	PW	1979,80
◊	Erwin	Nuclear Fuel Services	fuel processing	
○	Hartsville	A: 1&2; B: 1&2 (TVA)	BW	1983,84,83,84
◈	Jonesboro	Tenn. Nuc. Specialists	fuel processing	
○	Kingsport	Phipps Bend (TVA)	BW	1984,85
®	Memphis	Memphis State	HS	1977
○	Oak Ridge	Cinch River Breeder (DoE)	sodium	indef.
■	Oak Ridge	Y-12 Plant (DoE)	uranium components for weapons	
◆	Oak Ridge	Y-12 Plant (DoE)	waste mgmt./disposal	
◈	Oak Ridge	Gaseous Diffusion Plant/DoE/Union Car.)	uranium enrichment for weapons and reactors	
◆	Oak Ridge	Gas Diff. Plant	waste mgmt./disposal	
®	Oak Ridge	Oak Ridge Nat. Lab (DoE/Union Carbide)	research reactors	1950,58,60,62,65
◈	Oak Ridge	Oak Ridge NL	reactor research	
◆	Oak Ridge	Oak Ridge NL	waste mgmt./disposal	
◈	Oak Ridge	U.S. Nuclear	fuel processing	
○	Spring City	Exxon Nuclear	poss. reprocessing plant	
	Spring City	Watts Bar (TVA)	PW	1980,81

TEXAS

	City	Facility	Type / Notes	Date
▲	Abilene	Dyess AFB	SAC base	

(TX)

Location	Name/Owner or Contractor	Description (reactor:type, startup)
Amarillo	DoE/Pantex Plant (Mason & Hanger-Silas Mason)	testing, final assembly, disassembly of hydrogen bombs
Amarillo	DoE/Pantex Plant	waste disposal/burial
Amarillo	Hydro Jet Ser.	uranium mine/mill
Austin	U. of Texas	U-Zr 1963
Benavides	2 companies	uranium mine/mill
Bruni	2 companies	uranium mine/mill
College Station	Nuclear Science Center	pool, triga 1961
College Station	Texas A&M	HS 1968
Corpus Christi	2 companies	uranium mine/mill
Falls City	Continental Oil	uranium mine/mill
Fort Worth	Carswell AFB	SAC base
George West	US Steel	uranium mill
Glen Rose	Comanche Peak (TUG)	PW 1981,83
Jasper	Blue Hills (GSU)	PW 1989,91
Karnes County	Continental Oil	uranium mine/mill
Killeen	Defense Atomic Support	weapons storage
Matagorda	South Texas (CP&L/HL&P)	PW 1980,82
Pawnee	Intercont. Energy	uranium mine/mill
Panna Maria	Chevron	uranium mine/mill
Ray Point	Susquehanna Western	uranium mine/mill
Sulphur Creek	Wyoming Mineral	uranium mine/mill
Tuleta	IEC Corp.	uranium mill
Wallis	Allens Creek (HL&P)	BW 1985

UTAH

Location	Name/Owner or Contractor	Description (reactor:type, startup)
Big Indian Wash.		uranium mine/mill
Bingham	Wyoming Mineral	uranium mine/mill
Blanding	11 companies	uranium mine/mill
Blandwood	Plateau Resource	uranium mine/mill
Cahone	Laura Mining	uranium mine/mill
Ford	Dawn Mining	uranium mine/mill
Greenriver	Jack Watterson	uranium mine/mill

(WA)

Location	Name/Owner or Contractor	Description (reactor:type, startup)
Richland	Henford Prod. Op./DoE (United Nuclear Ind.)	fuel fabrication
Richland	HPO/DoE (UNI)	reactor R&D
Richland	HPO/DoE (Atomics In.-Rockwell)	waste management/ storage/burial
Richland	HPO/DoE (AI-Rock.)	reprocessing
Richland	HPO (DoE)/WPPSS: N Reactor (UNI)	plutonium production & steam (+4 standby prod. re.) graphite 1966
Richland	Henford Eng. Dev. Lab./DoE(Westinghouse)	breeder reactor R&D
Richland	HEDL: Fast Flux Test	sodium cld. breeder 1979
Richland	HEDL: Neutron Rad.	U-Zr 1977
Richland	HEDL	fuel fabr. research
Richland	DcE Critical Mass Lab. (Battelle/Pac. NW Lab)	waste mgmt. research
Richland	CML (Batt./Pac. NW)	plutonium processing
Richland	Exxon Nuclear	plutonium processing
Richland	WPSS: 1,2,4	BW 1982,80,84
Satsop	WPSS: 3,5	PW 1984,85
Seattle	U. of Washington	graph./water 1961
Sedro Wooley	Skagit (PSP&L)	BW 1986,88
Spokane	Fairchild AFB	SAC base
Spokane	Western Nuclear	uranium mine/mill
Wellpinit	Western Nuclear	uranium mine/mill

WEST VIRGINIA

WISCONSIN

Location	Name/Owner or Contractor	Description (reactor:type, startup)
Carlton	Kewaunee (WPS)	PW 1974
Durand	Tyrone Park (NSP)	PW 1985
Haven	Heven (WEP)	PW 1987, indef.
La Crosse	La Crosse (DPC)	BW 1969
Madison	U. of Wisconsin	pool, triga 1960
Two Creeks	Point Beach (WMP)	PW 1970,72

	Location	Organization	Description
△	Hanksville	3 companies	uranium mine/mill
△	Le Sal	Rio Algum Mines	uranium mine/mill
△	Marysville		uranium mine/mill
△	Midvale	Cimarron Mining	uranium mine/mill
△	Moab	3 companies	uranium mine/mill
△	Monticello	5 companies	uranium mine/mill
△	Norwood	CW Bunker	uranium mine/mill
▲	Ogden	Hill AFB	AF Logistics Command
△	Orangeville	Minerals West	uranium mine/mill
△	Price	Utah West	uranium mine/mill
®	Provo	Brigham Young	H 1967
®	Salt Lake City	U. of Utah	U-Zr, HS 1975,57
®	Salt Lake City	2 companies	uranium mine/mill
△	San Juan County	Homestake Mining	uranium mine/mill
△	Thompson	Golden Mining	uranium mine/mill
△	Tooele	Doran Hunt	uranium mine/mill

VERMONT

	Location	Organization	Description
●	Vernon	Vermont Yankee (VYNP) BW	1972

VIRGINIA

	Location	Organization	Description
▲	Arlington	Pentagon	plans nuclear war
®	Blacksburg	Virginia Polytech	graphite/water 1959
®	Charlottesville	U. of Virginia	pool 1960,61
●	Gravel Neck	Surry (VE&P)	PW 1972,73
®	Lynchburg	Babcock & Wilcox	pool 1958
□	Lynchburg	Babcock & Wilcox/DoE	critical assembly fac.
◈	Lynchburg	Babcock & Wilcox	fuel processing
●	Mineral	North Anna (VE&P)	PW 1978,79,83,84
■	Newport News	US Navy	nuclear shipyard
▲■	Norfolk	US Navy	nuclear sub base/shipyd.

WASHINGTON

	Location	Organization	Description
▲	Bangor	US Navy	nuclear sub base
■	Bremerton	Puget Sound (US Navy)	nuclear shipyard
△	Ford	Dawn Mining	uranium mine/mill
®	Pullman	Washington State U.	pool, triga 1961

WYOMING

	Location	Organization	Description
△	Albany	4 companies	uranium mine/mill
△	Bear Creek	Rocky Mtn. Energy	uranium mine/mill
△	Campbell	8 companies	uranium mine/mill
△	Carbon	4 companies	uranium mine/mill
△	Casper	7 companies	uranium mine/mill
▲	Cheyenne	Warren AFB	SAC base; ICBM field
△	Converse City	3 companies	uranium mine/mill
△	Copper Mtn.	Rocky Mtn. Energy	uranium mine/mill
△	Crooks Gap	3 companies	uranium mine/mill
△	Douglass	2 companies	uranium mine/mill
△	Fremont	6 companies	uranium mine/mill
△	Ft. Pierre	Johnson Brothers	uranium mine/mill
△	Gas Hills	5 companies	uranium mine/mill
△	Glenrock	Kerr-McGee	uranium mine/mill
△	Highland	Exxon Nuclear	uranium mine/mill
△	Irigaray	Wyoming Mineral	uranium mine/mill
△	Jeffrey City	3 companies	uranium mine/mill
△	Johnson County	2 companies	uranium mine/mill
△	Laramie	Power Comp.	uranium mine
△	Mills	Uranium Supply	uranium mine/mill
△	Natrona	7 companies	uranium mine/mill
△	Powder R. Basin	3 companies	uranium mine/mill
△	Pumpkin Buttes	Cleveland Cliffs	uranium mine/mill
△	Red Desert	United Nuclear	uranium mine/mill
△	Riverton	4 companies	uranium mine/mill
△	Shirley Basin	6 companies	uranium mine/mill
△	Sweetwater Ct.	Minerals Expl.	uranium mine/mill
△	Weston	TVA/Exxon	uranium mine/mill

PUERTO RICO

	Location	Organization	Description
®	Mayaguez	PR Nuclear Ctr./DoE	H 1959

THE OCEANS

▲⊛	124 Nuclear Submarines operating	
▲⊛	30 Nuclear Submarines being built	

War Resisters League
339 Lafayette Street
New York, NY 10012

APPENDIX D:

For Further Reading

PERIODICALS

Baptist Peacemaker. Deer Park Baptist Church, 1733 Bardstown Rd., Louisville, KY 40205.

The Bulletin of the Atomic Scientists. 1020–24 E. 58th St., Chicago, IL 60637.

Catholic Agitator. Los Angeles Catholic Worker, 632 N. Brittania St., Los Angeles, CA 90033.

Catholic Worker. 36 E. First St., New York, NY 10003.

Christianity and Crisis. 537 W. 121st St., New York, NY 10027.

Critical Mass Journal. P.O. Box 1538, Washington, D.C. 20013.

The Defense Monitor. Center for Defense Information, Capitol Gallery West, Suite 303, 600 Maryland Ave., SW, Washington D.C. 20024.

F.A.S. Public Interest Report. Federation of American Scientists, 307 Massachusetts Ave., NE, Washington, D.C. 20002.

Fellowship. Fellowship of Reconciliation, Box 271, Nyack, NY 10960.

FCNL Newsletter. Friends Committee on National Legislation, 245 2nd St., NE, Washington, D.C. 20002.

Freeze Newsletter. National Clearinghouse, Nuclear Weapons Freeze Campaign, 4144 Lindell Blvd., Suite 404, St. Louis, MO 63108.

God and Caesar. Commission on Home Ministries, General Conference Mennonite Church, Box 347, Newton, KS 67114.

Katallagette. P.O. Box 12044, Nashville, TN 37212.

National Catholic Reporter. P.O. Box 281, Kansas City, MO 64141.

The Peacemaker. P.O. Box 627, Garberville, CA 95440.

The Other Side. 258 W. Apsley, Box 12236, Philadelphia, PA 19144.

The Progressive. 408 W. Gorham St., Madison, WI 53703.

SANE World. SANE, 514 C St., NE, Washington, D.C. 20002.

Seeds. Oakhurst Baptist Church, 222 East Lake Drive, Decatur, GA 30030.

Sojourners. 1309 L St., NW, Washington, D.C. 20005.

WIN. 326 Livingston St., Brooklyn, NY 11217.

Year One. Jonah House, 1933 Park Ave., Baltimore, MD 21217.

BOOKS

The Consequences of Nuclear War

Adams, Ruth, and Cullen, Susan, editors. *The Final Epidemic: Physicians and Scientists on Nuclear War.* Chicago: University of Chicago Press, 1982.

Akizuki, Tatsuichiro. *Nagasaki 1945.* New York: Quartet Books, 1982.

Beres, Louis Rene. *Apocalypse: Nuclear Catastrophe in World Politics.* Chicago: University of Chicago Press, 1982.

Bertell, Rosalie. *Danger, Low-Level Radiation: The Story of Sister Rosalie Bertell, Her Research and Testimony on the Hazards of Nuclear Contamination.* Trumansburg, New York: Crossing Press, Fall 1982.

Committee for the Compilation of Materials on Damage Caused by the Atomic Bombs in Hiroshima and Nagasaki. *Hiroshima and Nagasaki: The Physical, Medical, and Social Effects of the Atomic Bombings.* New York: Basic Books, 1981.

DeGrasse, Robert, Jr., Murphy, Paul, and Ragen, William. *The Costs and Consequences of Reagan's Military Buildup.* New York: Council on Economic Priorities, 1982.

Gofman, Dr. John W. *Radiation and Human Health.* San Francisco: Sierra Club Books, 1981.

Goodwin, Peter. *Nuclear War: The Facts on Our Survival.* New York: W. H. Smith, 1981.

Hersey, John. *Hiroshima.* New York: Knopf, 1946.

Japan Broadcasting Corporation, eds. *Unforgettable Fire: Pictures Drawn by Atomic Bomb Survivors.* New York: Pantheon Books, 1977.

Katz, Arthur M. *Life After Nuclear War.* Cambridge: Ballinger, 1982.

Nagai, Takashi, ed. (Nagasaki Appeal Committee). *Living Beneath the Atomic Cloud: The Testimony of the Children of Nagasaki.* Tokyo: SAN–YU–SHA, 1979.

Oe, Kenzaburo. *Hiroshima Notes.* Tokyo: Y.M.C.A. Press, 1981.

Osada, Arata. *Children of Hiroshima.* Cambridge: Oelgeschlager, Gunn and Hain, 1981.

Rosenberg, Howard L. *Atomic Soldiers: American Victims of Nuclear Experiments.* Boston: Beacon Press, 1980.

Rotblat, J. *Nuclear Radiation in Warfare.* Cambridge: Oelgeschlager, Gunn and Hain, 1981.

Saffer, Thomas. *Countdown Zero.* New York: Putnam, 1982.

Schell, Jonathan. *The Fate of the Earth.* New York: Knopf, 1981.

Waserman, Harvey, and Solomon, Norman. *Killing Our Own: The Disaster of America's Experiments With Atomic Radiation.* New York: Delacorte/Delta, 1982.

Nuclear Arms Race/Nuclear Weapons

Aldridge, Robert. *The Counterforce Syndrome: A Guide to U.S. Nuclear Weapons and Strategic Doctrine.* Washington, D.C.: Transnational Institute, 1978.

Aldridge, Robert. *First Strike.* Boston: South End Press, 1982.

Born Secret: The H Bomb, The Progressive Case and National Security. Elmsford, New York: Pergamon Press, 1981.

Boston Study Group. *The Price of Defense: A New Strategy for Military Spending.* New York: Times Books, 1979.

Calder, Nigel. *Nuclear Nightmares: An Investigation Into Possible Wars.* New York: Penguin, 1981.

Clark, Ronald. *The Greatest Power on Earth: The International Race for Nuclear Supremacy.* New York: Harper and Row, 1981.

Ground Zero Members. *Nuclear War: What's in It for You?* New York: Pocket Books, 1982.

Hilgartner, Stephen, Bell, Richard, and O'Connor, Rory. *Nukespeak: Nuclear Language, Visions and Mindset.* San Francisco: Sierra Club Books, 1982.

Joyce, James Avery. *The War Machine: The Case Against the Arms Race.* New York: Avon/Discus, 1982.

Kaldor, Mary. *The Baroque Arsenal.* New York: Farrar, Straus, and Giroux, 1981.

Lens, Sidney. *The Bomb.* New York: E. P. Dutton, 1982.

Lens, Sidney. *The Day Before Doomsday: An Anatomy of the Nuclear Arms Race.* Boston: Beacon Press, 1977.

Lovins, Amory, and Hunter, L. *Energy/War: Breaking the Nuclear Link.* San Francisco: Friends of the Earth, 1980.

Morland, Howard. *The Secret That Exploded.* New York: Random House, 1981.

Office of Technology Assessment, Congress of the United States. *The Effects of Nuclear War.* Montclair, New Jersey: Allanheld, Osmun and Company, 1980.

Pringle, Peter, and Spigelman, James. *The Nuclear Barons.* New York: Holt, Rinehart and Winston, 1981.

Scoville, Herbert. *MX: Prescription for Disaster.* Cambridge: MIT Press, 1981.

Thompson, E. P. *Protest and Survive.* New York: Monthly Review Press, 1981.

U.S.-Soviet Relations

Barnet, Richard. *The Giants: Russia and America.* New York: Simon and Schuster, 1977.

Chomsky, Noam. *Towards a New Cold War.* New York: Pantheon Books, 1982.

Cox, Arthur Macy. *Russian Roulette: The Superpower Game.* New York: Times Books, 1982.

Kaplan, Fred M. *Dubious Specter: A Skeptical Look at the Soviet Threat.* Washington, D.C.: Transnational Institute, 1977.

Sivachev, Nikolai, and Yakovlev, Nikolai. *Russia and the United States: U.S.-Soviet Relations from the Soviet Point of View.* Chicago: University of Chicago Press, 1979.

Wolfe, Alan. *The Rise and Fall of the "Soviet Threat": Domestic Sources of the Cold War Consensus.* Washington, D.C.: Institute for Policy Studies, 1979.

Foreign Policy

Barnet, Richard. *Intervention and Revolution.* New York: World Publishing, 1968.

Barnet, Richard. *Real Security: Restoring American Power in a Dangerous Decade.* New York: Simon and Schuster, 1981.

Barnet, Richard. *Roots of War.* Baltimore: Penguin Books, 1971.

Herken, Gregg. *The Winning Weapon: The Atomic Bomb in the Cold War 1945-1950.* New York: Knopf, 1980.

Horowitz, David. *Containment and Revolution.* Boston: Beacon Press, 1971.

Horowitz, David. *The Free World Colossus.* New York: Hill and Wang, 1965.

Kolko, Gabriel. *The Roots of American Foreign Policy.* Boston: Beacon Press, 1969.

Mandelbaum, Michael. *The Nuclear Revolution: International Politics Before and After Hiroshima.* New York: Cambridge Press, 1981.

Sherwin, Martin. *A World Destroyed: The Atomic Bomb and the Grand Alliance.* New York: Knopf, 1975.

Biblical and Theological

Aukerman, Dale. *Darkening Valley: A Biblical Perspective on Nuclear War.* New York: Seabury Press, 1981.

Bainton, Roland H. *Christian Attitudes Toward War and Peace: A Historical Survey and Critical Re-evaluation.* Nashville: Abingdon Press, 1960.

Berrigan, Daniel. *Uncommon Prayer: A Book of Psalms.* New York: Seabury Press, 1978.

Cesaretti, C. A., and Vitale, Joseph T., editors. *Rumors of War: A Moral and Theological Perspective on the Arms Race.* New York: Seabury Press, 1982.

Douglass, James. *Lightning East to West.* Portland: Sunburst Press, 1980.

Douglass, James. *The Nonviolent Cross.* New York: Macmillan, 1966.

Douglass, James. *Resistance and Contemplation.* New York: Doubleday, 1971.

Ellul, Jacques. *The Presence of the Kingdom.* New York: Seabury Press, 1967.

Ellul, Jacques. *Violence.* New York: Seabury Press, 1969.

Ferguson, John. *The Politics of Love: The New Testament and Non-Violent Revolution.* Nyack, New York: Fellowship of Reconciliation, 1979.

Grannis, J. Christopher, Laffin, Arthur J., and Schade, Elin. *The Risk of the Cross: Christian Discipleship in the Nuclear Age.* New York: Seabury Press, 1981.

Heyer, Robert, editor. *Nuclear Disarmament: Key Statements from the Vatican, Catholic Leaders in North America and Ecumenical Bodies.* Ramsey, New Jersey: Paulist Press, 1982.

Jordan, Clarence. *Sermon on the Mount.* Valley Forge, Pennsylvania: Judson Press, 1952.

Kownacki, Mary Lou, editor. *A Race to Nowhere: An Arms Race Primer for Catholics.* Chicago: Pax Christi, 1980.

Kraybill, Don. *Facing Nuclear War: A Plea for Christian Witness.* Scottdale, Pennsylvania: Herald Press, 1982.

Lasserre, Jean. *War and the Gospel.* Scottdale, Pennsylvania: Herald Press, 1962.

MacGregor, G. H. C. *The New Testament Basis of Pacifism and the Relevance of an Impossible Ideal.* Nyack, New York: Fellowship Publications, 1954.

A Matter of Faith: A Study Guide for Churches on the Nuclear Arms Race. Washington, D.C.: Sojourners, 1981.

McSorley, Richard. *New Testament Basis of Peacemaking.* Washington, D.C.: Center for Peace Studies, 1979.

Rankin, William. *The Nuclear Arms Race: Countdown to Disaster—A Study in Christian Ethics.* Cincinnati, Ohio: Forward Movement Publications, 1982.

Rockman, Jane, editor. *Peace in Search of Makers.* Valley Forge, Pennsylvania: Judson Press, 1979.

Stringfellow, William. *An Ethic for Christians and Other Aliens in a Strange Land.* Waco, Texas: Word Books, 1973.

Swaim, J. Carter. *War, Peace and the Bible.* Maryknoll, New York: Orbis Books, 1982.

Taylor, Richard, and Sider, Ronald. *Nuclear Holocaust and Christian Hope.* Downers Grove, Illinois: IVP, 1982.

Trocme, Andre. *Jesus and the Nonviolent Revolution.* Scottdale, Pennsylvania: Herald Press, 1973.

Wallis, Jim. *The Call to Conversion.* San Francisco: Harper and Row, 1981.

Yoder, John Howard. *The Christian Witness to the State.* Newton, Kansas: Faith and Life Press, 1964.

Yoder, John Howard. *The Original Revolution.* Scottdale, Pennsylvania: Herald Press, 1971.

Yoder, John Howard. *The Politics of Jesus.* Grand Rapids, Michigan: Eerdmans, 1972.

Opposition to the Bomb

Brenner, Michael J. *Nuclear Power and Non-Proliferation: The Remaking of U.S. Policy.* New York: Cambridge University Press, 1981.

Dunn, Leslie. *Controlling the Bomb: Nuclear Proliferation in the 1980s—A Twentieth Century Fund Report.* New Haven: Yale University Press, 1982.

Freeman, Leslie J. *Nuclear Witness: Insiders Speak Out.* New York: Norton, 1982.

Geyer, Alan. *The Idea of Disarmament: Rethinking the Unthinkable.* Elgin, Illinois: Brethren Press, 1982.

Keyes, Ken, Jr. *The Hundredth Monkey.* St. Mary, Kentucky: Vision Books, 1982.

MIT faculty members, editors. *Nuclear Almanac: Confronting the Atom in War and Peace.* Reading, Massachusetts: Addison-Wesley, 1982.

Potter, William C. *Nuclear Power and Nonproliferation: An Interdisciplinary Perspective.* Cambridge: Oelgeschlager, Gunn and Hain, 1982.

Price, Jerome. *The Anti-Nuclear Movement.* Boston: Twayne Publishers, 1982.

Stockholm International Peace Research Institute. *World Armaments and Disarmament: The SIPRI Yearbook 1981.* Cambridge: Oelgeschlager, Gunn and Hain, 1981.

United Nations Educational, Scientific and Cultural Organization. *Obstacles to Disarmament and Ways of Overcoming Them.* New York: Unipub, 1981.

Zuckerman, Solly. *Nuclear Illusion and Reality.* New York: Viking, 1982.

Principles of Nonviolence

Cooney, Robert, and Michalowski, Helen. *The Power of the People: Active Nonviolence in the United States.* Culver City, California: Peace Press, 1977.

Fischer, Louis. *Gandhi: His Life and Message for the World.* New York: Signet Key Books, 1954.

Gandhi, M. K. *An Autobiography.* Boston: Beacon Press, 1957.

Gandhi, M. K. *Non-Violence Resistance.* New York: Schocken Books, 1967.

Gregg, Richard. *The Power of Nonviolence.* New York: Schocken Books, 1959.

Hentoff, Nat. *The Essays of A. J. Muste.* Indianapolis: Bobbs Merrill Co., 1967.

King, Martin Luther. *Where Do We Go From Here?* New York: Harper and Row, 1967.

Sharp, Gene. *The Politics of Nonviolent Action. Part One: Power and Struggle; Part Two: The Methods of Nonviolent Action; Part Three: The Dynamics of Nonviolent Action.* Boston: Porter and Sargent, 1973.

Stevick, Daniel B. *Civil Disobedience and the Christian.* New York: Seabury Press, 1969.

Contributors

Robert Aldridge served as a design engineer for Lockheed Missiles and Space Company for 16 years, working on the Polaris, Poseidon, and Trident missile systems. He is the author of *First Strike* (South End Press, 1982) and *The Counterforce Syndrome: A Guide to U.S. Nuclear Weapons and Strategic Doctrine* (Transnational Institute, 1978).

Dale Aukerman is a writer and long-time peace activist. He is the author of *Darkening Valley: A Biblical Perspective on Nuclear War* (Seabury Press, 1981).

Richard Barnet is a senior fellow at the Institute for Policy Studies in Washington, D.C. He is the author of several books, including most recently *The Lean Years* (Simon and Schuster, 1980) and *Real Security: Restoring American Power in a Dangerous Decade* (Simon and Schuster, 1981). He is a contributing editor for *Sojourners* magazine.

Danny Collum is associate editor of *Sojourners* magazine.

Gordon Cosby is pastor of the Church of the Saviour in Washington, D.C., and a founder of World Peacemakers. He is a contributing editor for *Sojourners* magazine.

James Douglass is a member of Ground Zero, a resistance community in Bangor, Washington, and the author of *The Nonviolent Cross* (Macmillan Publishing Company, 1966), *Resistance and Contemplation* (Doubleday, 1971), and *Lightning East to West* (Sunburst Press, 1980).

Lloyd Dumas is associate professor of political economy and economics at the University of Texas in Dallas. He is a member of the Nuclear Weapons Control Steering Committee of the American Association for the Advancement of Science.

Jacques Ellul is recently retired from his position as professor of history and sociology of institutions at the University of Bordeaux. A lawyer, theologian, and social critic, he has written numerous books, including *The Technological Society* (Vintage Books, 1964) and *The Politics of God and the Politics of Man* (Eerdmans, 1972).

James Forest is coordinator of the International Fellowship of Reconciliation (IFOR) and a contributing editor for *Sojourners* magazine.

Helmut Gollwitzer is a German theologian who retired in 1975 as professor of systematics at the Free University of Berlin. He is the author of several books and articles relating biblical perspectives to social and political questions.

William Greider was assistant managing editor and a columnist for the *Washington Post*. He is now national editor of *Rolling Stone*.

Howard Hiatt, M.D., is dean of the Harvard School of Public Health and professor of medicine at Harvard Medical School.

E. Glenn Hinson is professor of church history at Southern Baptist Theological Seminary in Louisville, Kentucky. He is a writer and the editor of *The Baptist Peacemaker*.

Raymond Hunthausen is archbishop of Seattle, Washington.

Robert Johansen is president of the Institute for World Order and author of *The National Interest and the Human Interest: An Analysis of U.S. Foreign Policy* (Princeton University Press, 1980).

Mernie King was formerly on the staff of Sojourners Peace Ministry; he now attends law school at the University of Mississippi.

Alan Kreider is on the staff of the Mennonite Center in London, England, and a peace advocate in the English churches.

Sidney Lens is a labor organizer, writer, and peace advocate. He is the author of many books, including *The Day Before Doomsday* (Doubleday, 1977), a comprehensive study of the arms race.

Richard Mouw is professor of philosophy at Calvin College in Grand Rapids, Michigan. He is the author of *Political Evangelism* (Eerdmans, 1973), *Politics and the Biblical Drama* (Eerdmans, 1976), and *Call to Holy Worldliness* (Fortress Press, 1980).

Henri Nouwen is a Catholic priest and a contemplative writer. He is the author of many books, including *Genesee Diary* (Image Books, 1976) and *Reaching Out* (Doubleday, 1975).

Ernest Regehr is director of research for Project Ploughshares, an interchurch educational program on Canadian military policies, researcher and lecturer for the Institute for Peace and Conflict Studies, Conrad Grebel College at the University of Waterloo, Waterloo, Ontario, and author of *Militarism and the World Military Order* (World Council of Churches, 1980).

Ronald Sider is president of Evangelicals for Social Action and the author of *Rich Christians in an Age of Hunger* (InterVarsity, 1977) and, with Richard Taylor, of *Nuclear Holocaust and Christian Hope* (InterVarsity, 1982).

John Stoner is executive secretary of the U.S. Peace Section of the Menno-

nite Central Committee (MCC) and a minister in the Brethren in Christ Church. He is the MCC representative to New Call to Peacemaking.

William Stringfellow is a theologian, lawyer, and author of several books, including *An Ethic for Christians and Other Aliens in a Strange Land* (Word Books, 1973) and *Conscience and Obedience* (Word Books, 1977).

Akahiro Takahashi is director of the Hiroshima Peace Memorial Museum in Hiroshima, Japan.

Elizabeth Wright lives in Salt Lake City. She is founder and chairperson of Citizens' Call in Utah, a group attempting to locate all persons, or their surviving families, who might have been affected by the atomic weapons tests conducted in Nevada.

John Howard Yoder is on the theology faculties of the Associated Biblical Seminaries and Notre Dame University in Indiana. He is the author of several books, including *The Politics of Jesus* (Eerdmans, 1972), and a contributing editor for *Sojourners* magazine.

INDEX